26933075

GOING GREEN: HOW TO COMMUNICATE YOUR COMPANY'S ENVIRONMENTAL COMMITMENT

E. Bruce Harrison

BUSINESS ONE IRWIN
Homewood, IL 60430

This symbol indicates that the paper in this book is made of recycled paper. Its fiber content exceeds the recommended minimum of 50% waste paper fibers as specified by the EPA.

Responsible Care® is a registered trademark of the Chemical Manufacturers' Association. Nexis® is a registered trademark of the Mead Data Service.

© E. BRUCE HARRISON, 1993

This publication is designed to provide accurate and authoritative information in regard to the subject matter covered. It is sold with the understanding that neither the author nor the publisher is engaged in rendering legal, accounting, or other professional service. If legal advice or other expert assistance is required, the services of a competent professional person should be sought.

From a Declaration of Principles jointly adopted by a Committee of the American Bar Association and a Committee of Publishers.

Sponsoring editor:	Cynthia A. Zigmund
Project editor:	Jane Lightell
Production manager:	Diane Palmer
Compositor:	The Wheetley Company, Inc.
Jacket designer:	Klyczek Design
Typeface:	11/13 Palatino
Printer:	Book Press

Library of Congress Cataloging-in-Publication Data

Harrison, E. Bruce.
    Going green : how to communicate your company's environmental commitment / E. Bruce Harrison.
        p. cm.
    ISBN 1-55623-945-9 (alk. paper)
    1. Industrial management—Environmental aspects—United States.
2. Public relations—Corporations—United States. 3. Business enterprises—United States—Environmental aspects. 4. Green movement—United States. 5. Environmental protection—United States. 6. Social responsibility of business—United States.
I. Title.
HD69.P6H37   1993
658.4'08–dc20   92-39264

Printed in the United States of America
1 2 3 4 5 6 7 8 9 0 BP 0 9 8 7 6 5 4 3

To Patricia de Stacy Harrison, who convinced me that I could write this book without quitting my regular job.

Contents

Preface   *x*

Acknowledgments   *xii*

Part I
THE BIG GREEN PICTURE   1

Chapter One
THE BIG PICTURE: WHERE YOU ARE IN THE GREEN WORLD OF BUSINESS   3
The globalization of greening, 4
Greening is Americanized, 4
Business owns greening, 5
Green failure has been criminalized, 6
Greening means good news, too, 7
The death of a movement, 8
Message received, 11
From top-down to bubble-up, 11
The international story so far, 12
Having writ . . . , 13

Chapter Two
HOW TO SHIFT TO A WINNING GREEN ATTITUDE   15
Going green is a habit, not a hormone, 16
Breaking the habit of negative mind-set, 18
Are you a "green" answer?, 19

Chapter Three
MENTAL GREENING: THE HABIT OF THINKING LIKE A GOOD GUY   21
The habit of taking charge of your emotions, 22
Visualize your green success!, 22
Positive thought starters, 24

Part II
CUSTOMER-PUBLICS   27

Chapter Four
GET TO KNOW YOUR VITAL CUSTOMER-PUBLICS   29
You can't fool—or please—everybody, 29

Forget about publics; create customers, 30
You need sustainable customers, 31
What kind of customers will you need?, 31

Chapter Five
MAKE YOUR COMMUNICATION PROCESS-DRIVEN,
NOT PROBLEM-DRIVEN   34
You need a wellness program, not an emergency room, 35
Benefits of a process approach to communication, 35
Envirocomm is an action avenue, 36
The QUALITY model, 36

Chapter Six
THE QUALITY MODEL TO MAKE ENVIROCOMM
WORK FOR YOU   38
Quantify your "publics", 38
Understand "what they want", 39
Ask questions, 40
Listen aggressively, 41
Interpret the data, 43
Take charge, 44
You, yes you, 45

Chapter Seven
TURNING ON THE POWER OF THE EMPLOYEES   47
Part I: Why, 47
Greening, safety, and quality, 48
Benefits of education and training, 49
What the law requires you to "tell your employees", 50
Reaching for 150 percent compliance, 54
Comprehensive program of ICI, 54
Part II: How, 56
Sideways, not down, 57
The supervisor role, 58
Means of communicating, 60
Training: Who and how much?, 63
The Doe Run example, 66
Leverage for company and planet, 66

Chapter Eight
RELATING TO GOVERNMENT   69
Relating to regulators, 69
Regulator blues, 71
Regulator green, 71
Politicians and regulators, 73
Regulatory ombudsmen, 75

"Reg-neg" instead of head-butting, 75
Government testimony, 76
Access to relationships, 77

Chapter Nine
TEN COMMON MISTAKES MANAGERS MAKE IN
WASHINGTON   81
Taking the "Man of La Mancha" view, 81
Detaching from "the public interest", 85
Not following codes of conduct, 87
Not telling the whole truth, 88
Getting hung up in politics, 88
Going it alone, 89
Complicating the message, 90
Not following up, 90
Not listening, 91
Planning behind, 91

Chapter Ten
INTERACTING WITH THE NEWS MEDIA   92
You can choose, 92
Your turn will come, 94
Be a "3" or a "7", 96
Person to person, 97
Be a teacher or a coach, 98
Get personal—and know who's interviewing you, 99
Basic interview tips, 101

Chapter Eleven
RELATING TO INVESTORS   102
Green heat of the '90s, 103
Valdez Principles, 103
How companies have responded to CERES, 104
Why talk green to your investors?, 106
What stockholders want to know, 107
Green raters, 108
Start those green interactions yourself, 110
Envirocomm tips for investor interaction, 110

Chapter Twelve
SUPPLIERS: THE *CRADLE* IN "CRADLE-TO-GRAVE"   113

Chapter Thirteen
INSPECTING AND CORRECTING THE PROCESS   117
"Inspect, don't expect" is a workable motto, 117
Looking for best practices, 118
Inspection from top management, 118
That will bring you back to *do*, 119

Part III
HOW TO . . .   121

Chapter Fourteen
TRAITS OF THE GREENING EXECUTIVE   123

Chapter Fifteen
LISTENING: BE A HEARPERSON   129
Reeducating your listening instincts, 129
What your customer-publics are asking, 131
They're asking: "Do you care?", 133

Chapter Sixteen
SPEAKING ON THE GREEN   137
Anybody can do it, 138
Don't make a speech, give a talk, 138
Get into their seats, 139
Get there early and stay late, 140
Write a speech that's right for you, 141
Write so you can talk it, 142
Write it so you can read it, 142
Practice, practice, practice, 143
Use your natural ability, 144
Beware the uncaring expert, 145
Take it from Abe Lincoln, 147

Chapter Seventeen
COMMUNICATING ABOUT RISK   148
Cardinal rules when talking about risk, 151
Above all: Remain credible, 152
Move toward a dialogue, 153
Confessing your sins: When internal environmental audit
reports become public domain, 153
WIIFM rules, 155

Chapter Eighteen
COMMUNICATING IN CRISIS CONDITIONS:
LESSONS OF THE *EXXON VALDEZ*   158
You don't have to be Exxon to have a *Valdez*, 158
It can hit your fan at any time, 159
You've got to have a plan, 160
The plan must be accessible, 162
People want to hear from the top, 163
The longer you wait, the less your opportunity, 165
Your short-term hesitation can have long-term impact, 166

Chapter Nineteen
DOS AND DON'TS OF CRISIS COMMUNICATION   168
If you're in charge, here are suggested steps, 168

Communication basics, 169
Crisis first-aid kit, 170
Prepare your own crisis communication profile, 172
Crisis planning questionnaire, 179

Chapter Twenty
WHAT TO DO WHEN YOU'RE ATTACKED BY
AN ACTIVIST GROUP   180
Know your attacker's motives, 181
Why me?, 183
Know yourself: Organize your information, 184
Talk to them if you can, 185
Get third parties involved, 185
Take control of news, 186
Inform your critical 20 percent publics, 186
Principles of confrontation, 188
A note on where activism is headed, 189

Chapter Twenty-One
CHOOSE YOUR GREEN PARTNERS   190
Partnering is required and desirable, 190
Examine your relationships, 191
Identifying partner candidates, 192
Who are the "leaders?", 193
Quantifying the leadership structure, 194
Relating to the "active opposition", 195
"Inspect, don't expect" is the guideline, 197
Open dialogue, with media coverage, 198

Part IV
MODELS OF SUCCESS   201

Chapter Twenty-Two
POLICY STATEMENTS: PUT IT IN WRITING   203
Intent: Statement with an attitude, 204
Content, 205
Implement: Take it to your customer-publics, 206
Highlights of environmental policy statements by leading
corporations, 208

Chapter Twenty-Three
BEST PRACTICES OF PARTNERING   216
McDonald's and EDF, 216
First Brands Corporation's Glad Bag-based system, 220
Clean Sites, Inc., 223
The Nature Conservancy's "Last Great Places", 227

Chapter Twenty-Four
MORE GOOD NEWS STORIES   231

Chapter Twenty-Five
ENVIRONMENTAL AWARDS: MORE THAN JUST
"GOOD PR"   242

Chapter Twenty-Six
CMA's RESPONSIBLE CARE PROGRAM   257
Reason for this program, 257
How the industry responded, 258
How it works, 260
The codes of Responsible Care, 260
Examples of company programs, 263

Chapter Twenty-Seven
HOW A CORPORATION COMMUNICATED A
NEW ENVIRONMENTAL ETHIC   266

Chapter Twenty-Eight
GETTING WITH THE PROGRAM: A SUSTAINABLE
DEVELOPMENT CHECKLIST FOR YOUR
ORGANIZATION   269

Part V
ISSUES AHEAD   273

Chapter Twenty-Nine
GREEN TRENDS POINT TO PRESSURES ON EVERY
BUSINESS   275
Greening is highly politicized, 275
No one is unplugged from greenism, 276
Green claims and "openness" can entrap business, 276
The "AMP" syndrome is in high gear, 277
Consumers and communities ask others first, 277
Increase in citizen suits, 278
Criminal penalties for company executives, 278
Rising stockholder activism, 279
Media coverage will intensify, 279

Chapter Thirty
HOW IT ALL STARTS: A GUIDE TO GREEN CRIME'S
HUMBLE ORIGINS   281
Raising the green-crime ante, 282
How green problems start, 286
Case A: The creative consultant, 287
Case B: The stumbling start-up, 288
Case C: Hidden discrepancies, 289
Case D: Technical creativity, 289

Chapter Thirty-One
ENVIRONMENTAL EDUCATION IS A KEY TO
YOUR FUTURE 292
Scares that shouldn't have been, 293
Envirocomm education, 295
Questions to address, 296
Environmentalism goes to college, 297

Chapter Thirty-Two
MARKET ENVIRONMENTALISM: BETTER FOR
BUSINESS, BETTER FOR THE ENVIRONMENT 301
The Austrian connection, 302
Environmental regs: Less is more, 302
Market options, 303
Communication via the market, 304

Chapter Thirty-Three
RELATING TO GREEN CONSUMERS: THE
MARKETING MINEFIELD 306
Shades of green consumerism, 307
Take my definition, please, 309
The G-men's green guide, 310
The benefits of clean language, 311

Chapter Thirty-Four
GREEN GOSPEL: THE INDUSTRY DILEMMA OVER
RELIGION, SCIENCE, AND THE ENVIRONMENT 313
Spiritual crisis?, 313
Science vs. policy, 314
Bridges, not moats, 315

Part VI
CONCLUSION 317

Chapter Thirty-Five
SUSTAINABLE COMMUNICATION: GOING
GREEN, WITH GUSTO! 319
Starting over, and winning, 320
Three steps to the green, 324
Key ideas of this book, 325

Footnotes 329

Index 334

Preface

The purpose of this book is to help your organization, and you personally, to "get on the green"—that is, a positive place with regard to environmental awareness, action, and improvement. This process is called "greening" and is rapidly becoming a top priority of American business.

While the burden of correction, discovery, and innovation has been carried largely by big companies thus far, there is now a cascade of green action that involves companies of every size.

Our emphasis will be on environmental communication, which I shorthand to *envirocomm* both for convenience and to signal that this is a special and in many ways unique new form of communication and public relations. Envirocomm is the necessary partner to your organization's environmental compliance efforts, to enable you to encourage green awareness and commitment, and then to communicate with vital publics.

We will start with a look at the urgent factors and trends that are encouraging you to take a role in the greening of your organization, wherever you are in it, as a rising manager or as CEO—and the fact that it is in your best interest, as well as the firm's and the public's, for you to be an informed executive and a good communicator.

Hangups—or pollutants in the channels of green communication in your company—need to be removed or you will obstruct your own effort to succeed.

I will explain a seven-step model for a QUALITY management approach to envirocomm. We will see that envirocomm is a *process*, and we'll shed two lingering misconceptions that can seriously handicap you as you try to get on the green. One is that "public relations" is something that you engage in only when and/or after you are in the wrong. Instead I'll urge you to base your communication efforts on desired results and not solved problems, to engage in building public relationships on a consistent basis. The second misconception is that "publics" can be successfully treated as audiences to be addressed. To overcome this myth—and any fear you may have of dealing with "the public"—I'll invite you to consider your key publics as *customer-publics*, to be created and sustained.

All of this will be set within the context of sustainable development, a concept of balancing environmental and economic goals that is sweeping the world—and that is on the agenda of leading business organizations and governments.

Going Green is a practical guide for the business executive or manager who wants to learn what winners are doing and how to be successful in communicating your organization's commitment in the rapidly arriving Green World of Business.

E. Bruce Harrison

Acknowledgments

When I have been ready to learn about environmental public relations, teachers have appeared. Allan E. Settle, director of public relations at the Manufacturing Chemists Association in the 1960s, was among the first. In the summer of 1962, when *Silent Spring*[1] exploded on the chemical industry, I was tapped by Allan to help him and the industry's management put together a rational, responsive program.

The chemical business, and particularly the agricultural chemical business, had been hit. Rachel Carson's thesis was not only that pesticides would wreak unintentional harm—the hypothetical spring when birds would not sing—but also that because it *knew* of the potential damage of chemicals to wildlife and humans, the industry was *evil*. She used the image of the Borgias, cooking up poison.

Allan Settle, who had come to the association from Monsanto and was a master of high-risk, high-profile chemical public relations, took leadership on the issue, and gave me responsibility for staff operations.

He gave the job to me for three reasons. One, I was available. Two, he and his counselors, the industry's public relations committee, considered me capable. Three, I was naive and teachable.

I had joined the staff less than a year before, coming from health-and-safety work on Capitol Hill, and had just been named Manager of Community Relations—to energize industry plant community "good neighbor" programs (including an annual observance known as "Chemical Progress Week").

Now Allan was saying, with understatement I did not then appreciate, "This is a hot issue and it may be around a while."

When I didn't impress him enough with my grasp of the significance, Allan drew me a picture. He was in full agreement with one of our associates' comparison of this attack on the industry by the Carson book to that of the Japanese bombers at Pearl Harbor in 1941. "We weren't ready for this, but we've got to come back fast. If we don't take charge now, we're going to be buried, pure and simple."

I said I was ready to go and within a week was delivering a draft of the strategy, put together in consultation with the committee's strong public relations professionals—people like Glen Perry of Du Pont, Bud Smith of

Dow, Dan Forrestal of Monsanto, Art Northwood of Shell Chemical, Bud Lane of Goodrich-Gulf, and Dick Moore of W. R. Grace.

For the new job, Allan invented a new title—Manager of Environmental Information, perhaps the first such title in corporate PR—and gave me three pieces of advice that I needed then and have never forgotten.

"Stay organized so you can find things fast and you don't forget anything." Allan had a system of putting things into three-ring notebooks —facts, documents, questions he received, questions he thought *could* be asked. I copied his system and use it to this day.

"Always stop after you've told the truth and you won't have to worry about what you've said and haven't said." Allan had been an Air Force information officer, and I had been the press secretary for a congressman, so we had both had had our share of talking too much and having to eat some extraneous words, so that advice hit home. I learned honesty is as important in the business world as anywhere else, and probably more so. In environmental communication, where confusion runs rampant, you stumble less if you stop when the facts run out.

"Go first class." Allan meant this in many ways—from travel (not so expensive in those days), to eating out, to producing a brochure or work paper. His rationale was that it only costs a little more—in money or attention or time—to do it right, and there's not only a lot more pleasure in quality than in expediency, *it also almost always pays off.* Quality work and a quality *attitude* turn time and money into an investment with a return.

Many times have I looked at the option of shortcut—whether to read that release again or to spend a few dollars more for a better printing job—only to recall Allan Settle's reminder to go for the first-class action.

It was also Allan Settle—a large, robust, optimistic man, whose life ended quickly when he was struck by illness while I was still at the association—who showed me that *taking charge is the only winning move after an attack.*

The chemical industry has the world's toughest job in public relations. It has to deal with public fears that are ignitable at will. While people absolutely require chemicals to live (every product is touched by chemistry; we ourselves are composed of chemicals), there is no end to the association of *chemical* to *danger*, and, therefore, no end to the communication challenge.

The industry's Responsible Care program is exemplary now, offering a practical, interactive means of building relationships with the key publics whose attitudes and actions affect the industry. The program is a commitment by companies to make environmental achievement a shared responsibility. The seeds for the modern program may have been sown when I was there in the early 1960s.

More than a decade after *Silent Spring* was published, Charlie Sommer, Monsanto's president, looked back on the forceful response made by his company and by the chemical association. "I've been asked in recent years whether Monsanto didn't overreact. At the time, it didn't seem so. Actually, I'm glad we spoke out. . . . [T]he major thing to remember is that the new era forced all companies to take a harder look at the way they and their products were impacting the quality of life. . . ."[2]

Industry has learned much about environmental public relations in the last quarter century. While some of the lessons have been, and may inevitably at times be, learned as the result of crisis—the tragedy of Bhopal in 1984 marking the extreme—most of the learning has come along a path of steady discovery, negotiation, and practical, enlightened management. The march of American business beyond mere environmental compliance and toward sustained, openly communicated progress owes much to the chemical process industry. When I think where the march started, I think of Allan Settle, my teacher. I am deeply indebted to him and to all my other teachers in the business community from whom I learned the lessons I now share in this book.

I am also indebted to all those who read portions of the manuscript and gave me advice, to those who responded to my inquiries (both formalized, such as the "greening executive survey" responses, and in conversation and letters), and to those who let me quote them and use their insights. Thank you, Frank Friedman, Harold Elkin, Charlie Sercu, Ernie Rosenberg, George Carpenter, Doug Wright, Jon Plaut, Ross Stevens, Norine Kennedy, Jim Rogers. I am grateful to the many chief executives from whom I have learned and who were generous in assistance as I prepared for this book: Robert Kennedy, Frank Popoff, Ed Woolard, Sam Johnson, Pete Silas, Reuben Mark, Al Dudley.

I want to thank the researchers, writers, and counselors of the E. Bruce Harrison Company for their dedication to this work, their belief in the value of capturing our experience and sharing our counsel, and their intelligence, patience, and extra hours put into this. This would not have been done without them. Thank you, Mary Mullins, Tom Prugh, Caroline Joyner, Jane Agate, Wade Gates, Anna McCollister, Bettina Lucas, Jim Plante, Brian Hertzog, Tim O'Leary. In addition, I drew freely on the advice and support given by Jeff Conley and Michael Petruzzello—and especially, my partner in all things, Patricia Harrison.

This has been a team effort. I take the blame for any mistakes and misinterpretations, but I give my mentors as well as my associates the credit for this book.

THE BIG GREEN
PICTURE

Chapter One

The Big Picture: Where You Are in the Green World of Business

You may be one of the many business executives who are asking now: How does my company—how do I *personally*—"go green" in the right way? How do I make the most of the time and money this is going to take? How do I avoid the problems that others have had? *If I'm getting into this game, what are the rules? What's in play? What's gone before that I need to know?*

Whatever the size of your operation—whether you're in manufacturing or a service business—and wherever you may be located or do business, you need to consider the reasons that business operations around the world are going green or are trying to respond to green conditions.

An international business executive, Stephan Schmidheiny, has given these reasons:[1]

- Customers are demanding cleaner products.

- Banks are faster to lend to companies that prevent pollution.

- Insurance companies are more eager to underwrite clean companies.

- Employees want to work for environmentally responsible companies.

- Green regulations are getting tougher.

- Clean companies are rewarded by relief from green taxes and charges, and by the ability to cash in tradable pollution permits.

You also need to know where your organization will sit in the new Green World of Business. What are the trends, the general conditions, and some of the impacts that may affect your organization in the immediate future?

THE GLOBALIZATION OF GREENING

The company going green today finds lots of company. Wherever it operates in the world, there is encouragement to operate with great regard for environmental effects. The level of tolerance for environmental degradation and the level of reward for environmental stewardship vary, but one condition is inviolable: There is no safe haven anywhere in the world for any polluter.

At levels consistent with local conditions, environmentalism has become institutionalized in governments in all nations, developed and developing. Green and growth are converging because government and commerce have come to accept the desirable political and social result of what is now called "sustainable development."

Greening has become a strategic political tool. Look at the NAFTA talks, where environmental issues were pushed onto center stage. Pollution became part of the agenda for negotiating a trade agreement. Or look at Europe. Current waves of green policy guidelines and legislation in the EC are part of a great game of catch-up. Britain is about to enact its first landmark pollution control act, near the same level of stringency as U.S. law. Germany looks to new energy taxes to pay for the cleanup of the filth acquired when that nation was united.

Eastern Europe is a classic case. As red moved out, green came in. The Czechs, Poles, and Hungarians immediately had to consider environmental moves that will help them qualify for trade in the upgreening European Community. Greening has become the lubricant to grease the machinery of government-sanctioned commerce.

GREENING IS AMERICANIZED

These worldwide developments follow the American model. Greening was able to get onto a fast track in the EC mainly because we have shown the way. EC green legislation pumped through the system in the last two years was greatly aided by principles and practices drawn from U.S. law and regulations.

Europeans are getting to know green policies such as "the polluter pays" and strict liability. The first links pollution and fines and opens the conceptual door to dealing in pollution credits. This is directly from the emissions-trading concept in the U.S. Clean Air Act amendments of 1990. Strict liability means that it may not be your fault, but somebody has to pay. Plaintiffs don't have to prove negligence—or even actual cause—for the defendant to be liable for cleanup. Compare this with our Superfund law for hazardous waste site cleanup.

These have been like swats with a two-by-four in waking up the business community in Europe. The trend is toward the American standard in many parts of the world, and it was this country that provided the most useful regulatory policy guidance when the documents were drafted at the United Nations Earth Summit in Rio in 1992.

International technology cooperation, with involvement of the U.S. government and American business, is hastening the spread of American know-how in greening.

BUSINESS OWNS GREENING

In the U.S. today, the green ball is in the court of corporate America.

Not only have many hundreds of chief executives and their senior business managers awakened to the fact that they have little or no choice, but in order to take the ball and run with it, they are convincing themselves and others that there is financial "green" in greening.

Part of the story is the success in marketing green products. Another part is the downside: the horror stories that show what can happen to the company that runs counter to the green concern that has matured in the U.S. An enforcement action, an accident or spill, or simply failing to communicate an environmental commitment has cost many an organization dearly in terms of both money and standing with various publics. In worst cases, executives have lost their jobs; some have gone to jail; others have had to appear in court or be questioned by government committees.

The larger picture discloses that executives of the major companies in this country are seeing the political, competitive, economic, and other values in taking charge of greening—or at least the part that controls their ability to perform successfully. They are realizing the benefits like those described by Schmidheiny.

"People expect the business community to make environmentally correct business decisions regarding products and processes," Samuel C. Johnson, the chief executive of Johnson Wax, told me as I was writing this book. "In many instances, the right environmental decision is the right decision for the bottom line as well."

At a great many U.S. companies, the chief executive or a very high senior officer has declared his or her personal commitment—and the company's—to a new green standard.

The forums are speeches, ads, publicity, policy statements. For counselors like me and public affairs people in many companies, the challenge used to be getting the attention of top brass. Not any more. Now the job is to channel the energy of the CEO in the right way.

GREEN FAILURE HAS BEEN CRIMINALIZED

Politicians and regulators have discovered that nothing gets the attention of a senior manager like the threat of doing time for environmental crime. A first-time environmental law violation will normally lead to jail time, says the head of the Justice Department's environmental division, referencing the current sentencing guidelines.[2]

In 1990, Justice Department environmental indictments totaled 134, up 30 percent from 1989. Four out of every five were against corporations and their executive officers. The department's conviction rate was 95 percent.[3]

It's the same story at EPA: A record number of environmental convictions in 1989. Half of these got jail sentences, and 85 percent of these actually went behind bars.

Civil penalties are huge; a total of $62 million was assessed last year. One company paid $7.5 million for a hazardous waste violation.

Jail time is increasingly common. A former vice president of a Missouri firm was sentenced to five years in prison for signing her name to a false report to the EPA.[4] A manager in Ohio thought he was acting reasonably during a flooding emergency caused by a downpour but a judge said he violated Ohio's waste law by failing to evaluate excess rainwater on top of a waste cell. He had pumped the rainwater into a creek. It caused no pollution, but the procedural violation got him a year in jail.

Bad publicity is rampant and damaging. Negative news stories almost always accompany enforcement actions. And there is more green news coverage, with more reporters and more media outlets—broadcast and print. Every newspaper or TV station looks for a green story that can be localized. Trials in the court of public opinion are obviating the need for prosecution—and eroding the option of defense—at the bar of justice.

GREENING MEANS GOOD NEWS, TOO

That's one set of trends impacting the situation as you consider going green. On the more positive side, companies and executives are seeing the good news in greening.

Organizations are developing a new green mentality. They are seeing green costs as investments that can eventually provide a profitable return. Maybe they have to treat their ROIs more elastically, looking beyond a return in the next quarter or even in the next year or two. Certainly they must quantify the costs of not going green with the costs of doing so. But when they look ahead and see that they won't be competitive, that their products may not be acceptable, that they may even be driven out of business in a few years without a strong, deep foundation of environmental responsibility—then the economic value of a green management mentality becomes more and more obvious.

Positioning in future world markets, to say nothing of the U.S. market, where government is providing a level green playing field, will require taking responsibility for transcending mere environmental compliance. There's a new green mentality in business. You can see it in commitments to *150-percent-plus* compliance and to zero pollution.

People in engineering and operations are thinking the same as the people in the regulatory community: Pollution is inefficient. Waste is a symptom of a poor operation.

When both engineers and regulators tell CEOs that story, you can understand why they move to learn all they can about greening. This explains the application of Total Quality Management (TQM) to environmental operations in manufacturing and the increasing number of recognitions given to high-level executives for environmental achievement.

THE DEATH OF A MOVEMENT

Finally, there's this: Getting on board with environmentalism is important because *there isn't any other train coming*. Not soon, anyway.

The American brand of environmentalism—an activist movement that began in the early 1960s, roughly when the use of pesticides was attacked in the book *Silent Spring*—has slowed down as a vehicle operating outside the institutions of America.[5] In a sense, this style of environmentalism died; it succumbed to success over a period roughly covering the last 15 years.

Here are the four key points at which the American, attack model of environmentalism slowed and stopped:

1. The presidential election of 1976. It began on November 2, 1976. This was the day that Jimmy Carter was elected president, helped into office by green activists. Shortly thereafter, representatives of these successful environmentalists became bureaucrats in Washington.

President Carter, a self-styled environmentalist himself, legitimated the movement. By helping to elect him, the environmental activists cemented their permanent government role. Afterwards, some went into politics, some even went to work for business. But few went back to the environmental movement after the Carter years in quite the same way as they had started. Those who did return did not find the movement quite the same as it had been.

The organizations themselves had changed. They were no longer the lean, mean, up-from-the-streets, risk-taking, reckless, and often rag-tag activists of the 60s and 70s. They were more polished, more knowledgeable about direct-mail marketing and moving in places of influence.

Environmentalists still spurred the media and politicians through activism, but the movement had arrived and was increasingly managed like a business.

2. Passage of the Clean Air Act Amendments of 1990. In November 1990, I sat in the East Room of the White House and watched President Bush sign into law new amendments to the Clean Air Act. With the stroke of a pen, the President placed environmental cleanup and enhancement on an unprecedented high level—higher than anywhere else in the world.

The historic Clean Air amendments were the result of more than a decade of compromise among government, environmentalists, and industry. It was the most convincing signal that the business community now embraced environmental protection, that *it* was to become the managing partner of the business of greening in America.

Everywhere business was making proactive green moves, including environmental policy statements, compliance-plus goals, high-tech solutions, and partnering with government and activist groups.

Environmentalists and businesspeople, as types, began to resemble each other a little.

3. Second World Industry Conference on Environmental Management. In the evolving death of the environmental movement, it was institutionalized, then accepted and, in April 1991, at the Second World Industry Conference on Environmental Management (WICEM II), it was given a new name: sustainable development.

Sustainable development is, even after years of debate, a theoretical concept. It's the green grail. It means growth plus greening, or greening plus growth. The definition depends much on where you live. Developing nations see sustainable development as economic strategy: using green concerns as leverage to boost their economies. Industrialized countries see it as a strategy for integrating very high environmental standards with highly competitive economic conditions. They have to make sure they can stay viable in their markets while they are reaching new green heights.

At WICEM II, 750 participants—governments from around the world, as well as business and industry, with the strong involvement of American CEOs (Frank Popoff of Dow Chemical was the cochairman)—all focused on the need for business to move aggressively on global greening.

And they decided that sustainable development was the goal that would get private and public interests pointed in the same direction. Out of this came *the drive to adopt an international business charter on sustainable development.*

CEOs Popoff of Dow, Edgar S. Woolard, Jr., of Du Pont, Paul O'Neill of Alcoa, Robert D. Kennedy of Union Carbide, and Pete Silas of Phillips Petroleum led the way in making a commitment that meets—and I believe exceeds—the most progressive agendas pushed by environmental activists over the last quarter century.

The concept of sustainable development is being interpreted by business and is being woven into the American business system's approach to greening.

4. The Earth Summit.   The 1992 Earth Summit in Rio de Janeiro was history's largest gathering of heads of state. They came to talk global greening, sign agreements, and begin to set up the bureaucratic machinery for putting it into practice. The institutionalizing process is now global.

The United Nations Conference on Environment and Development (UNCED) showed the world what the biggest and most progressive corporations are doing and what they plan, by way of setting green benchmarks for everybody else.

The fact is that while the Earth Summit was nominally devoted to putting the planet on the path to sustainable development, the world business community has gone ahead and blazed the trail. And U.S. businesses are leading the way.

As a concept, sustainable development has become ubiquitous. More than 1,000 companies have signed the Business Charter on Sustainable Development since it was introduced at WICEM II. These companies realize, as Schmidheiny, chairman of the Business Council for Sustainable Development, said at the International Chamber of Commerce Industry Forum prior to the Earth

Summit, that "business excellence and environmental concern . . . cannot be separated. . . . *Tomorrow's winners will be those who make the most and the fastest progress in improving their eco-efficiency* [emphasis added]."

MESSAGE RECEIVED

This message has been heard loud and clear in America. Union Carbide CEO Robert Kennedy, for example, said at the ICC forum that "some of the most innovative thinking on sustainable development is going on today within the business community. . . . Monsanto, 3M, Du Pont, AT&T, my company, and a host of others are working toward 'closed loop' manufacturing, a process that produces absolutely no discharges."

If there is a manufacturing philosophy more sustainable than that, I can't conceive it.

U.S. companies have a lead in this race because we've been waging the world's most aggressive war on pollution for three decades now. But the traffic in green ideas and policies is global. Kennedy's statement above is evidence of the fertility of ideas such as total-life-cycle responsibility for products and processes, which are rapidly becoming the international ideal.

And just as the traffic moves geographically, it moves hierarchically as well. Ideas that spring from the executive suites at large multinationals and become embodied in laws and regulations sooner or later begin to affect businesses of all sizes. Where clean-air legislation first targeted huge factories with belching smokestacks, now it's looking hard at neighborhood bakeries and the corner dry cleaner.

FROM TOP-DOWN TO BUBBLE-UP

U.S. business is also on the cutting edge when it comes to the evolution from green command-and-control techniques (rules imposed from the top down) to voluntary standards.

The process began with the Emergency Planning and Community Right-to-Know Act of 1986, which unleashed a flood of data about company operations to regulators, the public, and advocacy groups. At first it fed adversarial relationships, but it also created opportunities for dialogue and enabled progressive companies to connect with key customer-publics in ways that build support for mutually agreeable green progress.

It's this proactiveness in environmental management—Jon Plaut of Allied-Signal calls it "bubble-up"—that has given businesses some green running room. Commitments to internal audits, environmental education, and responsible disclosure help obviate imposed rules. Everybody wins: A program such as the EPA's 33/50 plan, in which companies pledge to help meet a national goal of reducing toxic releases 33 percent in 1992 and 50 percent by the end of 1995, relieves all the players of the odious, burdensome, and expensive machinery of bureaucratic regulation—and gets the job done better.

THE INTERNATIONAL STORY SO FAR

UNCED showcased two vehicles that carried the message of business's green proactivity to the world, even if—thanks to the 8,000 journalists who generally missed this most important story of the event—the world hasn't really heard it clearly yet.

The first vehicle was the Business Council on Sustainable Development mentioned earlier. It was created by UNCED Secretary General Maurice Strong and led by Stephan Schmidheiny and about 50 handpicked CEOs of major businesses and industries from around the globe. Its primary product was a book on sustainable development practices, *Changing Course: A Global Business Perspective on Development and the Environment.*[6] It is full of green success stories, too numerous to detail here, from companies of every stripe in every region of the world.

The second vehicle was the International Chamber of Commerce's Industry Forum, held the week before UNCED officially began. More than 400 businesses from six continents gathered to review progress toward sustainable development and to outline future challenges. The meeting noted some specific achievements:

- The ICC's Business Charter on Sustainable Development with its 1,000-plus signatories.

- The ICC's International Environmental Bureau book unveiled at Rio, *From Ideas to Action*, which provides a look at a year's international business progress toward fulfilling the ICC Charter.[7]

- A new UN Environment Program effort based on the Chemical Manufacturers Association's Responsible Care Program for local community awareness and emergency response.

- The Global Environmental Management Initiative's new self-audit, which helps companies measure their progress toward environmental protection objectives.

- ICC collaboration with UNEP on overseeing business progress on the charter.

- Public-private partnerships for environmental protection, such as the EPA 33/50 program.

HAVING WRIT . . .

So the green scene is dynamic. Top businesses worldwide, but especially in the United States, are charging ahead with plans for getting on the green and staking out the environmental-responsibility high ground. Their labors will inevitably set the mark for everyone else.

Smaller and mid-size businesses are more limited in resources than the Du Ponts and AT&Ts of the world, and thus may not always have to toe the same green line when it comes to performance. But any company that expects this wave of the future to quietly pass it by is in for a drenching. The world has changed and the handwriting—the road map, even—is on the wall for all to see. A global commitment to sustainable development and acting locally to make it happen are the new obligations of all businesses.

As Ross Stevens of Du Pont put it, clearly what went on at the Earth Summit defined a whole new world—a milestone in human history.

The challenge to any company is to communicate in a way that is compatible with the dominant, global theme of sustainable development, and that is integrated with the company's mission and its own specific operations, markets, and stakeholders.

If total-quality principles can be applied to environmental performance, how can communication also be made continuous (and continuously improving)? If companies can link to the principles of sustainable development, can communication be put to work to support this linkage?

Obviously, I believe the answers are available to these questions and I try to put them forward in this book.

The approach I suggest is what I call *sustainable communication*, which is a results-driven process for creating and sustaining relationships with customer-publics. It is continuous, open, interactive, and consistent. Its values are understanding, concern, and commitment.

I try to show in this book how the company can get on the green—that is to say, the place where you can score through involvement with the public—through this *sustainable communication* process.

As the environmental movement, as an external activist force, has changed, so has environmentalism inside the business community. Corporate environmentalism is now more lively than external activist environmentalism, I believe, and this trend will continue to grow.

Going green—or *greening*—is an implementation process. Getting on the green—or winning in your relationships with publics—is a business strategy that is in the company's as well as the public's interest.

Chapter Two

How To Shift to a Winning Green Attitude

The chief executive of Exxon had no time to prepare for the hot public scrutiny his company got when the tanker *Valdez* spilled its cargo of oil.

The CEO of Pennwalt experienced what I would consider an executive nightmare; having to stand up in open court to be excoriated by a judge because of an environmental incident involving his company.

And the head of Hooker Chemical, years after the devastating experience of Love Canal, looked back with remorse. He had listened too long to the lawyers who told him the company was in the clear—and he missed the chance to deal with public opinion.

Any of us can look back at a bad situation and learn from it. We can review our strategy (if we had one!) and see what worked and what didn't. We can almost always find ways that we *could* have improved the situation, if we had had the chance, if we had been in charge sooner or better, *if we had been prepared.*

Looking back is instructive, since hindsight is always 20/20. But this book is about looking ahead.

Senior management in any company today, large or small, is in real need of a map of Green World. With environmental requirements high and with public expectations even higher, the company executive wants to know: How do I move ahead, doing the *right* things—balancing the double green factors of environment and money—and avoiding the sand traps?

This book draws on real-world examples and the experience of real executives to help you improve your *foresight.* Getting on the green is not easy, but it's not that hard, either, because a lot of people are doing it.

Good green communication—the open, two-way exchange between parties with interest in a specific environmental matter (the process I call *envirocomm*)—is a vital part of positive green positioning, or placing the business person and the company squarely on the public-interest green.

GOING GREEN IS A HABIT, NOT A HORMONE

If you are an executive in a company that hopes to succeed anywhere in the world in the 1990s, you need to understand two things about the environment:

One, that it's an issue that is not going away. It is firmly rooted in politics, public policy, cultures, and free enterprise.

The chart on page 17 shows how far the environmental legal structure has developed since the River and Harbors Act was passed in 1899. Only eight more environmental laws were passed in the next 70 years. But after the 1964 passage of the Wilderness Act, the curve takes off and climbs like a mountain goat, with the enactment of dozens of statutes.

That's what entrenches environmentalism so deeply and ensures it a strong voice in the nation's affairs.

The second thing you should understand about the environment is that it is now mainly a *business* issue—some call it the #1 business issue of the decade—for at least two reasons.

First, *the cost of environmental compliance is now about $115 billion a year, and could rise to $200 billion by 2000.* About 80 percent of that is absorbed directly by the private sector. Ultimately, of course, consumers and taxpayers will get the bill for America's extraordinary, world-leading green laws.

Second, *business management is primarily responsible for the way the environment as an issue is perceived and the way it is handled.*

To be successful in business, from now to 2000 and beyond, you must be successful in environmental matters.

Environmental policy is climbing the corporate ladder to require the *continuous* attention of managers and executives all the way to the top.

No matter where you are in the organization chart, if you think of yourself as a manager, your success in the years just ahead will

FIGURE 2–1
Exponential Growth of U.S. Laws on Environmental Protection

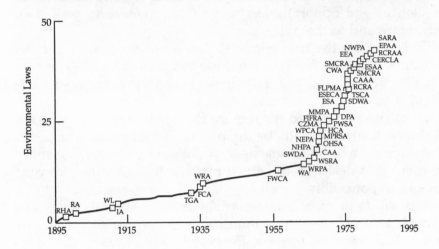

1899- River and Harbors Act (RHA)
1902- Reclamation Act (RA)
1910- Insecticide Act (IA)
1911- Weeks Law (WL)
1934- Taylor Graring Act (TGA)
1937- Flood Control Act (FCA)
1937- Wildlife Restoration Act (WRA)
1958- Fish and Wildlife Coordination Act FWCA)
1964- Wilderness Act (WA)
1965- Solid Waste Disposal Act (SWDA)
1965- Water Resources Planning Act (WRPA)
1966- National Historic Preservation Act (NHPA)
1968- Wild and Scenic Rivers Act (WSRA)
1969- National Environmental Policy Act (NEPA)
1970- Clean Air Act (CAA)
1970- Occupational Safety and Health Act (OSHA)
1972- Water Pollution Control Act (WPCA)
1972- Marine Protection, Research and Sanctuaries Act (MPRSA)
1972- Coastal Zone Managment Act (CZMA)
1972- Home Control Act (HCA)
1972- Federal Insecticide, Fungicide and Rodenticide Act (FIFRA)
1972- Parks and Waterways Safety Act (PWSA)
1972- Marine Mammal Protection Act (MMPA)
1973- Endangered Species Act (ESA)
1974- Deepwater Port Act (DPA)
1974- Safe Drinking Water Act (SDWA)

1974- Energy Supply and Environmental Coordination Act (ESECA)
1976- Toxic Substances Control Act (TSCA)
1976- Federal Land Policy and Management Act (FLPMA)
1976- Resource Conservation and Recovery Act (RCRA)
1977- Clean Air Act Amendments (CAAA)
1977- Clean Water Act (CWA)
1977- Surface Mining Control and Reclamation Act (SMCRA)
1977- Soil and Water Resources Conservation Act (SWRCA)
1978- Endangered Species Act Amendments (ESAA)
1978- Environmental Education Act (EEA)
1980- Comprehensive Environmental Response Compensation and Liability Act (CERCLA)
1982- Nuclear Waste Policy Act (NWPA)
1984- Resource Conservation and Recovery Act Amendments (RCRAA)
1984- Environmental Programs and Assistance Act (EPAA)
1986- Safe Drinking Water Act Amendments (SDWAA)
1986- Superfund Amendments and Reauthorization Act (SARA)

Source: National Academy of Engineering

depend in part on your understanding of greening as a business mechanism.

You must get ready personally for dealing with environmental challenges and opportunities, so you can manage to your own advantage and to the public's.

To be among the true winners, you must get in on the most advanced thinking that is being done by company executives and opinion leaders, and you must make sure your own green paradigm is adjusted for success.

Fortunately, this need not require too much work on your part. Technical matters will still be the purview of technical specialists. If you are not a technical manager, you won't need extensive study or training to deal with the green matters that will flow into your area of responsibility.

You *will learn* more and more about the technical areas—the same is true of legal and communication—as you go green. But this will be a natural process. Everybody will be doing it.

No, you won't need retraining and you won't be disqualified for green success because of your experience or talent. But your *attitude* can do you in.

If you have old-fashioned concepts and habits about public relations you may find yourself an alien in Green World.

If you are open to a new way of thinking—a habit of considering the positives of greening—you can run ahead of your competition and gain the encouragement of many publics.

Going green has much more to do with habits than with hormones.

BREAKING THE HABIT OF NEGATIVE MIND-SET

Green communication is so given to an "us versus them" scenario that, if you're a corporate executive, you can almost automatically fall into a defensive posture where you are trying to prove that you're not a villain.

It's a pernicious process. In your heart, you may start out believing you're in the right, with a good company and a good track record.

But then you start to look at the information you get from your own people—a problem the company had at an older facility years ago that you're still trying to solve, for example—and you undergo the constant bombardment of criticisms and accusations from people outside the company.

A lot of this, maybe most of it, is way off base—they've got the numbers wrong; it didn't happen that way; they don't know the whole story—but you also know that some of it has a kernel of truth that you could explain if you had to (and if they would let you).

And so you start to become logical and see both sides—or you become irritated or angry because of the unjustness of the criticism —and then you come home one day and for the umpteenth time there is a story in the paper that is negative, and your kid in school or your neighbor tells you what *they* heard about your company (or about companies in general)—and you either want to strike back or run away.

"Fix it!" the frustrated CEO may say to the environmental manager or the public relations person.

Unfortunately, that's not the end of it. Even if it seems to work for the moment, ordering others to "fix" the problem may be the most expensive, least effective, and shortest lived "solution."

As we'll discuss later in this book, executives in authority have many levels of legal and public responsibility that can't be delegated. The CEO who has to stand up in court and accept a verdict will certainly realize that he or she did not delegate the problem away—and that the answer is not flight or fight.

Both are off the green.

In an area with tremendous downside risk—companies can be badly wounded by the green sword—you find you have moved from a generally positive, or at least neutral, frame of mind to a negative, combative, or defensive mind-set.

When you are off the green, your competitors and antagonists may be very helpful—in ensuring that you don't get back on quickly. They may find it advantageous to keep you on the defensive, wearing the villain's hat.

ARE YOU A "GREEN" ANSWER?

I have a personal mission in counseling business executives, and that is to help them see that in environmental issues, as well as in many other areas concerning business and industry, business executives are part of the answer and not part of the problem.

No matter what anybody says, government and churches and activist groups don't actually solve the overwhelming majority of environmental challenges. Businesspeople do.

As everyone gets accustomed to Green World, this will be more true than ever. The technical know-how, the will to succeed, the ability to make a plan and follow through, the money and the way it is invested—all will come from the private sector.

Business will be one of the many sources of pollution—along with government, other people, and nature itself—but it will also be the leader in reducing *all* sources, preventing pollution, and sustaining environmental and economic development. Business will create the green tools.

This is under way and undeniable. Now businesspeople must make the mental leap to believe this inevitable state, and start to see themselves as part of the answer. Many are doing it. You need to know how to develop this mental greening.

Chapter Three

Mental Greening: The Habit of Thinking Like a Good Guy

When business executives ask me to coach them before a news conference or a speech, or to give them a warm-up or refresher course on presentation techniques, I always start by handing them a small card, which fits comfortably in the palm of your hand and looks like a business card. Printed at the top of the card are the following words:

WE ARE THE GOOD GUYS!

"Put this card in your pocket," I suggest to my executive friends, "and look at it whenever you feel challenged by any public on an environmental issue."

Let me use this card to coach you in the habit of thinking like a good guy. Obviously, this is not a cue card from which you read aloud. You won't win any points by saying aloud, "I am the good guy." This is not about arrogance but about standing.

The words on the card are to be felt within. They are a personal reminder to help you break the habit of starting on the defensive. They are your personal reminder that you have standing on the public-interest turf.

Because if you don't think you're a good guy, if you don't *believe* you're part of the answer and not part of the problem . . . well, there's a good chance you'll be fighting or defending more than you're communicating.

Later in this book, we'll talk about the objective of a *wise outcome* and the application of the Harvard negotiation project's very practical principles. For now, let's just focus on the point that the preconditioning required at this basic first step is one of being ready to communicate from a positive, confident, and *relaxed* frame of mind.

THE HABIT OF TAKING CHARGE OF YOUR EMOTIONS

When I help executives get ready for speeches, I have found most helpful the guidelines constructed by Dorothy Sarnoff, the actress who became a great coach of public speakers.[1] She developed a three-sentence exercise for mental preparation. The Sarnoff student was to repeat silently, before standing up, this mantra:

"I'm glad I'm here. I'm glad you're here. I know that I know . . ."

This is a good-guy mental adjustment. It's not flight or fight. It's a way to come to terms with where one is and what one is to do; to acknowledge that there may well be nonsupporting, doubting, even hostile people listening and judging; but to see this as an opportunity to communicate, to be "glad" for the opportunity.

The reason for the gladness is twofold:

(1) If "you" are here and I am here, at least we have the chance to look at the situation together. At least, for the moment, there are no potshots behind the back.

We have a chance, perhaps, of a lateral relationship.

(2) I have standing. I "know that I know," as Dorothy Sarnoff puts it, meaning that my information is my information; I know it; I believe in it; I am ready to share what I know with you because I think it may be helpful.

Green issues are sensitive and given to emotional communication. Your own emotions must be kept in check.

I have seen many business executives relax dramatically through the use of a silent attitude-adjusting device like this, ready for positive *envirocomm*.

VISUALIZE YOUR GREEN SUCCESS!

Great athletes and coaches have raised the "mental game" to a fine art. Some teams bring in consultants who teach visualization techniques.

Bruce Jenner prepared for the decathlon by thinking it through in advance. He said he visualized every part of the competition, every move and every muscle required. And he always ended his mental-preparation exercise by seeing himself crossing the finish line in that long race, circling the track in the stadium, hearing the cheers of the crowd.

Can you see yourself sometime in the future in one of the following situations?

- Presenting a paper with other representatives of business at a world conference on environmental management, leading toward a global green charter.
- Standing up at a press conference with some of your core customers and a formerly critical environmental group, announcing a packaging decision.
- Receiving an honor, along with fellow executives and employees, for your company's innovative success in recycling company and community waste.
- Sitting alongside fire fighters, city officials, and community neighbors as you draft the final stages of a local environmental emergency response plan.
- Hearing the verdict of a jury that has been convinced that the environmental class-action suit brought against your firm was unfounded and inconsistent with your performance and commitment.
- Participating in a working session of a high-level environmental advisory group with your fellow members from academia, environmental organizations, government, and the health profession.
- Being able to point to profits in key operations as the direct result of continuous environmental process improvement.

How does it feel, if you can imagine this happening to you? The business people *to whom each of these imaginings actually happened* will tell you it felt good. It felt the way you want to feel when you are part of the answer, a winner in Green World.

While I can't prove it, I would bet that some of the executives who lived the experiences sampled here had actually set their minds to these outcomes.

Robert Kennedy, the chief executive of Union Carbide, whose company suffered through the great tragedy of Bhopal and who resolved to rise from this tragedy and to gain new respect as an environmentally aggressive company, may well have visualized the situation in the first example.

That scenario occurred. It was a long, tough road, but Kennedy was there in Rotterdam in 1991 when, at the World Industry Conference on Environmental Management, he was one of the leaders in a business commitment to global environmental and economic sustainable development. I'd bet that Kennedy visualized an outcome like this, and that he's already set his sights on the next positive green milestone.

If you play golf or tennis, you know that mental preparation can help your game. There are books on mental golf and mental tennis. Some of the best skiers I know prepare for a good day on the slopes by thinking ahead; they use mental skiing before the physical action occurs.

Mental greening involves the habit of visualizing success in environmental matters. It's really more than foresight. It's a sort of *advance hindsight*—a way to think ahead to a desired outcome, so you can plan your moves to reach it.

The visualization need not be as grand-scale as some of the examples above. We are talking about a daily habit of practicing the positive art of seeing a successful finale to any environmental challenge. It can be a meeting with fellow workers, a financial commitment discussed with superiors, a newspaper interview, or a subpoena to testify before a government agency or to appear in court.

The important point is to break the habit of seeing a contentious, costly, long, or losing condition when the subject is green— and to build the habit that has a proven, uncanny way of raising the odds in your favor.

POSITIVE THOUGHT STARTERS

How do you get into the right frame of mind when you're trying to get on the green? I don't just mean during a crisis, but at any time at all: before a speech, before a board meeting, before you launch a project; when your company is planning a significant business move and the environment is involved; or simply when you are psyching up for another day of competitive challenges of all colors and shapes.

In this book are dozens of proven strategies and tactics to help you in mental greening. Here are a few thought starters, to put you on a positive path:

1. Think of green costs as investments. Look for the ROI. It may be farther out than you'd customarily like, but in Green World there are other cost considerations. Push your people to think differently about this. *Ask*: How can we make greening pay for itself over time?

2. Think of the interconnectedness. How are you part of the future already? Explore the sustainable-development idea of intergenerational equity—of doing it for the kids. Consider your connection to others—allies and challengers—through freely available computerized information. No latitude in dimension of time, space, or place.

3. Think of market advantage. Products vs. other products. Facilities vs. other facilities. Employees as a market. The political marketplace. Market positioning. Not necessary to always be the first, but to look at market data and not be so out of sync that you are hostile and disadvantaged.

4. Think of extension of corporate mission. How to extend basic values, this year's business strategy. Consistency, credibility.

5. Think of yourself on the same side of a picnic table with "victims"—with people who will be open to your ideas, concerns, and problems.

6. Think of a position—in a debate or an "us vs. them"—where your attitude is far removed from arrogance and apathy. You are reasoned, open, concerned, committed.

These are just flashes of light. Maybe some of them will mean something to you now—or later.

Taking charge of our emotions, seeing the road ahead clearly, getting our hands on the steering wheel and heading toward the outcome we want, as a way to maximize our advantage—these are, after all, typical behaviors for successful business executives, aren't they?

Why shouldn't this work when it comes to the environment? I can tell you that it does.

It can also help your frame of mind if you know you have begun a process with the intention of working cooperatively with others whose goals are similar. A good green policy statement, for example, is a comforting security blanket as well as a mat that welcomes open discussion.

Mental greening—attitude adjustment, purposeful self-conditioning, visualizing desired outcomes, and arming yourself with public-interest policies—can be the basis for greater success in your business and a more meaningful participation in physical, planetary greening.

If you are personally thinking on the green, you can now consider a practical system for green communication in your organization.

II

CUSTOMER-PUBLICS

Chapter Four

Get To Know Your Vital Customer-Publics

You won't get onto the green by "doing public relations" in the traditional sense.

In fact, I recommend that for the moment you forget entirely about "publics" and consider something you may know much more about—what it feels like to deal with customers or to be a customer.

In this chapter, we begin to explore the idea that a workable way of going green is to identify, and then create win-win relationships with, vital customer groups.

YOU CAN'T FOOL—OR PLEASE—EVERYBODY

The biggest trap in public relations is the seductive notion that you can achieve the nirvanic state of universal applause—when everyone loves you and approves of what you are doing.

That is a fantasy, dangerous in any business situation and anathema when it comes to the environment.

Greening involves so many sensitive subjects and people that it's virtually inevitable that you and your company will turn off, offend, or overlook some "public" group or individual at some time.

Focusing only on pleasing people—being eager to do everything others' way and fearful of any criticism—is not the way to get on the green. In the extreme, it's tantamount to dropping your mission and going out of business.

But focusing on creating customers—that is, attracting people to your side because you've plugged in to their interests—is to focus on future business opportunity.

The companies that are successfully establishing themselves on the green, with solid and positive environmental positions, are companies that have thought first about their corporate mission and then have found ways to modify first their mental attitude, and then their commitments, processes, and products, so that the mission and the public interest are more compatible.

They have not found it either necessary or desirable to satisfy all the people, all the time.

FORGET ABOUT PUBLICS; CREATE CUSTOMERS

Management writer Peter Drucker advanced the idea that the first goal of company management is to create customers. Nothing else matters—the goals of profitability, employee relations, quality, production goals, safety—if customers are not the focus, said Drucker in his big book on management.[1]

If customers don't come first, asked Drucker, what does? With customers, all the rest is possible. The *management* goal of creating customers makes possible the *operational* goal, whatever it may be. This idea can be applied to any organization.

Members of Congress must create customers (whom they call voters or constituents) to enable them to do their job. Legislating may well be the *operational* goal, but if the focus is on legislating and not getting re-elected (the *management* goal), the job disappears.

A newspaper must create customers (subscribers, readers, advertisers) so it can do its reporting and editorializing job.

An environmental group must create customers (members, donors, supporters) so it can stay in the greening business. The goal is not to green, but to ensure the wherewithal that enables it to green.

To summarize: The management goal—that of attracting people to the organization—gives the organization the ability to pursue its chief purpose. People will judge the operation by the demonstration of its purpose. But the organization will live or die on the effectiveness of the number one management function: creating customers.

YOU NEED SUSTAINABLE CUSTOMERS

To maintain a place on the green in the next decade, you will need to attract a sustainable core of people who believe as you do and who believe in you, when it comes to environmental action.

A lot of public relations counselors will talk to you about the publics you need to reach with your environmental message. You may hear about "delivery mechanisms" and "audiences" to "hit."

This is okay, up to a point. *Publics* and *reach* and the rest are useful terms of art in public relations and advertising, and they can have value in program strategy and tactics. But they can be sand traps when you're trying to get on the green.

Unless you're really careful, this orientation can mire you in egoism. You can become preoccupied with the "reaching" and delivery of the "message," and find yourself thinking you actually have publics, people waiting to hear from you, like an audience for a stage performance.

In fact, when it comes to the environment, the surveys confirm what you already know. *In general, people don't trust business.* They believe companies cause most of the pollution and that almost anybody is more trustworthy when it comes to green talk.

As the sustainable development era takes hold, the idea of reaching publics will have less and less relevance. The challenge is not to reach, but to relate.

Starting now, you must look at the kinds of relationships (customer relationships—in the sense that there is an offer and an acceptance involved) that will get you on the green and keep you there.

As your organization goes green, you will need more kinds of *customers*—sustainable *relationships*—than you or anyone else in business needed in the past.

WHAT KIND OF CUSTOMERS WILL YOU NEED?

By taking a new look at publics as customers to be created and sustained, we can see that most companies need several kinds:

• Consuming customers who buy products and services, and give you sales revenue, reputation, referrals.

FIGURE 4–1
Recasting "Publics" as "Customers"

"Public"	As Potential "Customer" They May:	
(E) Employees	Buy in to your value system...	Build and support your green performance and reputation.
(S) Suppliers	Buy in to your value system...	Give you resources and spread your green reputation "upstream."
(P) (R) Politicians, Regulators	Buy in to your perspective...	Provide a more level playing field for your green performance.
(M) Media	Buy in to your perspective...	Give you a fair representation of your green record, commitment, and views.
(N) Neighbors	Buy in to your values and perspective...	Support & partner in your green performance and build your green reputation.
(T) (D) (R) Transporters, Distributors, Retailers	Buy in to your values and commitment...	Extend your green influence and reputation "downstream."
(A) Activists	Buy in to your record and commitment...	Support & partner–or give you a fair opportunity with your other "customer–publics."

Source: © E. Bruce Harrision Company 1992

• **Employee customers who buy values, and give you output, service, support.**

• Stock customers who buy stock, and give capital, support, referrals.

• Supplier customers who buy into the company's production and delivery systems, and give you resource support, reputation.

• Neighbor customers who buy your community/family values, and give you reputation, standing in the community.

• Political customers who buy your public values, and give you government support (or level playing field).

• Media customers who buy your news and insights, and give you fair representation to their readers and viewers.

In here are the vital 20 percent of your publics.

FIGURE 4–2
Vital 20% of Customer-Publics

Source: © E. Bruce Harrison Company 1992

The attitudes, expression of opinions, and decisions (small and large) made by people in these *customer-public* categories will determine your organization's success or lack of success in the arriving Green World of Business.

Chapter Five

Make Your Communication Process-Driven, Not Problem-Driven

Former Governor of Louisiana Earl Long once said to his public relations man, "I don't need you when I'm *right*!"[1]

Unfortunately, public relations professionals are sometimes considered to be fixers, problem-solvers, people to call in for protection when the going gets tough.

Of course, the public relations adviser or officer is needed when there is trouble and the company (or politician or public figure) is either "wrong" or is *in* the wrong—that is to say, off the public-support green.

If the "problem" has to do with the company's environmental record, performance, or public perception, the public relations adviser has an important role on the team with technical specialists, lawyers, and other advisers.

The PR adviser has current media contacts, experience in responding to interest and inquiries from various publics, and the ability to write and to deliver information in a clear, usable form. No question! These are valuable skills in solving communication problems, routine or during urgent, unfavorable circumstances. But these are only the minimum skills of the public relations professional engaged in envirocomm.

PR professionals are often underutilized when it comes to environmental communication. Your envirocomm team can go beyond reactive tactics. You can get, and should expect, from them strategies for creating and sustaining public relationships that will keep you on the green in the sustainable-development era.

YOU NEED A WELLNESS PROGRAM, NOT AN EMERGENCY ROOM

If you only scramble to communicate when problems come up, you deny yourself the benefit of *avoiding* them. It's like the doctor who only deals with patients when they get sick and never gets the chance to help people prevent illness.

You should expect from your public relations or communication capability some of the same quality management characteristics you put into your technical pollution compliance and prevention capabilities.

Qualified public relations people have strategic, planning, and operational skills that should be a continuing part of management's greening decisions and practices.

Envirocomm is the partner of the organization's technical program. As with the engineering and operational commitment to achieve and extend beyond compliance, envirocomm shifts the emphasis from problems to *process*.

BENEFITS OF A PROCESS APPROACH TO COMMUNICATION

Think of the benefits of a process that continuously communicates with core publics: It can provide an early warning system to head off (or make it easier to deal effectively with) public relations problems; it can provide ideas and feedback on your environmental initiatives and partners or allies in other green initiatives or issues; and it can save you money by helping to ensure that you make your green moves efficiently and with public support.

Envirocomm—results-driven, not problem-centered—will continuously *improve* your communication to build better internal and external customer-public relationships, and it will reinforce your *technical* program.

If your organization believes in total quality management, you will not want to overlook the importance of applying this concept to green communication along with the other company greening areas.

Patrick Jackson, publisher of the respected weekly newsletter *PR Reporter*, observes that total quality management is largely a communication function, and can benefit from the skills of public relations.

In my opinion, the organization's overall success in greening—whether or not management has adopted a formal TQM approach—depends on a quality approach in public relations and communication.

ENVIROCOMM IS AN ACTION AVENUE

Unless you want your environmental policy to gather dust on a bookshelf somewhere, your environmental program must be evolutionary, benefiting from feedback-driven adjustments. *That suggests you should consider a continuous-process environmental communication program.*

Envirocomm contributes strongly to the creation and maintenance of the public relationships that will make or break your overall greening effort. It protects you and your organization from isolation. Standing alone is the opposite of standing on the green. Isolated, you are vulnerable; allied with some core publics, you escalate your odds of being part of win-win situations.

In the sustainable development era, business will be asked not only to solve its own environmental problems but also to help others solve theirs.

By beginning now to exchange information and points of view with critical publics, you will be better positioned to be part of the answer to green challenges, not viewed from the outside as part of the problem.

THE QUALITY MODEL

Your green communication program must continuously create and sustain public relationships, so that your environmental commitment is not unilateral and therefore unlikely to enjoy the necessary public support.

It is essential in envirocomm to be market-oriented. You must think first and continuously about the primary customer-publics your organization needs to satisfy as you green up.

As the result of my firm's work with greening companies and organizations, we have been able to recognize and develop the essential steps of the market-oriented, envirocomm process. There are seven steps, and they can be remembered easily as the Q-U-A-L-I-T-Y Communication Model.

QUALITY Communication Model

Q = Quantify (carefully count) your key customer-publics, internal and external.

U = Understand their points of view as well as you understand your own.

A = Ask questions that show your interest and draw out their questions.

L = Listen attentively to their answers as well as their questions.

I = Interpret this information so you can initiate appropriate actions.

T = Take charge of the communication process in a way that empowers your publics.

Y = You, your organization, and your management have key roles to play.

Chapter Six

The QUALITY Model To Make Envirocomm Work For You

Let's start by removing two communication pollutants. You will clog up the envirocomm process if you're stuck with the notions that (a) you have to communicate with 100 percent of all possible publics; and (b) that you are actually "talking *to* the press" instead of *through* media *outlets.*

Now here is the seven-step, QUALITY process that can make your environmental communication pollutant-free:

Q: QUANTIFY YOUR "PUBLICS"

The *Q* in our model reminds you to break the mind-set of monolithic monologues. You need to transact with *specific* individuals—or groups of individuals—and that means identifying them. This is the person-recognition step. Beware the old notion that anybody can ever again stand on the mountaintop and hand down chiseled stone tablets to the masses. In the new green world, this is a waste of tablets, time, and money.

Instead, quantify your "audiences." Count and catalogue them, as you would customers, which in fact they are. Envirocomm means focusing on your core constituencies—orienting your communication at the outset toward your "customer-publics," the roughly 20 percent of the possible publics whose actions and attitudes can most directly affect your ability to succeed.

The envirocomm QUALITY process starts, and lives, by detailed and accurate lists. By category, you need names, addresses, and, in some cases (certainly with regard to the news media), telephone numbers of people with whom you will have contact and dialogue. (See Chapter Four for suggested categories.)

Go for the details. Don't generalize about publics or the media. If you're selling ideas, you need to know precisely to whom you are selling. If you're going to create sustainable relationships, you may well find yourself needing to know specific individuals by name. That requires counting noses.

As for the media, they are not an audience but a collection of outlets. (The only way you might be "talking *to* the press" would be if you owned that particular news media organization and you were communicating with the employees.)

Mental greening requires you to see yourself talking *through* the press. Think of your media list as a pipeline to customer-publics. As we discuss in Chapter Ten, this is not a pipeline you own, and it's a channel subject to its own forms of pollution, but it's the pipeline that's available. You will need to identify the right pipelines, by category, names, and numbers.

U: UNDERSTAND "WHAT THEY WANT"

An industry executive stood at the window of a conference center in Chicago a few years ago, watching a street rally against a public policy position taken by his industry. Frustrated and a little resentful, he said to an associate, "I don't understand them. What do they want us to *do*?"

A bit of advice attributed to St. Francis of Assisi—*Seek first to understand, not to be understood*—makes sense when it comes to green communication.

In order to move surefootedly onto green turf, you need to understand:

- your company's current and potential environmental risks and opportunities; and
- the attitudes and potential actions of publics that affect your ability to perform.

Envirocomm can help break the organizational fixation on problems, such as crises, environmental incidents, or shortcomings that are to be avoided, explained, or "managed."

A problem-driven communication approach turns the company public-relations function into a tactical response to blowups.

Since the goal of a continuous-process approach is to build positive relationships with people and groups identified as core publics, public relations becomes a *strategy*—part of an overall management process that creates answers and helps keep you positioned to deal with problems.

You can build these positive relationships only if you know what "they" want. You need a current reading of the changing expectations, desires, concerns, and fears of the various publics vital to your organization.

Mental greening suggests that you see envirocomm as you would see the marketing and sales process if you were creating a customer for a product.

Obviously, you can only sell the product that people decide to buy. Most customers make the buying decision based on the product's potential to fill a need. Successful salespersons know that needs—or benefits that satisfy needs—fall into four predictable categories: pride, pleasure, profit, or protection. The sales process actually starts with good market research into potential customer needs or desires in one of these areas. This provides understanding that leads to the sale. (See the First Brands example in Chapter Twenty-Three.)

Your publics are like customers. You will make a "sale" or a productive connection if you can first understand and then address the needs of a given customer-public.

A: ASK QUESTIONS

To win in Green World, you need honest information from people whose opinions are most important to you: the vital 20 percent, the core customer-publics that you have identified and quantified.

The best way to get that information is to go to them and ask questions.

Al Ries and Jack Trout have pointed this out in their book, *Bottom-Up Marketing*.[1] They suggest "going down to the front, into the minds of customers and prospects" and asking *what* and *why* questions, to provide a basis for sales tactics. (We deal more with this—asking questions as well as listening to the questions that are asked—in Chapter Four.)

For now, let the *A* in QUALITY remind you to ask your very important publics *What?*, *Why?*, and *How can we do better with you?*

But there's an earlier stage in this part of the QUALITY communication process—and that is for the questioner to answer some questions.

Unlike the protest-riled executive who resentfully asked, "What do they want?" the successful executive in the sustainable development era will be asking positive, green-mentality questions like these:

"With regard to pollution and the environment, what do my customer-publics need? What do they value? What do they know about our organization? What do they really know about environmental issues, especially those that relate to us? Where do they learn what they 'know?'

"If we commit to a particular green strategy or program, will we get public support? Will our own managers and employees be satisfied and supportive of what we do?

"Exactly how much should we even say about our green rollout? What's the prospect for it to be challenged, and who will do the challenging? *Will it get us on the green or will it put us in the rough?*"

Questions like these make sense if the company has decided that its commitment to greening or sustainable development requires openness and partnerships. The questions put to vital stakeholders must show them you care, that you are committed to a positive outcome, and that you want to be part of a solution *they* can support.

With this self-interrogation, you haul yourself down off the mountaintop and into the market, where you can begin to build honest, lateral relationships with customer-publics.

L: LISTEN AGGRESSIVELY

Tom Peters has said that at least two pages of any strategy document ought to be titled The Listening Strategy.

FIGURE 6–1
7-Step Q.U.A.L.I.T.Y. Model

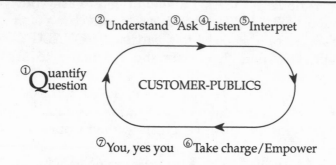

Sustainable Communication

Source: © E. Bruce Harrision Company 1992

You can't form a communication strategy until you have listened. General George Patton, asked about his battle strategy, replied, "I never start with a strategy. I start by going to the front and looking around." He needed first to know about battlefield conditions.

The conditions in your customer-public marketplace will tell you much, if you know how to listen.

Peters says his listening strategy would include questions for management like these:

How are we going to listen? How are we going to get feedback? How can we use listening to gain a clear-cut strategic edge?

The sustainable development era will still have need for business spokespersons, but the greater need will be for business *hear*persons. Ask questions and listen to the answers, and listen to the core concerns behind the questions raised by others.

Listening will give you information to process. Just as important, it will show that you care.

Your customer-publics are no different from your traditional customers. They will reject you more often for indifference than for any other reason.

Your intentions may be lofty; your commitment positive; your information accurate; your message well-structured and timely— but if you are perceived by any customer-public as uncaring or indifferent, you will fail to build the relationship you both need.

People don't want to hear from experts; they want to hear from people who care. Put another way, *people won't care how much you know until they know how much you care.*

I: INTERPRET THE DATA

The *I* in our model stands for *interpret* but it could also remind you to "incubate" what you've learned so far.

Before moving to the strategic action steps, you will need to sort through the data you've accumulated.

If you are a rising young manager, or if you are a public relations professional accustomed to the essential matter of analyzing public-opinion information, or if from your position in the organization you are frequently called on to evaluate test results and construct best- and worst-case scenarios, then you should have no trouble doing this.

All you have to do is look at what you've learned, compare it with your company's mission—including the corporate greening mission—and come up with an overall strategy and some tactical options to try in the customer-public marketplace, with corrections to be made as you get feedback.

But if you're up near the top of the ladder, if you are in fact the CEO, I predict that this step will be more than a little difficult for you.

Survey after survey shows that chief executives trust very few people to give them advice. More often than not, a CEO will say, when it comes to making a decision, "I trust my gut."

I take nothing away from the reliability of gut-instinct decisions. I've been running a business for a long time, and I make them myself.

But business instincts are made, not born. We come to rely on gut instincts because, over time, we have stored up the experiences that we value for the lessons they have taught. We remember *personally* what worked and what didn't. We tap into that carefully developed, personal core of belief every time we make a decision.

We rely on our gut instincts because we have *educated* guts. Now, in the sustainable development era, we need to reeducate them.

The business of business will more and more require executives to put aside traditional, comfortable, even *successful* gut instincts, such as "A cost must deliver an offsetting economic benefit," or "An ROI must be in this year's timeframe," or even "In our free-enterprise system, a lot of information is highly proprietary and must be kept confidential" (for example, an internal environmental inspection is a management tool for self-correction only).

Trusted experience, stored in our guts, now must deal with what our minds are telling us about Green World.

In Chapter Three we talk more about the green mentality required in an era when a company's technical data, once the province of engineers and operations people, is now available to all employees, neighbors, competitors, newspapers, and groups whose main purpose in life is to challenge business.

A shift in gut instincts is necessary in a Green World where agitating publics tell you to put environmental considerations ahead of economic facts, where competitors say they are *doing* this, and where some are showing how to be successful at it.

When stockholders, churches, government, and business employees are going green together and are ready to condemn the business that seems to be off the green, it's time to give our guts a crash course in the new realities.

So incubation is in order and is of greatest importance to the veteran, high-level executive. This should be the breakthrough step (what some have called the "Aha!" point) where you adjust your thinking, and in time, your gut, in response to the valuable new information now in your hands.

T: TAKE CHARGE

Now it is time for action—or, more accurately, interaction.

The *Q, U, A, L,* and *I* steps have brought you to the *creation of public relationships*—the heart of envirocomm.

Now you and your organization can establish the sustainable communication process that makes those relationships beneficial.

Envirocomm is an active process on three levels. It is *proactive*, in that it takes the initiative in relationship construction and maintenance. It is *reactive*, in that it responds to and comes to terms with the actions (and attitudes that presage actions) of customer-publics.

And perhaps most important, it is *interactive*. This means that the communication climate is open and information can flow freely in all directions. You go beyond dialogue—one-to-one communication —to *multilogue*, or communication in which a number of two-way transactions are handled simultaneously, with the goal of harmonizing perspectives and organizing partnerships.

An example of this process is the Responsible Care program pioneered by the U.S. chemical industry, in which local groups of people from all walks of life come together to discuss environmental conditions and problems, to plan cooperatively for handling environmental emergencies, and to implement agreed-upon programs (see Chapter Twenty-six).

Responsible Care is a best-practices case of the sustainable development principle of balancing green and growth needs, recognizing that there are interregional and intergenerational equities to consider.

Your green communication process must now be made evergreen —a continuous operation that is constantly improving and self-enriching.

Y: YOU, YES YOU

The "radio station" you should be most tuned in to is WIIFM— What's In It For Me?

The public relations professional who has examined the envirocomm process up to this point will see the benefits in it, and may already have something like it in operation. If so, go on to the next chapter; you already know what's in it for you.

If you are not "in public relations" (i.e., you are not responsible for this management function in your organization), you may be saying, "Well, this seems to make sense, but I'm not going to take on PR personally."

Without flogging the truth that you probably have heard a million times—that *everyone* in the organization has a role in creating public relationships—let's just summarize some interesting benefits of an effective envirocomm process:

- It offers a practical, measurable system of communication support for your company's technical environmental compliance and risk-avoidance strategy.
- It gives you a mechanism for anticipating and managing the terms, timing, and tactics of public interest projects and issues. You get a handle on situations before they turn into conflicts and litigation, and you can sort out what public programs make sense.
- It provides a competitive edge in marketing and sales by systematically focusing attention on process, markets, and vital customer-publics.
- And finally, it equips you superbly to be the spokesperson for your organization on green issues, whether it's talking informally to family and friends or on the record to media, industry peers, or government. Envirocomm is designed to feed you the information you need and to guide you in its use.

Chapter Seven

Turning On the Power of Employees

Someone asked Max De Pree, the author of *Leadership Is an Art*, to describe the role of a leader. De Pree said it was similar to that of a schoolteacher who repeats the basics day after day. "When it comes to vision and values," De Pree said, "you have to say it over and over again until people get it right."[1]

When it comes to greening in your organization, you can't get there without your associates and employees. But I am sure De Pree would agree that "saying it over and over" will not suffice. It takes continuing education and training for environmental awareness and on-the-job performance.

The environment, as an employee-relations subject, can and should mean three things:

1. A validation of the employee's right to know.

The greening firm shows that it agrees, without reservation, with the legal requirements to inform employees about environmental factors, hazards, and risks. This agreement fits perfectly with a company attitude of openness: *We have nothing to hide.*

2. An opportunity to improve understanding.

In the greening transaction with its employees, the firm is given an opening that can be used to permit management to better understand its employees and to help employees better understand the information they are now privileged to receive. *Let us understand each other.*

3. An acceptance of responsibility.

Beyond the responsibilities accepted by management for legal and other reasons, the company has the opportunity to enlist its

employees to work both internally and in certain external relationships to help the company in its greening efforts. *Let us reason and
work together.*

Employees know, and you must remind them, that with rights
come responsibilities. The company that understands its employees' desires, fears, and level of acceptance, and understands the
opportunity built into its new green obligations, will advance with
its employees as allies against the competition.

GREENING, SAFETY, AND QUALITY

When it comes to successful environmental communication, both
within the company and outside, employee involvement is absolutely critical to the company, large or small, trying to get onto the
green. Openness and dialogue—the keys to communication compatible with spreading ideas like *sustainable development, total quality management,* and *pollution prevention*—must start with the firm's
own people, and they must continue day after day.

How is this best accomplished? If the company already has a
safety communication effort or one that encourages quality, can it
simply add an environment module to one of these established
employee programs? Is education and training mostly for technical
or environmental people in operations, or is this for everybody?

Safety (accident prevention) and quality (defect prevention)
have much in common with greening (which begins with pollution prevention) in many organizations.

Environmental, health, and safety are knitted together in some
companies, under the direction of a single individual or department. The pursuit of quality often brings safety and environmental actions and attitudes into play.

But the leading-edge companies that are combining action in
the green and other dimensions also recognize that the greening
road branches off into new territory.

These companies find that greening efforts must consider laws,
technology, costs, public policies, competition—*and* the opinions
of peers, employees, consumers, opposition organizations, and
stockholders. I can think of no other area where management
must deal with more factors, more sensitivities (economic, health,

and others) and more uncertainties. With the environment, internal and external factors are constantly changing.

These changing, special circumstances, which subject the company to unique vulnerabilities but also offer it unique chances for success, suggest a special approach to employee education and training.

"We have made environmental protection a central element of our quality process," said Robert D. Kennedy, Union Carbide's chief executive, "and we have reinforced its top priority status by upgrading the level of all employee training and education in safety, health, and environmental affairs. Our plant employees attend training sessions and classes regularly to learn about environmental issues, internal standards, and government regulations—including penalties and liabilities—that affect their particular site."

Many large companies regularly measure employee attitudes, so top management can study employee perceptions of the company's seriousness about environmental performance and commitment. This approach is adaptable to smaller operations. This is a sustainable communication approach that recasts employees as important customer-publics with whom the organization is engaged in continuous, open, and positive interaction.

BENEFITS OF EDUCATION AND TRAINING

Why should you treat employee greening in a special way? Let's examine the *benefits* of successful education and training in the greening company:

1. To keep you in compliance and out of jail. Yes, "technical and legal" are Job #1! If you fail to reap this benefit, the others will seem very minor indeed. Interaction with employees must include *education* and *training* about on-the-job actions necessary to comply with regulations. You must do all you can to weed out those "humble origins" from which grow the infractions that knock a company off the green and bring criminal proceedings against company executives.

2. To plug the holes in your greening machine. If you consider pollution to be *inefficiency,* as more and more companies do, you'll need to do everything possible to promote efficient operations and attitudes. Bad habits, bad attitudes, and lack of training are signs

of *communication inefficiency* that can spike your company's efforts to get on the green. The result can be the loss of time, money, markets, and public reputation.

3. To be prepared for emergencies. The greening company's internal environmental communication program covers not only routine practices to prevent accidents, defects, and pollution—in effect, *the inefficiency prevention program*—but also rapid, responsive, and efficient individual and team effort during an emergency.

4. To make your greening "organic." Since greening is first an inside job, management and employees must be interacting, arriving together at the same points of commitment and responsibility. When company and employee concerns are aligned, each learns when and how to solve green challenges for mutual benefit.

5. To make it "everybody's job." The greening company knows the truth in this statement by Edgar Woolard, chairman and CEO of Du Pont: "As long as environmental protection remains in a special category assigned to certain people—instead of part of the mental checklist with which each person approaches every task—then our environmental accomplishments will remain reactive and corrective rather than proactive and innovative."[2]

6. To leverage your green position. Employees are not only internal implementers of company greening; they are external *interpreters*. They not only tell the company's story (or air the company's laundry) to families and friends; they also reach other customer-publics (potential friends and opponents) of the company. The employee view, expressed openly, affects how the firm is accepted in the community and marketplace. It can either strengthen or foul the company's relationships with other customer-publics.

WHAT THE LAW REQUIRES YOU TO "TELL YOUR EMPLOYEES"

As you know by now, I'm not big on *telling* any customer-public anything that they either (a) don't want to know or (b) will not understand, because you have not first completed the requirement of *understanding their needs and questions*.

Still, green rules and regulations now in place in the United States and spreading throughout the world *require* employers to convey information to employees. We need to look at these requirements and consider how they can be turned into chances to improve company-employee relationships.

As your lawyers and technical specialists may have already advised you, there are two federal laws that have spurred much of the action on environmental risk reporting and communication in the workplace.

First, the Occupational Safety and Health Administration (OSHA) has developed a hazard communication standard to protect workers handling chemicals. It requires companies to have an active program to inform workers about hazardous chemicals in the workplace and how to deal with them.

Second, the Superfund Amendments and Reauthorization Act (SARA) and the Pollution Prevention Act require companies to gather a lot of information on hazardous chemicals. This is reported to the federal government and then incorporated into a national computerized data base. Workers and the general public have ready access to this information.

Here is more detail on the requirements of these two U.S. laws, which are apt to be copied in other countries over the next several years:

OSHA Requirements

The OSHA hazard communication standard (HCS) aims to make sure that the hazards of *all chemicals produced, imported, or used in the United States* are evaluated and that information about them is known to affected employers and to the employees exposed to them. Originally these requirements applied only to the manufacturing sector, but have now been expanded to include all *non*manufacturing employers as well.

The HCS action starts with the manufacturers who either make or import chemicals. They are required to review available scientific data on the chemicals they handle and to determine what hazards they pose.

The manufacturers and importers then must get the hazard information to downstream employers by marking the containers (with labels, tags, or other approved marks) and through material safety data sheets (MSDSs), which must be displayed at the work site. Container labels must identify the chemical, display hazard warnings appropriate for employee protection, and identify the chemical's manufacturer or importer. MSDSs must include the specific chemical identity, its common name(s), physical characteristics and hazards, known acute and chronic health effects, exposure limits, characteristics of exposure, precautionary handling and control measures, emergency and first-aid procedures, and the identity of the organization that drew up the MSDS.

The information stream continues, as the law requires all downstream employers—i.e., any firm that receives these regulated chemicals—to communicate.

If you are one of these companies, you are required to display the above information so it can be read by everybody who works for you or who may be affected or exposed. The law says you must set up comprehensive, written hazard communication programs for your employees and conduct specific warning and training programs.

The greening company's employee information and training program must cover the following points, at minimum:

- an explanation of the HCS program and requirements
- proper operations in employees' work areas where hazardous chemical are present
- the hazards of chemicals used in the work areas
- measures employees can take to protect themselves from the hazards
- where at the work site to find the written hazard evaluation procedures, and how to obtain and use other available hazard information
- specific procedures put into effect by the employer to provide protection, such as special work practices and the use of protective equipment
- methods workers can use to detect the presence of a hazardous chemical

The OSHA standard also discusses labeling exemptions, protection of trade secrets, and disclosure requirements in the event of a medical emergency.

SARA Requirements

The SARA requirements that affect employers and employees are in Title III of the act, also called the Emergency Planning and Community Right-to-Know Act. The main focus of the law is the community: neighbors near a plant where there is a potential chemical hazard.

This law has a lot of power and a benefit for the greening company. It is stimulating an aggressive national effort toward community-level and state-level emergency planning. It is also providing some companies with a logical, positive route to the green: local citizen committees that work with the plant or groups of plants to consider both emergency plans and pollution prevention options.

SARA affects the company-employee relationship in at least two ways:

1. The law requires *public* access to information about facilities, specifically, information about the quantities of hundreds of toxic chemicals (as defined by various EPA and other agency lists of regulated chemicals) that are routinely released by the facility into the environment each year. This is the basis for the *Toxics Release Inventory*, a national data base accessible by anyone with a personal computer and a modem.

The law also has requirements for company planning on pollution prevention. Employees of a given firm are, for this purpose, part of the public, with legal rights to know. They may not have previously known about these so-called toxic releases. They may or may not understand the numbers, the names, or the relative risks involved.

Obviously, first attention goes to the company's front line, to make sure that people who work at the company get the information and understand it. Likewise, pollution prevention plans covered by SARA are a matter for employee involvement.

2. SARA requires companies to develop emergency response plans with help from communities.

Developing the on-site portion of an emergency response plan requires input from employees as well as considerable communication in the form of training and orientation. As community residents, employees and their families are affected just like other neighbors.

REACHING FOR 150 PERCENT COMPLIANCE

Now that you know some of the requirements of the law, I hope that you will consider two observations that your lawyers and technical people may have missed:

1. Obeying laws that *require* you to communicate with employees is essential to keep the organization out of trouble, but is not enough.

2. Built into these requirements are good opportunities to team up with employees and, through them, with other customer-publics.

Sustainable communication on environmental matters means going beyond mere legal compliance, to reach the concerns and interests of all customer-publics.

Successfully handling the demands of the worker right-to-know and emergency planning regulations means going beyond the bare bones of the regulatory requirements to communicate with employees.

It means developing training, orientation, and ongoing information programs that are accessible, readily understood, up-to-date, and interactive—responsive to changing worker needs and flexible enough to allow for input from them.

COMPREHENSIVE PROGRAM OF ICI

To show you an example of an intensive employee communication program, I am indebted to ICI, one of the world's leading chemical companies, with more than 130,000 employees and 100,000 customers at the time the following report was prepared for the Earth Summit in 1992.

At ICI, implementation of group policy is the responsibility of operating units wherever they are in the world. Because of the wide range of products involved, implementation details differ significantly, but a great deal of effort has been expended in the building of environmental training modules that can be used virtually everywhere.

Senior levels (up to CEOs of the group's major component businesses) have regular conferences that include environmental elements. These cover international issues, external pressures, and policies needed for the future, as well as dissemination of internal and external best practices.

Line managers with profit responsibilities learn about environmental issues in conferences relating to products (cradle-to-grave), packaging and recycling, and external pressures, including those from customers and pressure groups. Conference material is widely circulated in hard copy and video for further use at the local level at home and overseas.

Environmental and technical specialists have a one-week practical course on clean technologies, recycling, and energy saving, which includes information on the regulatory and political background.

Communication specialists have training on environmental issues and the growing demand for more information by the public at large, including reporting on achievements against published targets.

New recruits to the company are put through detailed induction courses designed to develop maximum professional effectiveness. There is a strong environmental element in the courses for those joining manufacturing functions. They learn that standards set by the company are an integral part of every decision and action. Marketing recruits are introduced to the concept of life-cycle analysis of products, and every effort is made to integrate environmental considerations into all aspects of business training.

In common with most companies, ICI's environmental programs have strong support from top management. *Middle management is often more of a problem. It is up to management in operating units to send middle managers on appropriate courses inside or outside the company.* In the UK there is a mobile ICI team offering a participative one-day seminar in the workplace or nearby on the issues, legislation, ICI policy, external pressures, and management issues. This includes discussion on whether environmental issues are a threat or an opportunity and questions relating to communications with insiders and outsiders. This program is designed as a "training for leaders" event.

Employees at all levels have been put through a trial "Environmental Awareness" package designed to enable participants to better understand the global environmental issues and the company's policies and to evaluate the issues in a balanced and realistic manner. This includes the development of the individual's environmental perception of values.

As the ICI experience shows, the requirements and the resulting opportunities for employee communication can add up to a mechanism that empowers employees to do something good for the planet, *within the context of their jobs.*

PART TWO: HOW

Environmental communication is an interactive process. The greening company strives for communication that is sustainable because it is open, two-way, and continuous, and that goes beyond what the law requires to reach the areas where concern, lack of information, and lack of understanding still exist. This is the area beyond compliance, the extra 50 percent in our formula for green success.

In this context, effective communication with employees has as much to do with the nature of the process as with the content of the information. What employers say will have the most value if delivered in the spirit of creating a better work environment in which each employee is a valued member of the team.

As in other areas, it makes good sense to apply the QUALITY approach to environmental communication with employees. To do that, the company needs first to *quantify*—that is, to really think about the people, the individuals with whom you need to have a positive, green interaction.

While you must reach *all* employees, there will be some order of contact. For example, senior managers or supervisors may need to be involved before other employees, if for no other reason than to give top management advice on what other employees are most likely to be interested in and suggestions on approach. People directly involved in environmental controls or in specific environmental programs (for example, customer relations) will probably need a communication mechanism specific to their jobs. The point is to think through the process of beginning to communicate with employees about environmental matters and to approach this in a logical manner, so each step reinforces the previous one.

Companies with whom we have worked have found that one place to start is at the senior management level, interviewing individuals to discuss policy and communication options.

When lists of names (or titles or job areas) are compiled—the quantifying or Q step—the rest of the Q-U-A-L-I-T-Y process is ready to roll:

The organization now seeks to *understand* employee interests, needs, and level of awareness. It accomplishes this by *asking questions* and actively *listening* to employee concerns, inquiries, and suggestions.

In the process of gaining understanding, the firm is already interacting constructively with the vital customer-public that is its employees, and it is prepared to *interpret* what it now knows. The firm puts the information and input from employees into relevant contexts. It fits employee interests and insights into the context of the company's operating mission, of its legal requirements, and of its commitments for the future.

The company is now at the *take-charge* point. It can institutionalize the interaction on greening with the employees. This means opening up channels for continuous involvement, not only with regard to compliance greening, but also with regard to the company's green policies and any action plans.

The goal is total company involvement, from board and CEO level through every responsible employee. The ideal is an intensive, interactive commitment involving as many people as practicable to create and sustain corporate greening. As challenges arrive, management and employees tackle them as a team. Together, they create options and interactively consider them. Jointly, they conduct dialogue and partnerships with others outside the firm. Feedback mechanisms are created, so the company knows how to adjust its communication for sustainability: an early warning on misunderstandings and other potential problems, as well as on partnerships and other potentially positive options. Greening becomes evergreen.

SIDEWAYS, NOT DOWN

The goal is as much horizontal communication as possible, and as little hierarchical.

Robert Haas, chairman of Levi Strauss & Co., has described the kind of shift that may be needed when top management begins to practice interactive, sustainable communication:

"It's difficult to unlearn behaviors that made us successful in the past: Speaking rather than listening. Valuing people like yourself over people of different genders or from different cultures. Doing things on your own rather than collaborating. Making the decision yourself instead of asking different people for their perspectives. There's a whole range of behaviors that were highly functional in the old hierarchical organization that are dead wrong in the flatter, more responsive organization that we're seeking to become."

It may not be necessary for you to reorganize your structure, and it's not necessary to reinvent employee communication. It *is* necessary to apply the simple basics of communication logically and continuously. Basics such as these take on new meaning when applied to sensitive, changeable subjects like pollution and emergency response planning:

Talk *with* employees, never *down* to them. Raise any issue in terms of how the employees benefit. Don't ignore the negatives; share the facts and their potential impact. Always strive to make communication clear and timely. Elicit questions, comments, and suggestions to make the communication interactive. Keep access to information open.

The SARA, OSHA, and other requirements are a great opportunity to put openness and shared responsibility for greening into effect. And when we look at a law like SARA, we are reminded of a practical benefit: *Effective employee communication is both the hallmark of the successful greening company and the best defense against external attack or emergency.*

Should a crisis or environmental incident ever occur, it will be managed most successfully if employees are familiar with the facility's policies, operations, and procedures and if they have been interactive with management in anticipating the potential for problems and the right way to handle them.

THE SUPERVISOR ROLE

I want to underscore a point made above. Unless your employee communication system is just not working and needs an overhaul, you do not have to do a major reconstruction. This is especially true with regard to certain traditional ways in which information is exchanged between management and employees.

Studies show, for example, that (despite comments such as "I want to hear from the CEO!"), employees prefer to receive information from their supervisors. That is, people like to hear from people close to them, people they have come to know, people who are accessible frequently. To avoid gaps in the line of communication, there needs to be a comfortable, highly interactive connection for every employee. If the supervisor understands his or her role and has an equally comfortable and interactive relationship with *higher* management, the environmental communication process has an extremely valuable channel.

The greening company must do all it can to break out of the old mentality of "handing down" information and mandates from on high (if for no other reason than the fact that information is no longer voluntary; it's required by still higher authorities). While management messages and questions must flow through the organization from some point of origin, the traditional, top-down actions (sending out a memo or issuing guidelines) may serve to create more confusion than clarity, and isolate management from their own best customer-public. Our firms need input, support, and contribution from all employees if we are to get on the green together.

A department supervisor, well-trained and suited to the task, is the ideal person to present new environmental, health, and safety information affecting the department, as well as to provide a route for employee input and information updates. He or she can be an agent for horizontal communication that erases some of the hierarchical roadblocks.

The departmental supervisor can provide more room for management-employee interaction for efficient green performance and communication. The greening company will put its officers (and outside specialists) into the communication process, but it will take care not to undermine good employee-supervisor relationships.

This means special training to develop supervisors into a positive force for management and employees in the greening program. This is worth the time and investment. Supervisors should be given both the responsibility and suitable incentives for improving employee awareness and participation.

MEANS OF COMMUNICATING

Group meetings within a department offer a good way to raise and discuss issues affecting employees. Besides providing an efficient flow of information, they can provide instant feedback, reveal feelings and attitudes, and give rise to options that are mutually beneficial.

Meetings should be planned. Management, supervisors, and employees, in any equitable combination, can do the planning. All should agree there is a reason for the meeting. This purpose should be stated at the outset. If presentations are to be made, there should be an agenda or outline. Presentations should be brief, open to questions, and provide time for group discussion.

Printed materials can help meeting participants focus on topics and keep the topics around for follow-up. For this reason, it helps to use simple, photocopiable pieces and looseleaf notebooks that can be updated easily. Audiovisuals—overheads or flipcharts— also focus meetings and stimulate discussion, and these can be converted to take-aways.

Have follow-ups, distribute additional printed materials, design feedback channels, and add *one-on-one discussions* with supervisors.

The point is to create and sustain communication. This requires paying attention to the process. If it closes a door or closes a mind, any element in the process is counterproductive. It is an inefficiency, a waste to be avoided.

Quality control circles, originally designed to solve plant production and customer service problems, can be adapted for environmental communication.

The basic idea as applied to productivity is simple: eight to ten workers serve on a team or circle, with the task of collecting, generating, and conveying to management new ideas for increasing productivity. Members meet periodically on company time with their supervisor (and, frequently, with a person trained in group dynamics or industrial relations). They learn how to talk the language of management and to present their ideas to executives using business-school methods.

The synergism and the sense of ownership of the production process these circles generate has returned sometimes startling benefits. Similar benefits should be transferable to the emergency planning communication process. Employees could be expected to observe potentially troublesome work practices and conditions or safety information gaps and inefficiencies. Circle meetings or buzz groups can provide the logical forum to discuss potential solutions and ways to disseminate them.

Beyond face-to-face communication, the traditional tools for written employee communication are well suited to conveying environmental risk information to workers. Newspapers, newsletters, magazines, and tabloids can all be effective.

Which vehicle to use depends on objectives and budget. A newsletter is fast, timely, and relatively inexpensive if produced on a word processor with only a rudimentary masthead (the name, logo, volume number, and other information at the top of a newsletter). A newspaper uses low-cost newsprint and has a newsy feel that draws readers into the text. A magazine can contain more elaborate photos, art, and feature stories, but at higher cost.

Recent trends in the uses companies have made of employee publications make them more appropriate than ever as vehicles for environmental risk communication. Many companies are reducing the "bowling and babies" sections in favor of more space devoted to clear explanations of issues that affect worker well-being.

The messages in employee publications should include ongoing information from appropriate company officials and department heads. There is more freedom here than in face-to-face meetings in deciding who in management ought to deliver which messages. Perhaps a number of different people in different positions of responsibility will have pertinent information to share.

Environmental risk issues within the facility and outside in the community that affect workers or the firm should be examined honestly and thoroughly. Pertinent company policy statements should be printed. If the firm has a "correspondent network" for its newsletter or other periodical, it might be useful to create one or more positions for "environmental safety reporters" to dig up and report on relevant success stories. Correspondents can be kept involved by: (1) outlining responsibilities; (2) establishing deadlines; (3) spotlighting those who do outstanding jobs; (4) providing questionnaire-style forms for gathering news (who, what, when, where, why, and how); and (5) using feedback from the "editors" on why their material was or wasn't used.

Though perhaps old-fashioned in an electronic age, employee bulletin boards can be a useful link in a green communication program. A few tips on making them work as well as possible: place them where they can be seen under relaxed conditions—in the break area or near a water fountain. Pay attention to appearance; keep them neat and use colored paper to categorize materials. Put boards under glass for limited access and less clutter. Keep information brief and fresh, and change it on a set day each week. Assign responsibility for board maintenance to a department or individual. And, if you have the option, put your electronic bulletin board—a computer log-on banner or mailbox—into the *envirocomm* process.

The average American spends less than 35 minutes a day at home with the newspaper, but in the average home the TV is on more than five hours a day. Many companies now have in-house video networks that do everything from teaching job skills to providing a corporate news show at break times. Packaged hazard training programs often rely heavily on videotape in cassette form, making video capability a must for in-house training.

If you decide to develop your video capability, start with basic equipment and simple shows, then gradually expand. Do not invest heavily in a system that might prove wrong for your needs. Try renting or leasing services and equipment before buying. Try to make your productions as professional as possible. This is the standard people are accustomed to and they may not pay attention to anything less; worse, they may ridicule amateurish productions and reject the information they contain. Don't forget to consider as a substitute the simpler medium of slide shows; they are much less expensive and more flexible than video productions.

Should information be sent home or distributed at work? If it would be of value to family members as well as workers, such as information conveying the care and thoroughness with which the company works to prevent accidents, send it home. If the news is fast-breaking, in-house distribution is probably better. (If it is distributed during working hours, be prepared for on-the-job reading, or distribute it during breaks or at the end of shifts.) Direct mail to homes can be an ideal way to spotlight important information and keep attention focused on it. A frank, cordial letter from a company's CEO can often generate more good will and understanding than volumes of policy manuals and brochures.

A few simple guidelines can increase the impact of a direct-mail campaign:

- Develop a theme to unify and enliven the overall objectives.
- Send mailings at regular intervals.
- Get the help of company marketing, public relations, or qualified outside consultants to assist with copy and visuals.
- Begin the campaign with a personal letter from the CEO to give an overview of the issue or benefit program.
- Focus on just one aspect of your message per mailing, or just hit the high points.
- Provide a contact person's name or a feedback card with each mailing.

In sum, the greening company needs to use any and every communication device needed to keep employees and management on the same line, talking to each other, with as much horizontal communication as possible.

No matter what the size or scope of your operation, you will need to consider changes appropriate in the communication program as you go forward, so you are always attuned to the level of employee understanding and the impact of changing external factors. A communication channel that works today may be inadequate or superfluous tomorrow. You may need to add a rumor hot line or to drop a publication or to conduct a survey of employee opinion.

Our QUALITY model reminds you that the sustainable communication process is *never over*. When you've completed the Y (you—yes, you—are involved) step, that will bring you back to Q—and the next time around, the Q stands for *"question everything you've done so far, and see how you can improve this time."*

TRAINING: WHO AND HOW MUCH?

As with total-quality management programs, the company wishing to derive the most benefit from its environmental-awareness management program must invest time and money in training and education.

An intensive green-awareness program in a larger firm can involve hundreds of hours of instruction. A typical program would start near the top of the organization, with an orientation and strategy focus for the executive management team, and would reach through all levels to the general work force.

Step one—for senior executives—might well be a two-phase endeavor. Let's say XYZ Inc.'s CEO decides the company needs an environmental policy and the right kind of commitment and rollout within the company. For some of our clients, phase one has consisted of a series of interviews conducted among senior managers, key corporate staff, and heads of business units. These individuals are asked, one at a time or in small group discussions, how they perceive the greening process in their company.

Why should the company do more or differently? What does each individual personally believe and support? What is her or his opinion of competitors' efforts in greening? What are employees likely to want to know or want to achieve?

Answers to these questions are sure to vary. What you learn, in this phase, is how different people at the top of the organization view the needs and options of the company, with regard to environmental positions and performance.

In phase two of this first step, you bring these people together in seminars, briefings, and discussions, and you work in the information and opinions gathered in the interviews. Senior executives learn more about what laws require, what other companies have done, how green policy is made and what has the best potential for working within XYZ Inc.

In some cases, it makes sense to have a policy or strategic team put together in this step, and for this team to have responsibility for an environmental policy draft that will be refined to incorporate insights and realities discovered in subsequent steps. But let me emphasize that the immediate goal is not to nail down another policy at the top, but to open up thinking. Any agreement or tentative consensus here is good, but it should not be binding; this is not the place to make decisions that cut off further input. You want to create openness and dialogue: a model for the overall company greening program.

The time required for the first phase is about one hour for each interviewed executive. In addition, each executive will need to commit from six to eight hours over a period of a few months to briefings and seminars, with designated team members engaged for a good many more hours before and after the greening program moves into subsequent steps.

Step two focuses on middle-level managers and supervisors—the vital people for interaction between other employees and top management. They also need information on environmental issues, policies, strategies, and tactics that affect the company. However, the emphasis of training is on the tools and techniques that accomplish greening.

Relating to environmental performance on the job, they need much more detail from qualified interpreters (such as technical consultants and attorneys who specialize in environmental law).

Relating to environmental communication, they need training not only in what is required by law to be communicated, but also in the processes and techniques that make communication truly effective and productive. Here, for example, is where supervisors can learn to use a process such as the QUALITY model and tools like those described in this chapter.

Initial training at this level, over a period of three months, can require 20 or more hours.

Step three, in effect, trains the trainers. It takes the greening education program a little more intensively to a relatively few individuals—those who will be specifically charged with keeping the greening process alive and well. In this group will be selected supervisors and technical and professional staff, who will act as trainers, facilitators, and troubleshooters. They will educate or train new employees through teams, and they will keep teams current and energized. They will be a continuous resource and will identify other resource needs.

For these few people, a lot of time is required. For some, this may be a full-time job. In a two-month training program, count on more than 100 hours per month in training.

The final step rolls out the program to the general work force. Training and education is a continuous process. Meetings or seminars to present the program, to put it into perspective, and to get feedback will require several hours (up to about 20 or so over a three-month initial period).

The process can become self-encouraging and self-sustaining; once started by management, a good program will show workers the stake they have in the organization and will tend to increase their contribution to it.

THE DOE RUN EXAMPLE

Jeffrey Zelms, president of the Doe Run Company, a large producer of lead headquartered in St. Louis, credits work teams that combine management and front-line employees for his company's success in reducing air emissions.[3]

After spending $10 million on capital improvements, including expensive pollution-control hardware, Zelms was certain that either more money or cuts in production were the only way for the company to meet federal standards—unless it enlisted employees to help.

Zelms hired an outside consulting firm to manage a program to involve employees. "Our only technology was a box of crayons and a lot of butcher paper to chart the flow of the plant," recalled Zelms. "We simply sat down and developed natural work teams that addressed certain systemic activities, such as communication. Just getting teams talking and listening to each other made a significant improvement in emissions."

In a 1992 report to The Executive Committee, a national network of company executives, Zelms reported that over a two-year span Doe Run had cut airborne lead emissions by 50 percent—without spending additional money on equipment and maintenance. And there was a dividend to Doe Run's investment in environmental training and team-building. "The work teams have translated into improvements in other areas," said Zelms. "The mere fact that people are communicating better for a specific reason (greening) will peripherally offer improvements in other areas."

LEVERAGE FOR COMPANY AND PLANET

Employees can (and *will*) leverage your green position. Studies prove that workers who trust what they know about their workplace are not only more satisfied and more productive, but they also contribute to the processes of change.

Philip Lesly, the sage Chicago counselor who has helped companies manage what he calls "the human climate" for many years, has said, "So long as people understand the reasons for what is done and the consequences of not doing it—and feel that their interests are being considered—they will be more amenable to management's efforts."

Lesly says that to engage the employee's receptive mood (he uses the example of tough economic times as an opportunity to get closer to employees), *management must carefully involve employees "in the processes of change."*

This is certainly true with regard to environmental matters. Companies are in dynamic and changing relationships with the environment and with people. The process of change within the firm is a responsibility that management can fulfill only with its employees' involvement.

The benefits are both in the firm's self-interest and in the public interest. If employees understand and believe, they will come up with ways to help the company move onto the green. They'll attract support from others outside the company for this move. They will be a dynamic, positive factor in the creation and sustenance of relationships vital to the company and, in turn, beneficial to the planet.

As individuals, at home and in the community, they will, because of commitments and understanding developed on the job, do more for the environment, and they can help the company get into partnerships and alignments that are beneficial, from both private and public perspectives.

Checklist for Greening Employees

Awareness, training, and motivation in the greening company are critical. Business International Corporation studied U.S. companies and found the following traits of the successful firm, with regard to employees:[4]

- The CEO and other senior managers have established far-reaching goals in the spirit of continuous improvement.
- The firm has several kinds of environmental programs in place so that every employee can become involved.

- The company provides environmental awareness training designed for each level and function.
- There are several prestigious award and recognition programs to praise employees for outstanding environmental contributions.
- Computer and MIS support are provided to help the EHS function directly.
- Systems exist that keep employees not directly involved in the EHS function informed about regulatory and social EHS trends at home and abroad.

Chapter Eight

Relating to Government

The goal of this book is to get you *on* the green as you *go* green. The key strategy is to interact continuously and consistently with all customer-publics. This is the best way to avoid surprises and to attract support. And of all your customer-publics, none is more critical than government.

Government *has* to look at you. It's the law. Public opinion requires it. Not only does the new Green World of Business leave no place to hide; it moves companies, large and small, into the spotlight. Only the most naive of companies (or those who don't plan to be around very long) would ignore the prospect of new government scrutiny with regard to the environment.

Going green can redefine your company's relationship with government. *You* win when you anticipate and act to control the relationship between your firm and government. The desired result is interaction. This creates a relationship that helps both you and government people to be informed. The risky condition is one that puts you always in the position of having to be responsive or compliant or (worst case) contentious.

The opportunity (which, I contend, should equal if not exceed the necessity) to interact with government can be found at many levels. Our QUALITY approach urges you to concentrate on two big categories of customer-publics within government: regulatory officials and politicians.

RELATING TO REGULATORS

"Compliance" is what your firm's technical and legal people handle. These are the people who know exactly what the law requires and the latitude your firm may have in precisely obeying the law. They know about flexible deadlines, approximate standards, and loopholes. Therein lies the rub. It's the loopholes that can hang you.

The *appearance* of being "not in compliance"—for example, getting on an activist hit list or giving a reporter something negative to write about, *even though you are precisely legal and are not exceeding pollution limits*—may cause you more trouble than you need or want.

This book is neither technical nor legal; my point is that if you want to get on the green with others in the public interest, you must obey the law *and be perceived as a law-respecting citizen*. This means that if you are not in compliance, you need a plan to get into compliance. And you need to make this commitment publicly known.

You must hinge the letter of the law to the spirit of compliance. Here's the winning formula: $C + A + C + C = R$. Spelling it out, companies on the green will be in strict *Compliance*; they will *Acknowledge* past faults; they will *Commit* to a positive future goal; and they will engage in open, interactive, and consistent *Communication*. This will yield mutually beneficial *Relationships* with customer-publics, including government as a direct customer-public as well as those other customer-publics (such as employees, neighbors, and consumers) whose attitudes and actions shape what government thinks and does about the greening company.

It all starts, I believe, with move #1: *get over the noncompliance hurdle*. Now I know this may mean doing what other firms have not done. Some very large and high-profile companies have been out of compliance with green rules for years. Entire cities are out of compliance with some federal regs. This is because of the great difficulties encountered in meeting the numbers in federal laws such as the Clean Air Act.

Some firms, while not in compliance, are not in serious trouble because of it. However, you may not have their latitude. Your firm may get on an enforcement hit list *before* you have the needed support from your core customer-publics. Your firm may be singled out by a hostile group for the simple reason that you're in noncompliance, despite the complicated explanation. The point is that to win with other customer-publics, you can't let this loser situation haunt you. Comply—others will call it "not breaking the law"—and you're not disabled. And while you are *not* complying with every detail of a rule, be sure to show every sign that you are trying to get there.

REGULATOR BLUES

Let's put worst things first. The worst-case relationship between a company and a regulator is one that is routinely formal and potentially contentious. You know such a relationship if you see it. Contact is usually by mail or courier; reports are rendered by the firm, notices and requests by the agency. Instead of dialogue, letters are exchanged, with the lawyers signing them or looking at the drafts. The postal carrier or courier has more personal contact with the people at the agency than do the people at the regulated firm. If there are meetings, the sides are composed of lawyers and technical staff who gather in stiff, formal sessions or proceedings.

All very businesslike, certainly legal, and not that unusual. From the business side, after all, we are *busy*. Why take time away from what *we* must do, to get involved in what *they* are charged to do? Getting to know regulators is not that easy, is it? Won't they get in touch when we need to do something? And besides, we know what they want and what they'll say. And there is always the chance that if we don't raise our profile we won't be noticed— isn't there?

REGULATOR GREEN

Two characteristics describe normal regulatory transactions in this new Green World of Business: data and dialogue.

The legally required exchange of data, now common with regard to environmental matters, shines the green spotlight on firms large and small, high profile or low. SARA Title III, the continuous inquiry built into the federal Toxics Release Inventory, as well as a number of other federal and state data-hungry devices (and the hyperactive enforcement mechanisms ready to ride these numbers), make it less and less likely that any firm will be unnoticed. Out of the blue, this green spotlight can land on virtually any firm in America.

The second characteristic is that because of this accumulating green data exchange, there is greater need in the regulatory agency for understanding the data and its practical impact. At least in some cases, there is still latitude for regulatory discretion in interpreting the current waves of green laws and their application. To turn green theory into practical rules requires knowledge of the market. This suggests room for dialogue. One happy result is that your technology exchange can start very close to home, if your regulatory official is willing to learn.

How do you move toward this better-case scenario? That is precisely the purpose of the QUALITY communication model. The predication is that, with specifically identified regulators (personified and recast as customer-publics), you may be able to move through mutual understanding to a continuous-improvement condition.

Communication between the firm and the regulatory agency should be *interactive*, not just responsive. In most cases it is in the firm's interest to move this communication onto a person-to-person basis, to build bridges over time and not during conflict. Most often, this communication link is well achieved by the firm's environmental specialist—a person who can speak the language of the regulator. For example, a manufacturing facility that is frequently under scrutiny by a state regulatory agency may have its top technical person spend time periodically at the agency, personally responding to questions, raising questions for clarification, and otherwise promoting understanding.

Any representative of the firm can be the facilitator of the company-government dialogue; it is a matter of fitting the person to the situation. Who is qualified to establish common ground (and interested in doing it)?

Agency staff and officials can be invited to participate in seminars or other programs with your firm's technical specialists or with others in management, when the subject is appropriate. For example, a small company's president, on the program committee for a solid waste seminar, suggested and personally invited the state's chief regulatory official to participate.

Inviting regulators to company open houses, tours of operations, and other get-to-know-us occasions are among the options to be considered as ways to create and sustain open relationships. And the contact need not be confined to visits. Copies of papers, reports, and articles relating to areas of known interest can be sent to staff people at the agency, once you get to know them. Feedback to agency officials on talks they give in public, which you heard or read about, can show interest and keep communication flowing.

Testimony at hearings and participation in other proceedings will continue to require legal and technical counsel and presentations, but there will be benefit even here from the insights resulting from a continuous approach.

To be avoided at all costs, obviously, is the zero-sum game where the agency can win only if you lose. The most lonely position in the Green World of Business is to be on an agency or enforcement hit list; worse still is to have this materialize as a surprise because of poor communication. When a crunch comes, you don't want to have allowed a condition to develop so the company has no open channel for communication and therefore no leeway and no leverage. Isolated, scrambling for understanding when relations are adversarial—this is like learning to swim in a shark tank.

POLITICIANS AND REGULATORS

There are subtle but important differences between *politician* and *regulator*, the terms used to describe the two categories of key government customer-publics in our model.

Harry Truman said a politician is simply someone who understands government. "It takes a politician to run a government," Truman stated. Under a broad view like this, regulators would always be politicians. This is not the case. While all politicians have the potential to be regulators, not all regulators are potential politicians. Many regulators are bureaucrats.

Just keep in mind that, throughout our QUALITY approach, after you've decided *who* your key customer-public is, the critical next step in the process is to *understand* who this individual is.

What is this person's connection to you? What motivates his or her questions, concerns, interests, desires, and preferences, with regard to you? When it comes to government, you will be especially interested in understanding *the potential for control and influence over you and your operations and efforts in greening.*

For our purpose, the term *politician* refers to those elected or appointed to public office and those who actively seek to hold such a position. The term *regulator* is used to describe individuals in government who construct and, usually, have the power to enforce government regulations. Regulators interpret the law enacted by the professional politicians in Congress; they write the regulations and administer the program. But when is a regulator also a politician? When a bureaucrat? And what difference does it make in a relationship effort aimed at improving communication?

Let's call in a specialist in political language. William Safire is a Pulitzer Prize–winning columnist who served in the Nixon White House as senior speechwriter. His columns in *The New York Times* and books such as *The New Language of Politics* and *Safire's Political Dictionary* have been for me a source of fun and education.[1]

Safire (in *Political Dictionary*) quotes sociologist C. Wright Mills on bureaucrats: "The executive bureaucrat becomes not only the center of decision, but also the arena within which major conflicts of power are resolved or denied resolution."

This suggests that the bureaucrat is an expert in procedure that creates a power center. This is a breed in ascendancy as the green rules roll over business. One of the most serious problems companies have with laws such as the Clean Air Act is *permits*. This is a regulatory area, with the regulator given options to do more (or less) than the writers of the law may have intended. By standing at the intersection of economic activity and turning on red lights or green lights (or applying red tape or green tape), the bureaucrat regulator becomes a force to be reckoned with.

The bureaucrat regulator—that is to say, the career professional with authority over regulatory matters—can be a tool of, or a pain to, the regulatory politician—the professional who has been elected or appointed to run the agency or bureau. (The pain is sharpest when the bureau shifts leadership or when there is a change in political party, and the career bureaucrats stay on, protected by law and tenure. This "self-stopper" potential is noted by Safire in quoting Alben Barkley, the 1948 Democratic convention keynoter: "A bureaucrat is a Democrat who holds a job a Republican wants.")

REGULATORY OMBUDSMEN

Chances are, if you reach out to regulators, you will find them open to discussion. Unfortunately, this is not always the case. Some regulators have decided, on their own or under political pressure, to take a confrontational stance. Some take on the mantle of the aggressive environmental advocate who wins through formal, publicized action against business. Procedure and process, akin to litigation, seem to be preferred over the quiet and expedited resolution of problems. However, these situations are not in the majority. Regulators and the regulated alike are increasingly aware that public sparring over rules and creating costly regulatory bottlenecks are not in anyone's best interest.

Consequently, some regulators are ready to meet you halfway. Connecticut is one of the states trying to streamline its permitting process. With a backlog of close to 3,000 permit applications in 1992, the state department of environmental protection restructured its bureaucracy. It created an ombudsman to assist business and the public in meeting regs and properly filing for permits.

If your state has a similar service, see if you can make it work for you and your customer-publics.

"REG-NEG" INSTEAD OF HEAD-BUTTING

Instead of escalating the risk of failure that both sides court when they butt heads over green rules, some regulators are encouraging dialogue before the rules are written. Regulatory negotiation—reg-neg—is an example.

Reg-neg was used in developing definitions of reportable health and safety studies under the Toxic Substances Control Act and in writing the "significant new use" rule under that federal law. A good example of reg-neg was the Carpet Policy Dialogue at the federal level. The process was put to work to enable those with a stake in the manufacture, installation, and use of carpet to find the best ways to reduce exposure to chemicals released by new carpets.

How does it work? Government usually takes the initiative when reg-neg seems likely to head off confrontation on a new rule. The agency will bring together as many stakeholders as possible: business people, labor unions, environmental and consumer groups, and representatives of other government agencies who have related experience or who will be impacted by the regulation. Together, the participants list issues, concerns, and action options. A facilitator within the group, or one hired to conduct the negotiations, leads toward the draft of a proposed regulation.

It if works, you get a rule that is as fair as possible to all concerned and therefore one not likely to be seriously challenged. This obviously saves a lot of time and money for the public and the private sectors involved. If it doesn't work, at least some insights were aired, and the chances are that both the regulated and the regulators learned something in the process.

GOVERNMENT TESTIMONY

Whether you are giving testimony before a legislative or regulative body, three rules are common:

Do your homework. Tell the truth. Keep your cool.

If I can add another commandment to head off frustration—namely, don't expect too much too soon and don't expect anything right away—I've told you all I know about being a government witness. Having said that, let me elaborate:

You neither start nor stop with writing the statement for the hearing. Naturally, you'll know your subject. Presumably, you'll have something to say. But getting ready to testify is a lot like getting ready to make a sale. You want to know the territory. You want to know the context in which you'll be pitching—what's happened before, who else will be testifying, who's on the agency panel (names, titles, responsibilities), what's the agency's or committee's mission. You want to anticipate the reaction you'll get. You want to be ready for the questions. Try the Ted Williams at-bat test. Think: "What would I throw to me if I were the pitcher?" Williams took the Boston Red Sox to the top by thinking that way. He was never surprised by a pitch.

Getting ready means researching, organizing the information that will make up your testimony, drafting your comments well in advance. (See Chapter Sixteen.) Some of my clients have overcome stage fright and avoided surprises by trying out their testimony in a mock hearing in which our staff play the roles of specific members of a government committee.

Your statement should be short. Put into it the headlines, the meat and potatoes, the real-life examples you know about; put all the backup information you have into a document that you file for the record.

The statement has to be based on truth. You get no chance to catch up to lies or misinterpretations. It has to be an expression of a true belief, supported by facts, cases-in-point, relevant evidence.

What about your personal appearance and demeanor? Transparency (that is, honesty with your evidence on display) and accountability are your strongest personal traits. You need to show that you're qualified to be there, that you have a legitimate point, that you are confident and helpful.

It's a plus if you're a natural—if you're attractive, articulate, or known to the agency panelists. But I wouldn't let too much ride on these factors; they're not the foundations of effective testimony. In fact, I have seen them get in the way of the message if they turn into mere entertainment or grandstanding or hostility. Careful preparation, composure, courtesy, a commitment to a positive value are the sturdy stuff to bring into the hearing.

P.S. Don't let it end with the statement presented for the record. Consider other customer-publics. You may want to send a copy of your testimony to your senator, as many House members as you care to, to state government officials, and to the news media. Depending on the subject, it may be useful to let employees, stockholders, customers, suppliers, and others know what you've said. You may even want to use this as a means of creating a constituency for your point of view. You've spent a lot of time getting your message together. You may as well get some mileage out of it.

ACCESS TO RELATIONSHIPS

My colleague for many years, Ernie Wittenberg, made the point in his book, *How To Win in Washington*, that there's a difference between entry and access.[2] Entry, says Ernie, is getting into the outer office. Access is getting time with and attention from the government official who can act in your behalf.

There are several routes to relationships with politicians, such as members of Congress and state legislatures. Veteran lobbyists and veteran counselors like Ernie Wittenberg and his wife Elisabeth point to three primary access routes:

Route #1: *Be a constituent.* "All politics is local," said Thomas P. (Tip) O'Neill, former Speaker of the House. Politicians must create customers, just as people in business do, in order to be allowed to function. So if you need to reach an officeholder who needs to reach you, the communication channel is open. No route is better than being a voter. Unless it is . . .

Route #2: *Represent lots of constituents.* Every politician wants to know how many other people feel the same way that you do. Here is where your success in creating numerous customer-public relationships can be leveraged. If you are seen in the eyes of the officeholder as representative of many voters—for example, you are the head of a local business organization or you represent senior citizens or another active citizen group—you will get face time. One of the great rights of America is the citizen's right not only to vote but to build constituencies. Grassroots organization and expression are powerful weapons in participative democracy. The politician will want to have a relationship with someone who can deliver support or messages. This can come quicker if you can travel . . .

Route #3: *Personal friendship.* "If you've gone to school with the [politician], if you're on the same board for a charity, if you're her doubles partner, or if you were the sponsor of his membership in your country club," says Wittenberg, "your calls will be answered and it will turn out that someone has unexpectedly canceled an appointment that you are welcome to fill."

And, always, the money road, or . . .

Route #4: *Political giving.* Even if you enjoy one or more of the foregoing advantages (and *especially* if you don't), you and your organization will want to consider the opportunities and benefits of political fund contributions and Political Action Committees (PACs). While I won't get into the wholly foolish discussion as to the "influence" that political contribution in itself "buys" in this country, I do believe that contributions can create awareness.

Business people who give and/or raise funds get into the political process. Events sponsored, tickets bought, functions attended—all serve to open channels of communication. Company and industry PACs stimulate political awareness among employees and other stakeholders, and contributions from the PACs are acknowledged by politicians. Giving to chosen parties and candidates is an acceptable, legal, and, I suggest, desirable route to get in front of people in government.

However you gain access, your success in building an open and mutually respectful relationship will rely largely on your ability to sustain communication.

(Laws at federal and state levels govern political communication, which is frequently connected to lobbying, and I urge you to check with your lawyer to see what's allowed. My general observation is that companies are confused about what they can and can't say to employees and other publics when it comes to politics and government issues, with the result that some companies don't do anything at all. This is too bad, because it shuts down a channel that is powerful and uniquely useful.)

Here, our QUALITY process model is a workable guide. You will need to understand clearly the motives, desires, and practical restrictions of the politician and build your relationship and your case within this context.

Generalizing, a politician wants: Support for candidacy, security in office, recognition of value, minimum public criticism (except when criticism builds support in a more important, more vocal, richer, or more active constituency), to be right, not to be wrong, to be smart, not to be dumb, not to set up traps that will get him later.

The politician's job is high-profile and very public, and he or she depends on others with similar job enhancers to be successful. This explains why the politician is often in league with activists and the news media: the synergizing A + M + P (activists, media, politicians) syndrome, outside of which business has traditionally stood.

Regulators, like all entities, must also create constituencies. But their need for the support of people who influence their ability to succeed is commonly less high-profile, less subject to popular alliances. They do not run for office, but they depend on those who do—their political bosses in the agency, for example, as well as legislators who give them laws to work with and then oversee their work. They do not ask you to vote for them, but they can benefit from your relationship if your cooperation, data, or expertise helps them in their work. If being wrong about you damages the regulator's relationship with enabler politicians, it is in the regulator's interest not to be wrong about you. That's the win-win-win move you will do well to explore.

Chapter Nine

Ten Common Mistakes Managers Make in Washington

Washington, D.C., sometimes makes me think of Cervantes' classic, *Don Quixote*. When the Man of La Mancha rides on his horse out to the plain and the windmills, he turns to his squire and says: "Look there, where thirty or more monstrous giants present themselves, all of whom I mean to engage in battle and slay . . ."

Too many people in business come into Washington and seem to take the same attitude. The place is awesome, with frightening foes to be engaged. The Capitol looks like a monster, but in they go, ready to fight. Like Quixote, they tend to get knocked off their horses.

The rise of green lawmaking, and its companion green rule-making, over the last several years has brought a lot of company people to Washington. Many of these people are very successful. They know the ropes and they operate as efficiently as anyone else in the federal maze. I learn from these folks every day.

This chapter is for those who want to win in Washington, but who are not accomplished lobbyists or even experienced constituents. I want to help you avoid some common mistakes business managers make in Washington.

MISTAKE #1: TAKING THE "MAN OF LA MANCHA" VIEW

Looking at the capital as an awesome system of unapproachable forces can lead to wrong approaches to the wrong people and assorted other stumbles.

The correction is seeing D.C. as something more familiar to you. Look at this big political and bureaucratic establishment as a sort of rambling company, maybe a conglomerate. It's a system, run by managers. You know what managers do. They plan, motivate, and regulate the activities of others to reach *their* objectives, just the way business managers do.

So the way to avoid mistake #1 is to recognize that this is not a battleground but a conglomerate. You're not out to fight foes who are lurking in the system, but to find the *manager* who holds a key to your success.

Three groups of resident managers have a lot to say about how Washington works: the activists, the media, and the politicians—the A + M + P synergy that drives the the public opinion process that results in green rules and regulations.

Activists. Green activists in Washington can include any advocate or power broker. There are activists for environmental groups and activists that represent business interests—activists for action and activists for *no* action. Lawyers, lobbyists, and others who lean on government and each other are tossed into this category—at least for the purpose of this chapter's discussion.

Media. Washington is the political news center of the world. Every country, state, and major city, a great many smaller cities and towns, and every conceivable specialty area—from *Aviation News* to *Zoo Journal*—are represented in Washington. One building in Washington, the National Press Building (where I opened my office 20 years ago), houses services for approximately 4,300 editors and reporters.

It's not a good idea to generalize, but *generally*: Washington journalists are active, inquisitive, intelligent, and fairly jaded. Jaded because there is such a richness of news! There are so many *sources*, so many *surprises*, so many *secrets*, and so much boring stuff that has to be covered. All in all, there is simply *too* much news.

There are too many press events, too many government actions, too many spokespersons. It's a free country! Anybody can put out a statement or try to call a news conference. The day book issued by the wire services, calendars and news releases from every conceivable company, association, and organization, faxes and phone calls—these offer a steady stream of options that almost literally swamp Washington media desks every single day. Washington has a daily news flood.

What does this mean to you, if you're a business manager and you want to meet the press, in one way or another, when you're in Washington?

The news flood creates two conditions. The first is indolence. Obviously a journalist in Washington does not have to work very hard to find things to write about or people to interview. The second condition is killer instinct. To succeed over time in Washington, a journalist *must* work hard to push aside the less important to get to the greater. He or she must sort the options and dig through the obvious to find the real thing: the news or source specifically relevant to his or her beat, media outlet, or geographic area. The journalist must move the story ahead, past his or her own previous story, and past the competing media outlet in his or her market. Freshness, new insight, quotable statements—each original and *interesting*—are the daily prey of the Washington press.

If you want to make news, you can. If you can stand and deliver, you have a chance to be captured, on tape or in ink, in Washington. If you get in front of the "right" journalist—that is to say, the *manager* in a media outlet who can *use you* to fulfill his or her objective—you can make news.

Politicians. These are the people who bring you to Washington. In this chapter, I use the term *politician* instead of *government official* to make the point that these are people concerned about getting elected or appointed to office. This lets me differentiate *politician managers* from such other government managers as those bureaucrats and judicial officials who do *not* aspire to higher (or different) office. Some bureaucrats and judges *are* politicians; some are not.

You may need to deal with others, but as a constituent and business manager, you are likely to have your best shot with the political types. Your representatives in Congress, for example, are certainly more open to folks from home than anyone else in Washington. And there is a greater chance for your transacting, manager to manager, with others in the politician group if you understand how *they* manage.

Let's continue the management system analogy. As noted, the politician group—which includes elected, appointed, and (especially in the case of Congress and the White House) hired staff managers—is the dominant group. But also be aware that managers within the group are constantly being dominated by events and by each other. A clean air law enacted last year can be amended next year; new laws can be passed; rules can be appealed and revoked; orders can be canceled.

No matter who's in the White House and who's on the Hill, there is always some degree of jockeying for control. It's like a conglomerate with competing divisions or a division with competitive managers. One manager can overrule another (president vetoes Congress, but Congress overrides vetoes). One manager's actions can be changed by another (for example, a regulatory manager turns an environmental law into a regulation that is different from that intended by the manager on the congressional staff who drafted the original bill).

This is a system where the politician managers differ along numerous lines (party, geography and makeup of constituencies, and jurisdictional) and exhibit various styles in managerial organization. It comes as a surprise to some Washington visitors to discover that a senior staff person on a Senate committee may have more to say about the content and management of a particular bill than a senator on the committee. More experienced businesspeople realize that this is good delegation. As with a corporate executive, the senator has determined that it meets his objectives to empower subordinates with certain managerial responsibilities.

The top executives in the company have the top goal of creating customers. The senator may be the manager of a general objective, say of creating constituents, while yielding to the management of an aide whose objective benefits the senator. To draw this finer, we can see a situation in which a committee staff counsel is the manager: planning, motivating, and regulating the activities of committee members (senators, in this case) to reach the objective of clearing a bill.

Similar situations occur in congressional offices. There the assistants are the day-to-day managers, driving toward objectives, involving and reporting to the senator or House member as may be desirable.

All this makes for a lively system. It has room for scoring by the businessperson who goes to Washington and makes the right moves. Here's the key: After locating the manager who holds a key to your success, find out how to *identify with his or her management purpose.*

Just keep in mind that in business, the top management purpose is *to create a customer,* according to gurus like Peter Drucker. In politics, the purpose is *to create a voter.* For aggressive bureaucrats, a voter is anyone with a say in how long they keep their present jobs or what their next jobs will be. The successful pursuit of *voters* enables politicians to do the things they wish or are pressed to do, just as the successful pursuit of *customers* enables the company to produce goods, hire people, pay taxes.

If your purpose (which has to trace back to creating customers) aligns with theirs, you are more apt to get their attention and work with them effectively. What I've seen, time after time, is the industrial representative who marches into an immediate stalemate with a politician (on the Hill or in an agency). Such a representative often gums up the works for the company because he or she did not bother to think through a way to tie in to a politician's management purpose. If, after doing your homework, it is clear that you are at cross-purposes with the manager you've targeted for an approach, you may be able to alter your approach or go to another manager.

MISTAKE #2: DETACHING FROM "THE PUBLIC INTEREST"

Politician managers in Washington are sensitive to public criticism, but this should not be construed to presume they fear *all* criticism. No manager—and certainly no politician—pleases everybody all the time. The successful manager keeps working toward his or her objective, with the public good in mind, without *unnecessarily* raising resistance. Most Washington politicians know before they come to Washington whom they need to please and whom they can afford to displease. It can be troublesome to be criticized by a hostile constituent or by another politician. It can be costly to provoke the enmity of a superior, of a particularly influential politician, of a significant press manager, of a significant group of voters, or of any other significantly opinion-shaping social, worker, economic, or "public-interest" person or group.

What Washington politician managers rightfully fear is the *irretrievable* loss of support (voters or sponsors) needed to enable them to pursue their objectives.

Politicians need public approval. They do not, however, expect or need unanimous approval. They are rarely—as a group or as individuals—appealing to the *same* public (and even more rarely, at the same time). They work and produce for maximum favorable exposure among those publics whose attitudes and actions affect their ability to meet their objectives. Benefiting from favorable spotlights, politician managers share some objectives with press and other managers (including some in industry) who can influence exposure possibilities.

For example, there is a special affinity with television. A politician may want to gain followers by presenting himself as a personable, active leader. Similarly, a TV manager may want to enliven a show with a leader or potential leader being personable and active. Their objectives align. Likewise, politicians and the press, joined by some "public-interest" organization managers, have opened formerly closed doors through "sunshine" rules and televised proceedings. The new openness has caused some anguish among bureaucrats and politicians. Some still feel that meetings open to all comers and sessions covered by TV are "posturing" for the public—a handicap to efficient management.

Just the same, the trend will continue, because the objective of exposure is shared by so many Washington managers and because it is in line with prevailing public interest. *What is "public interest"?* As Citicorp of New York once observed in full-page ads in Washington newspapers, "Probably no phrase in the English language affords more ambiguity or opportunities for demagoguery than 'the public interest.' Aside from the obvious question of who has the right to speak 'for' the public, there is the still larger problem of just whose interest is being protected, and from whom." Self-appointed public-interest groups have no lock on either the *representation* or the *definition* of the public interest.

Viewing public-interest groups as a component in the Washington management system, we see them as units run by managers. Those managers must create *customers* (members, contributors, sponsors, followers) to enable them to carry out management objectives. (As Citicorp's ads noted, "Even the noblest cause can at length become a vested interest [which] may attract at least a few who are perhaps more interested in doing *well* than in doing good.") These managers will succeed to the extent they can convince politician managers that it is best (coinciding with their purpose of creating a voter or follower) to support the self-styled public-interest group position. The politician manager, to hew to his or her management purpose, must consider whether the position being offered conforms with the interest of a big portion of the public that elects him or her (or, in the case of a bureaucrat, the administration manager or congressman who supports him or her).

Industrial managers are members of the public, too. They have rights to pursue their objectives. They have the right to agree or to disagree with any other manager's definition of *public interest.* They have the right to represent that portion of the "public" which is operating as a company, and to suggest that other "publics" would benefit from their objectives.

The mistake many industrial managers make in Washington is either *abdicating* or *fighting* public interest.

The winning way is to look for the logical, justifiable, factual attachment of your objective with a definable portion of the public interest. The larger the portion, the better. Keep in mind, as you approach a politician manager, that he or she is thinking "public interest" from a personal perspective of creating support. A member of Congress is particularly sensitive to the fact of being an elected representative of the public interest, and will not wish to turn off a significant base of influence among the public to which he or she is responsive.

MISTAKE #3: NOT FOLLOWING CODES OF CONDUCT

What are the laws and rules? As with public interest, they are changeable. Laws about lobbying are written. They are fairly clear, although not entirely. And there is an advanced effort on Capitol Hill now to change them. It would be tougher to contact a congressman without telling the public about it, for example. Rules of conduct are unwritten and constantly under revision.

Conduct befitting a successful manager includes all the courtesies and behaviors that prevail in any society, plus some that seem distinctive to Washington. You don't criticize one bureaucrat to another bureaucrat, or one congressman to another (even though the bureaucrat or congressman may do so). You don't call on an editor at deadline time. You don't interrupt a congressional staff manager while he or she is running a hearing. You dress for business (you don't wear jumpsuits, tennis shoes, or loud sport coats) when you are working. You don't mispronounce names. You don't mix enemies at a social affair. In short, you behave, talk, and dress in a manner that will enhance rather than impair your chances to be an effective manager.

The advice I gave to one industrial manager was this: "We are not out to draw attention to ourselves but to our viewpoint. When we do gain the attention of a congressman, we want him to look forward to the prospect of working with us. He should have no doubts that we will do our part in an appropriate way, without embarrassments or surprises."

MISTAKE #4: NOT TELLING THE WHOLE TRUTH

I single this out from other manager performance characteristics because it is preeminently important in Washington. There is generally no room in business for misrepresentation, lawful or not. Lies catch up with and compound themselves. In Washington as in no place else, now as at no other time, there are many risks in telling less than the truth. The industrial manager will do well to go overboard on the side of candor and disclosure.

It is a good practice to make sure that the manager whom you are approaching is at least generally aware that there is another side (and perhaps many other sides) to the situation in which you have an interest. You are making your case in the honest belief that facts support you.

MISTAKE #5: GETTING HUNG UP IN POLITICS

Some industrial managers come to town thinking they can only talk to Republicans or to Democrats or to specific varieties of politicians.

Successful lobbyists say the trick as an outsider is to avoid being either a bitter partisan or a political neuter. The partisan alienates the other party. The neuter has, in this political city, the respect of no one of importance.

My experience is that for many effective managers, the question does not arise very often. If you are working toward an objective, identifying with the public interest and the interest of the manager you are approaching, politics need not become partisan. A new Democratic senator from a given state is going to be just as responsive to your suggestions for solving a problem in his state as was his Republican predecessor. The problem, after all, affects the "publics" that remain the same no matter who represents them.

The fundamental mistake for the manager to avoid is to become attached so securely to one party that the company's interests are compromised.

MISTAKE #6: GOING IT ALONE

Some company people come to town thinking they cannot talk to labor unions, public-interest groups, competitor company people, or even their own trade association. Whether from fear of being found guilty by company superiors of not knowing how to do *every*thing, or from "company secret" conditioning, they make the mistake of assuming they can do it themselves—that they *must* go all alone, a Don Quixote up against the Washington windmill giants.

The manager is rare who can "do it myself" better, either in business or in government. The Age of Coalition has dawned in Washington. Groups of managers from industry, labor, associations, agriculture, in any and all combinations, are getting together "ad hoc" to share knowledge, multiply strengths, and avoid duplication.

The value of coordination is recognized by members of Congress and bureaucrats who often appreciate being able to hear from and deal with many advocates through a united front. It saves everybody's time.

A common, impressive device is for one of the advocate managers to hand to a member of Congress a list of organizations that feel the way the manager does. This is particularly useful if the manager doesn't happen to have a direct link (say, a company operation) in the member's congressional district, but others on the list do have such connections.

When novice public affairs people ask me how they should get started, trying to solve a problem for their company, I tell them, "Call your association headquarters first." Somebody there will know something about the subject and can give you a lead.

MISTAKE #7: COMPLICATING THE MESSAGE

Washington is a combat zone of advocates vying for attention. The hard-to-understand message loses valuable time and support. This is a challenge to managers who must work for action on a complex issue, but it can be done. It can mean simply breaking up the issues into manageable, understandable pieces.

A device of many Washington managers is the one-page fact sheet providing a simple, one-sentence (or at most, one-paragraph) opening statement about the action that is needed, with the balance of the page giving the reasons why. Naturally, these reasons need to align with the public interest to the extent possible; they may also include a frank statement of any particular interest that would benefit (one hopes, justifiably) from the requested action.

MISTAKE #8: NOT FOLLOWING UP

The industrial manager who envisions breezing into town one day and out the next, mission accomplished, is more apt to be disappointed than not. Convey your simplified message, along with any needed supporting information, as frequently, as continuously, and in as many forms as necessary to gain the attention and understanding of the government or press managers whose actions you need, while not becoming a nuisance. Once or twice is usually not enough. Be prepared to follow up, at home and in Washington, as necessary.

MISTAKE #9: NOT LISTENING

The message of the opposition and responses to your approach are valuable raw materials. You can use them to be more effective. They can keep you from making the same mistake twice. Casual or ill-considered reactions are not cause for tossing out a sound management plan, of course. But there are always ways to improve your product. And *listening* is to the Washington manager what *test-market surveys* are to the product marketing manager.

MISTAKE #10: PLANNING BEHIND

Begin with planning and continue to plan, to think ahead, to adapt to changing conditions and circumstances. The process involves analysis of results and the development of new objectives as you reach—or fail to reach—former objectives. Implicit in this, and in all of these, is the unavoidable burden of intelligence, or keeping up with what you have to keep up with to do your job of managing.

In Washington, as in your company, objectives stay in focus, and the system, with all its flaws, is more understandable when you think and function as a manager.

Chapter Ten

Interacting With the News Media

Phil Silvers, the actor, once said, "I've never won an interview yet." And many business executives would agree. For some of us, there are few things more fearful than being interviewed by a reporter.

You do it when you have to; it's not too bad if you're talking about your area of expertise, and it may even be satisfying if the news is good-to-neutral and the publication and the reporter are friendly.

But get me up before a TV camera to explain our environmental commitment? Sit me down with an environmental reporter? Now, in these crazy times? Now, when our operations are not all perfect and I'm not exactly sure when they will be perfect? Too risky. No fun! No way, if I can avoid it . . .

Fact is, you *can* avoid press interviews most of the time. You can beg off by sending others to speak for the company, experts who may know far more about the subject—for example, the technical side—than you do. Or you can toss it to "the PR guy (that's his job!)."

You do have a choice. So let's consider the options.

The question is: When is it *better* for you to handle the public statement on environmental matters—a phone call inquiry, a public statement, an interview? When is it a necessity and an advantage to be the news source? And, if you go for it, how do you improve your chances to "win" the interview, so you actually enhance your position on the green?

YOU CAN CHOOSE

There are conditions that favor your being the news source. For example:

• Whenever you are the best person to *reassure others* that you and your organization are on top of a crisis or a seriously challenging situation.

John Hall, the CEO of Ashland Oil, put his company way ahead of the negative news curve when he hopped on a plane and traveled to the site of a water-pollution incident. Instead of turning it over to other spokespersons, Hall showed the world—and all the company's customer-publics—that he personally was concerned about the environmental effects. By talking directly to the press, he demonstrated unusual openness and candor that won over a lot of skeptics and reassured a lot of concerned people.

Could a vice president or an environmental specialist have met the press? Of course. And it might have been okay. A lesser officer might have handled interviews as well *technically* (known how to parry and thrust with reporters), but none could have displayed more commitment and caring than that personified in the chief executive.

Nothing beats seeing the person in charge showing up at the scene soon after the incident. The press shows enormous respect for the executive who is brave enough and open enough to actually make himself or herself available at the time that editors and reporters need information and perspective. You should not expect hugs and huzzas, but you can expect your willingness to be interviewed to be met by a willingness to listen.

There's also a side advantage to being the news source if you're the "final authority." The chief executive can actually say *less* than others might say, and the press will be more likely to accept it. He or she will enjoy some credit for having become the news source, and a statement such as "We're looking into that and I expect we'll have a report tomorrow" will have more face value than if it came from a lesser official.

So if an environmental incident occurs or troubling green news breaks, and if it's on your watch or if you're the logical key executive, go ahead. Volunteer to talk to the media.

• Whenever you are *modeling a perspective*—presenting a new message in a manner that you and your organization want to see repeated and developed.

The chief executive of United Technologies, Bob Daniell, personally met the press when the company unveiled its strong, company-wide environmental policy. By personally presenting the fresh information concerning the company's commitment to waste reduction and pollution prevention, he set the tone for others in the company.

Plant managers and heads of operating divisions are the best people to make announcements about green developments in their areas. By statement and example, these key executives model the behavior they want to achieve.

So if the news is *yours*—coming from your area of responsibility— and if you want to set the tone and level of expectation for follow-through, you are the best news source.

• Whenever you will benefit from *media interaction*.

While it is true that you are always speaking *through* the news media to reach other customer-publics, it is also true that editors and reporters are themselves customer-publics with whom you need to interact. How else can you know personally the depth of interest in you and the level of understanding of your operations and issues? How else can you have a personal, one-to-one relationship with those whose attitudes so powerfully impact you and your business?

You may, if you have the chance, make a friend of a reporter or editor. You have the skills and the interest to do this, and *your* attitude of openness and commitment may make a real impression on a reporter who is even the least bit objective and willing to listen to you.

Yes, there are risks in this; some reporters are not objective or willing and you may or may not gain any ground through the interaction. But if you don't make a friend, you should at least build some respect and the possibility of future interaction. At minimum, you will learn something—how the process is working, how the questions are being phrased—that you can learn no other way.

So it may be that just the fact that you have not talked to a reporter in a long time (ever?) is reason enough for you to decide, on your own, to become a news source at the next opportunity. You can benefit from the interaction.

YOUR TURN WILL COME

An editor, like nature, abhors a vacuum. The news editor's job is to manage the production of stories that will fill space in newspapers, silence on radio, and blank screens on television. There may be slow news days, but there are no no-news days.

This means two things. Sometime, like it or not, your turn will come to make the news. The great, insatiable news machine will end up in your face.

It also means that when a reporter calls you to talk about your organization or facility, there will almost certainly be a story— whether you participate or not. This should be your signal not to dodge but to choose. Your choices are: Help determine the content of the story, or leave this to the reporter and to others who respond to the reporter's calls.

To a reporter, the term *good story* really means the *one* element that will help him or her tell the story. A good story is one that has the necessary dramatic elements to capture and hold the audience's attention. The reporter must use dramatic elements to expose a conflict or show a conflict resolved in order to capture the audience.

Steve Friedman, the executive producer of NBC Nightly News, has often told aspiring broadcast journalists that if they want to know how to construct a good TV news story, they should look at TV commercials as their model. They have everything. They expose and resolve conflicts six times a half hour in a nice, neat 30 seconds.

Print journalists quickly learn to incorporate dramatic elements into writing, if they want to land on page one with a by-line. They learn to search out the most colorful, pathetic, or telling quotes. And journalists are very aware of the importance of seeming to meet their audience needs. For years, local television news programs have been produced according to tried and true formulas. More and more, national network news programs follow similar formulas. In recent years a growing number of newspapers have adopted similar formula approaches under such titles as "Project 2000."

Reporters are people doing a job, and they are looking for what will allow them to do it with the least difficulty. To the extent possible, you need to help the reporter meet those needs.

My experience is that it's better to be the news source, and a good one, when you and your organization are selected for press attention. The question is, how to make the most of the situation?

BE A "3" OR A "7"

Let me help you see yourself through the eyes of a reporter or editor.

You will be sized up on what might be called "The News Source Ruler." Instinctively, after listening to you state your views or position, the journalist places you, as a potential news source, on a scale of quotability. Imagine this scale as a ruler numbered from 0 to 10.

At the far ends of the ruler—at the 0 and 1 positions, and at the 9 and 10 positions—are the extreme viewpoints. Radical or reactionary statements, incoherent comments, unexplained, unjustified polarized positions are expressed here.

Typically, reporters give short shrift to 0, 1, 9, and 10 because these views are too extreme to be credible. They are covered as messages from beyond the fringe, if they are covered at all. (You may think some pretty bizarre viewpoints get respectful media attention, but you should see the people reporters decide to ignore.)

At the middle of the News Source Ruler—at positions 4, 5, and 6—are the equivocators. The media also pay relatively little attention to statements that are too central, too wishy-washy to make good copy. How do you build a story out of "Further research is needed"? Or "We're working on that"? They may be the voice of reason and balance and thoughtful appreciation of the issue's complexity, but that usually translates to *boring*.

So most of the news consists of the viewpoints of positions 2, 3, 7, and 8.

Reporters turn to sources that give direct, reasoned, precisely stated, and supportable statements. They will try to get quotes from 2s and 3s on one side of an issue and 7s and 8s on the opposite side. Each side will typically get alternating paragraphs in the same story if the issue is hot, or separate stories as each side creates and dominates its own news events.

Objectivity to the journalist means giving both sides their chance and reporting accurately what they said. It doesn't mean filling in the boring middle. If you're a 5, you'll lose out to the 7 on the other side of the story. Don't let yourself be pushed to a position that is not yours, of course, but recognize that journalists don't trust 0s and 10s, and have little use for 5s.

Therefore, if you've decided you want to get into the story—which means you've come to the conclusion that you want to take charge of your own position, and not be left to the mercy of others—aim to be a 3 or a 7, a credible exponent of an identifiable viewpoint.

PERSON TO PERSON

Reporters want two things: *conflict* and *simplicity.* You will often have little interest in helping meet the reporter's need for conflict, but you can help keep the story simple and understandable. You can *educate* the reporter who is interviewing you about a technical, environmental subject, making the reporter smarter and thereby better able to write a good story.

You have to decide in advance what your main points are, then stress them consistently and repeatedly, even if you have to hook them onto your answers to irrelevant questions. Leave out the technical qualifiers that your colleagues might insist on but the general public doesn't need and won't grasp. Stay away from jargon, and find simple ways to explain the technical terms you can't avoid.

The most important thing I can tell you is: *check continuously to make sure the reporter understands what you are saying.* If the journalist never asks you what you mean, you should *not* assume you're being understood. Most of the time this is a signal that they are not getting your message—and either don't care or don't know what to ask you. So if the reporter gets glassy-eyed while you're talking or if he or she scribbles furiously, apparently taking down every word you're saying, as though you were dictating, call time out!

Ask, "Does this make sense to you?" or "I know some of this is complicated, so I'll be happy to slow down or back up" or "Could I give you an example to clarify what I've just said?"

Take charge of the interaction. Clear the way for a horizontal exchange. Don't put up barriers of jargon, technical terms, stiff language, run-on delivery, and the like. Get on the green together, where you have the best possibility of a productive interview.

If you don't simplify and explain on the spot, the reporter, back at the office, will try to do it for you, or will turn to another source. That could be a serious mistake. It's the reason for a lot of "misquotes" and "stupid stories." The journalist and the interviewed person simply didn't communicate effectively; there was not a productive interaction.

BE A TEACHER OR A COACH

Bear in mind that journalists—especially general assignment reporters—may have limited expertise and they always have limited time. At all but the largest general media organizations or the environmental specialty publications, reporters covering environmental stories are unlikely to have any special preparation for the assignment.

A typical reporter at a news conference or in an interview will try to bone up for questions, but often has neither the time nor the technical understanding sufficient for more than a cursory scan of available information. He or she will take a look at your press release, background kit, or fact sheet, if handed these in advance, but you shouldn't be surprised if they have a weak grasp of the meaning of developments.

Reporters covering an environmental emergency such as a leak may be drawn from a police beat or from general assignment. They reach the scene without time even to scan related stories, much less a technical handbook.

I have to believe that a lot of reporters are like I was when I was in journalism school. I suffered—and so, it seemed, did most of my friends who were writers—from science phobia. We went into writing because we were turned off by chemistry, physics, and the other sciences. I am told that today the typical college journalism major takes only one or two science courses, and chooses those carefully. (You may be able to do something about this. If the idea appeals to you, you can offer to teach local journalists about what you are doing, through a local high school or graduate course.)

My point is that you shouldn't expect general assignment reporters to find much time (or to have much inclination) for technical training they will use only a few times a year. A reporter who covers your facility regularly, of course, is a good candidate for "continuing education," or some helpful coaching, if you can offer it with respect and no pain.

It's a good idea to train yourself and your staff in the best way to interact with the media. Hiring good public information specialists can help, but the suggestions in this chapter are for the business executive not necessarily in public relations to learn to interact with reporters.

I strongly recommend a good media training program or executive presentation coaching, for you and your fellow executives. But remember, journalists by now all know that business executives get media training, so you don't want to flaunt the "tricks" you pick up in the training session. Just relax and let the relationship develop easily, working in the guidelines we've talked about in this chapter.

GET PERSONAL—AND KNOW WHO'S INTERVIEWING YOU

What happens when you actually agree to an interview? First of all, as we've discussed before, remember that you have some rights. And while you exercise them, you can improve the climate for the interview interaction.

Your most basic right is the right to know who is interviewing you. Expect identification, but then I suggest that you take charge and "get personal."

It is always appropriate, even if the reporter gives name and identification, to ask, "What is your name again? And the name of your publication (or station)?" Slow the questioner down long enough to turn him or her into a person so you can have a person-to-person interaction. Smile; if it's not a simple name, ask how to spell it. Ask, "What are you working on?" or "Are you on deadline now?" or another friendly question to show you are interested, that you care about his or her work.

When you get a phone call from a reporter ready right then to ask you questions, you need to exercise special care. I recommend that clients *always* slow the process down and *not* launch into the interview at that time. Instead, take the name and number of the person who calls and says he or she is a reporter, and then call back, even if it is only a few minutes later. (Just say you need to clear something out of the way so you can give the reporter your attention.)

Two major benefits accrue to you. One is that you verify that the reporter is with a real media organization. You may find out he or she is a free-lance writer, which is okay, but you wouldn't have known that if you hadn't placed the call yourself.

And the second major benefit is that you give yourself at least a few minutes to organize yourself and decide what *you* want to say. I suggest that you write on a three-by-five card at least one point that you want to make and that you have this card in front of you at the phone when you call back. Then, during the conversation, make your point, in so many words, at least three times.

And again, the two phone calls—one from the reporter, one from you—have the effect of improving the relationship. Each of you has already put a little effort into this interview. It puts things on a little more even footing.

You also have the right to control the length of the interview. Feel free to say at the outset: "I wanted to get back to you now, because I thought you might be on deadline, but I'm afraid I only have a few minutes to speak with you now." Tell why, if you care to. The point is to establish that there is a time limit (you may want to say, "I have until 4 o'clock" or another specific time). This puts the reporter on notice that you will expect the important questions to be asked up front and not sprung on you after a few easy, intentionally disarming comments or questions.

Incidentally, knowing your questioner should go deeper than just name and phone number, if possible. It's to your advantage to get to know local journalists. A reporter will often appreciate your attempts to create a dialogue, and even if he or she doesn't write something immediately, may remember those features on a slow day.

Beyond that, while there isn't much you can do about the nature of journalism, you can certainly try to understand journalists and figure out how to deal with them. This can improve your own performance as a source and lead to better coverage.

It doesn't have to be complicated. You can invite a reporter for a background tour and meeting. You can suggest feature stories—

noncontroversial stories that may or may not involve current news—and make yourself available when he or she is looking for information.

This proactive approach can help ensure that your other publics will read and see your side of the story. It may also help soften media coverage of unfavorable events as well.

BASIC INTERVIEW TIPS

As for the interview itself, here are some tried and true guidelines:

- Keep your message simple and use examples.
- State your most significant points up front and continue to stress them.
- Speak in the first person if appropriate; it strengthens credibility.
- Always tell the truth. Admit wrong when you know it exists and explain why it is wrong.
- Admit it when you don't know something. Offer to find out if you can.
- Avoid argument. Remain courteous and positive.
- Do not be led from your message.
- Do not repeat insulting or leading questions. Acknowledge them but steer the interview back to your own points.
- Listen carefully to questions and responses to your answers.
- Ask if the reporter understands specific parts of what you are saying.

These tips and the interactive approach outlined in this chapter can help you create respectful relationships with the media. I'm not saying you will necessarily become a particular journalist's best friend—though it could happen!—and I am saying that this is the critical place to add value to your green communication. By building and sustaining relations with this customer-public, you are also creating open channels to the rest of your vital customer-publics.

Chapter Eleven

Relating to Investors

Attention, greening company! Stay in step with your owners! Now *that* may be a tough marching order.

What is the drill? Consider the paradoxes of stockholders. On the one hand, they are the easiest customer-public to reach. If you have stockholders, you have open channels for communicating your green commitment. Law requires you to tell them what you're up to—and prudence says tell them often. The channels are annual and quarterly reports, special letters, publications, annual meetings, and other occasions.

Reaching is no problem. The publicly held company is constantly in touch with its owners (as well as prospective owners). It's relatively easy to plug in green messages as appropriate to reach stockholders. *Relating* may be another matter because, on the other hand, stockholders are not entirely available to the same kinds of interaction your company uses to get into relationships with other customer-publics. Establishing any kind of relationship requires a certain degree of definability. Characteristics vary in every customer-public group, certainly; but employees have many traits in common, to which the company may relate; so do community neighbors, suppliers, even regulators and politicians. At least you know pretty much where the great majority of these customer-publics stand most of the time, or you can fairly easily find out, using an approach such as our QUALITY model.

Stockholders, especially in the big company, are another case altogether. They are individual people, and they are institutions. Some are in for the long term, committed to the company as much as any employee, maybe as much as family. Others are short-term and detached—in today, out tomorrow. Some are influenced by the company and its friends. Some are influenced by opportunists, competitors, and enemies of the company.

GREEN HEAT OF THE 90s

It is this paradox—the bed of opposite and conflicting opinions and what's in it for me?—that has made the area of investor relations the corporate hotseat of the 90s. Long gone is the (probably mythical) stockholder who is unquestioning, mostly widows and heirs and other nontroublesome types. Institutional investors, global ownerships, shifts in economic power globally, electronic transactions, and a seemingly endless cascade of mergers and acquisitions have created volatility never before known. The shifting of social responsibilities from government to the private sector and the rise of social questions such as environmental responsibility as corporate topics have made the investor relations seat even hotter.

Some of the heat comes from the investment community— brokers, advisors, funds, and individual stockholders. Interest among institutional and other investors in the dollar payoff of green rules and green sentiment has become a steady influence in stock buy-and-sell decisions. The rules that require pollution prevention equipment purchases, the sentiments that cause consumers to buy green products, the pocketbook, as well as the emotional influences that come into play as a nation goes green—all these have risen in the last several years to impact shareowned companies.

Opportunism, when greening means a higher ROI, as well as agitation within stockholder ranks about green obligations, have been driving factors in getting management's attention to environmental issues.

VALDEZ PRINCIPLES

A primary source of green contention at the social level, affecting company-investor relations, is the green activist group. While many activists over the years have needled management, often with staged publicity tactics, like picketing a stockholder meeting or bulling inside to hand the president a "dirty" award, it was a special kind of group, arising from the investment community, that seized lion's share credit for stirring up stockholders and management on the subject of environmental disclosure and accountability.

The Coalition for Environmentally Responsible Economies (CERES) was stitched together in the late 1980s with people from investment firms, government pension funds, and church groups by social activist and financial advisor Joan Bavaria. Together, the members represented millions of shares of stock in major corporations.

CERES's main leverage on management was the unveiling in 1989 of its proposed 10-point code of corporate environmental conduct. With intent to shock, the group called its code the *Valdez* Principles, reminding publics and the news media of the (then-recent) Exxon tanker *Valdez* accident, which released millions of gallons of crude oil in Alaska's Prince William Sound. The suggested principles (listed below) were not related to tankers or Alaska. The title signaled attack and conveyed a point: roughly, that companies harm and don't care about the environment. Any company approached to sign on to the *Valdez* Principles would obviously start in a reactive, if not defensive, mode.

FIGURE 11–1
Valdez *Principles 1990*

1.	Protection of the Biosphere
2.	Sustainable Use of Natural Resources
3.	Reduction and Disposal of Waste
4.	Wise Use of Electricity
5.	Risk Reduction
6.	Marketing of Safe Products and Services
7.	Damage Compensation
8.	Disclosure
9.	Environmental Directors and Managers
10.	Assessment and Annual Audit

HOW COMPANIES HAVE RESPONDED TO CERES

Some companies, mostly smaller companies with already established green-market orientation, adopted the *Valdez* Principles. Some saw the pledge as a marketing advantage and used it competitively. Others recognized an opportunity to make a commitment to a cause that would grow and have an influence on both the business community and public policy.

CERES members—owners of stock—took their *Valdez* Principles to many large corporations. None signed, but almost all felt some impact. Some companies were required to entertain stockholder resolutions asking management to adopt the *Valdez* Principles. Votes for the resolutions were predictably small, but at Kerr-McGee the total vote in favor reached a significant 16.7 percent in 1990.[1] At several companies' annual meetings, stockholders raised the issue and asked management to support the pledge or explain their resistance. For any number of companies, responding to direct contact from CERES or merely anticipating the possibility of shareholder interest in the *Valdez* Principles, envirocomm was kicked into higher gear. Companies communicated heavily about environmental commitment, with and without reference to the proposed code, and made sure the subject was covered before, during, and after the annual meeting season.

How did companies say no to CERES? When asked by the news media if they would sign the *Valdez* Principles, companies answered generally in the same way: *No, we are not signing. We have our own set of principles regarding environmental protection and stewardship. Here is what it says . . .*

Companies without readily available policy statements were given incentive to put these position pieces together and to examine closely the company's green strengths and vulnerabilities. Media inquirers could usually get a package of relevant materials quickly.

By mid-1992, as companies jostled to be engaged in discussions raised by the United Nations Earth Summit, the *Valdez* Principles no longer stood alone, nor necessarily led any discussion on corporate management's environmental commitment. The business community's aggressive greening actions in the last few years have put companies in better charge of their public positioning and into better communication with the investment community and others interested in green issues.

In addition to their individual company green policy statements (see Chapter Twenty-Two), many companies have signed on to progressive codes of conduct within their own industries, trade groups, and communities. The chemical industry's Responsible Care program is the key example (see Chapter Twenty-Six). Associations in the forest products industry have developed a comprehensive code of environmental and forest management principles for its members' use. The textile industry's Encouraging Environmental Excellence program, requiring chief executives to commit to 10 principles, allows participating companies to use the program's seal in its advertising and marketing.

The International Chamber of Commerce's Business Charter on Sustainable Development, signed by a variety of companies in several countries, has become preeminent in corporate green guidelines worldwide. Activity in the business community among the more advanced companies who have signed pledges is now toward the next stage: measuring progress, benchmarking for specific improvements, and reporting results.

Some stockholders will be satisfied with moves such as these. Others will keep pushing management on green issues. An area of continuing challenge from skeptical stockholders and others will be that of adherence to pledges and enforcement. Many companies will need to be transparently open to answer such challenges—to prove their intentions by making their evidence easily available. The message—inspect, don't expect (or track us, don't trust us)—will need to be delivered constantly, with full awareness that this puts an obligation on the company to be constantly communicating with investors about greening.

CERES itself has evolved from attack toward dialogue. With industry input, the group's proposed principles have been amended to be more practicable, more acceptable to the businesses they once attacked.

While, at the two-year mark, none of the principles' signatories included the major, transnational, publicly held companies that were the initial objective, CERES and its shocking code have had an impact on shareholders and the companies accountable to these vital, and sometimes volatile, customer-publics.

WHY TALK GREEN TO YOUR INVESTORS?

The envirocomm lesson of the *Valdez* Principles is not much different from that of the *Valdez* incident itself. You need to take charge of the dialogue with key constituencies. When the external hit comes, you benefit from ongoing relationships.

In the 1990s, the investor-owned company must communicate continuously with regard to its environmental commitment and performance. Some stockholders will want to know the company's positions and green results for purposes of protecting their investment in the firm. Others will use their shares for leverage toward company action and public policy. Some may not seem to be very interested, so long as the stock price and dividends are satisfactory. But they, and others who are not so trusting or committed, may be influenced by negative green news associated with the firm or by prodding from activists.

To repeat an earlier point: It is neither necessary nor possible to please all the stockholders all the time. Or to communicate with 100 percent of this changeable, diverse customer-public.

Building a base of investors who understand the total corporate condition, and the green role in it, is the best way to prepare for sudden challenges from inimical forces. And it is the best way to attract additional stock customers who may add both value to the company and strength to the company's customer-public relationships.

Shortly, we'll discuss ways to get in touch with the vital investor-support group.

WHAT STOCKHOLDERS WANT TO KNOW

One study of stockholders quantified the level of general interest in greening. Marc Epstein, professor of accounting at Yeshiva University, surveyed a random sampling of stockholders with 100+ shares in any stock listed on the NYSE or American exchange, across 50 states.[2]

Epstein's results rattled against any stereotypical view of shareholders as conservatives interested only in financial return. He said social concerns were high in the minds of his survey respondents. Of these, said Epstein, in 1991, shareholders' number one interest was that the companies in which they were investing were controlling and reducing pollution. Second, he said, was interest in product safety.

Not particularly revealing. You knew that. It does confirm that you're not alone if you sense greenism in your investor ranks. But because of the diversity in this customer-public, the green interest among stockholders of a given company may be all over the lot.

Stockholders interested only in a return on their invested dollars will want to know: How will environmental problems affect the price of the stock, company performance, dividends? What is management doing to minimize the problems? How much will environmental costs be? If you're selling green products or green services (for example, cleanup technology or process consultant work), what's the market like and what will be your share next year or some reasonable time in the future?

Shareholders who are more social-minded will seek a range of data, pledges toward action, and results that are audited and proven.

Before I go on to some specific green-interest areas, let me remind you that *all* customer-publics, wherever and whoever they may be, want to know one thing from you and your company. And that is: *Do you care about me?* They ask that question in a lot of different ways—Will you protect my money? Will you protect my planet?—but that's what it boils down to. Keep that in mind for later, when we talk about communicating, and remember that they don't listen if they don't believe you care about them.

GREEN RATERS

Investment firms—advisers, as well as entrepreneurs who put funds together—have been active in the last several years, trying to quantify corporate greening.

For example, in Switzerland, attorney Robert Chanson established Eco-Rating International to rate firms on environmental risk. He sees this as a kind of green Moody's, to serve green-fund managers.

Chanson proposes a universally applicable assessment method that allows an "Indonesian textile company to be measured against a British steel company," but at this writing, the system was limited to businesses within like industries. Admitting to more subjectivity than one finds in a financial rating system, Chanson nonetheless believes his system is fair and logical. To give you an idea of what green raters look for, here are the categories for judging as given by Eco-Rating:

- *Environmental impact*—emissions, use of natural resources, disaster risk.
- *Logistics*—methods of transporting personnel, materials, and finished goods.
- *Infrastructure*—construction of buildings, equipment.
- *Ecological profile of products.*
- *Compliance with environmental laws and guidelines.*
- *Environmental risks from research and development.*
- *Management*—delineation of responsibilities, qualifications, allocation of resources.
- *Soft issues.*

Another group, the Investor Responsibility Research Center (IRRC), uses the Standard, and Poors directory; it assesses listed corporations, rating them on six environmental factors:

1. Environmental disclosures in securities filings.
2. Liabilities resulting from past contamination of specific sites.
3. Reports of significant accidental spills of oil or chemicals.
4. Estimated routing emissions of toxic chemicals.
5. Environmental enforcement actions under nine environmental statutes that resulted in monetary penalty assessments.
6. Companies' *descriptions* of their environmental policies and programs.

While receiving a favorable profile from green raters may be helpful, ecorating, of ALL types, is a subjective art form; greening is in the eye of the beholder. When ratings clash, who is believed? Private green product rating systems, similarly subjective, have not fared well, with the result that government green rating is entirely possible.

Meantime, on the business side, organizations like the Global Environmental Management Initiative are trying to help companies measure, benchmark, and report their individual green-process improvements. This, combined with continuing communication with shareholders, could provide the information and reassurance needed by the stockholders, if not the fund managers.

START THOSE GREEN INTERACTIONS YOURSELF

The point of our QUALITY model holds true. Take charge of the green communication process; *make it a process,* not an event or a response, with all stockholders.

Create interaction. Take responsibility for give-and-take with stockholders about the environment and the company's commitments. Interaction is not one-way communication; it requires feedback and opportunities for the stockholder to speak.

Identify and focus on the core constituency. *It is desirable to reach and to reassure the reassurable stockholder,* who cares about the company's green position. The goal should be *interaction,* fostered through communication, with stockholders who have more than a casual interest in the company's success.

Interaction occurs when the company asks questions, and when it listens to answers given and questions raised by stockholders.

ENVIROCOMM TIPS FOR INVESTOR INTERACTION

Following are some ways for the company to relate to stockholders more interactively. Note that security analysts are important in the QUALITY envirocomm process. Analysts and stockbrokers influence the opinions of stockholders.

1. ANALYST SOCIETY SPEECHES. *What happens*: Your president talks to security analysts and includes green information (look at the topics listed above and choose what's important). *Envirocomm tips*: You keep track of the questions, if any, related to greening. You consider the analyst who asked the green questions a good conduit to investors, or an influencer of general opinion about your firm. So you follow up with that analyst; you put him or her on a list to get green information later; you look for ways to interact with him or her; for example, an invitation to:

2. PLANT TOURS, OPEN HOUSES, SEMINARS. *What happens*: Your company invites several analysts (rule of thumb, no more than 8 or 10, to keep it personal) to go through facilities or take part in a company discussion. Environmental information is

available. Focus is on Q&A. *Envirocomm tips*: You note questions on greening and answers given. Follow up. Put them on a list. Give them your business phone number; call when you have green news.

3. STOCKHOLDER QUESTIONNAIRE. Some companies (or research firms hired by the company) survey stockholders periodically, asking if they understand financials, what they'd like to see in their annual report, what they think of management, why they acquired the stock, and so forth. *Envirocomm tips*: Put some green questions in. Scan all returns for green comment and questions. Use for improving envirocomm and for clues on ways to interact. Note that you may be able to survey certain categories of your stockholders (e.g., employee-stockholders, retiree-stockholders); this can help you quantify—identify and better understand—opinions and needs within your core groups.

4. STOCKHOLDER "CLUSTER" COMMUNICATION. You can zero in on high concentrations of stockholders—check the list and see where they are—for more interaction. Whether they are in a metro area or clustered near plants or headquarters, consider: *events*, such as open houses, homecomings, tours, mini-meetings (taking the company to the people); *publicity*, using local newspapers, radio, and television. The point: show off environmental progress and get input and understanding on green issues from those who have a stake in your success. This could evolve into something like an occasional *community advisory panel*, but different: These are people who own your stock.

5. OTHER TWO-WAY GREEN AVENUES. Publications that make it easy for the stockholder to get involved: a reply form with a phone number or order form for green information. Hot lines or toll-free phones with a recorded *envirocomm* message and a tape to receive the calling stockholder's message. Investment clubs that look at companies like yours and to whom you can relate.

Annual meetings can be a place to help stockholders feel part of the company's green commitment. When AT&T created a public information strategy for its highly successful campaign to reduce the use of CFCs in its manufacturing processes, its senior environmental and public relations executives outlined the process to its shareholders at the annual meeting before it ever went public. A special videotape was prepared to explain the campaign, as well as other environmental activities under way, and met with much success when shown at the meeting. AT&T and its shareholders were in step, moving onto the green.[3]

Chapter Twelve

Suppliers: The *Cradle* in Cradle-to-Grave

Most manufacturers take stuff—raw materials—and turn it into something else with greater value. The product is then shipped to other manufacturers who add some value of their own, or straight to market. This is elemental. But in the context of greening, it bears mentioning that if manufacturing is a chain with many links, you may be the only green link in a long stretch of brown. That is, unless you can help others in the chain green up as well.

In the emerging scheme of things, product design, formulation, and production must increasingly consider the environmental impact of manufacturing from cradle to grave. That's the essence of AT&T's "Design for Environment," says Environment and Safety Engineering Vice President David Chittick. The systems thinking program, based on Total Quality Management, was brought into play after government-mandated divestiture created a recycling problem for the company. Back when the phones were leased, the rate of return, reuse, and recycling was very high. But the new government regulations increased purchasing of telephones by consumers. Now all AT&T business unit managers are encouraged to think ahead to the total use of their products. "Environmental considerations are part of every design activity. Disposal, handling, energy and resource requirements, or recycling needs, are reviewed before a manufacturing process is created," says Chittick. It's critical, of course, that you look at the processes inside your own plants, but when it comes to raw materials, the cradle is upstream at your suppliers. Focused communication about greening is especially critical for them.

Your greening company benefits by working with suppliers to encourage their own progressive environmental policies.

First, it makes your own green goals easier to achieve. Everybody is pulling in the same direction. Second, if pollution is waste and waste is expensive, suppliers that reduce pollution may be able to lower their costs and save you money. Third, it extends your green influence upstream, which makes you part of a green chain, not a solitary green link. (McDonald's, by insisting on containers to save shipping and storage space, forced the dairy industry to change to boxy containers.)[1] Finally, it reinforces your credibility with other customer-publics, including consumers, activists, and media.

This is not to say all will always be sweetness and light. Sometimes communication will reveal things you wish you didn't have to know. For example, in *Changing Course*, Business Council for Sustainable Development Chairman Stephan Schmidheiny tells of the painful but valuable experience of Smith & Hawken, a California retail and mail-order company that made its name selling quality garden tools and equipment.[2]

The company learned in 1988 that the teak used in its line of furniture was being harvested unsustainably by its suppliers in Thailand and Myanmar (Burma). Smith & Hawken's commitment to ecoefficiency drove it to investigate alternate sources of supply and eventually to switch to a Javanese supplier. The cost, in research, higher materials prices, and lost business, ran to several hundred thousand dollars. But the company has kept its strong environmental reputation at a time when issues of sustainable forestry are prominent in the public mind.

The nature of your green communication with suppliers will depend on your business. Canadian Pacific Hotels & Resorts is pretty clear and specific about what it wants from its suppliers.[3] CP tells its hotels to buy in bulk to reduce costs and packaging waste. It also prohibits individual serving containers, items in packages that can't be reused or recycled, and disposables, and requires buying recycled items whenever possible. In general, CP tells employees to question every purchase—Is the product really needed? Does it damage the environment? Is there a greener alternative?—and to base buying decisions on the answers.

IBM also takes an activist approach. The company was once known for its confrontations with suppliers, but is now developing strong green policies with them and using their environmental performance as a criterion for continued business relations.[4] John Gillett, the company's procurement manager for northern Europe, notes that diplomacy and innovation are central to effective maintenance of the sometimes delicate relationships with suppliers. He recommends four steps to creating a credible green buying policy:

1. Build sound relationships marked by mutual respect.
2. Make sure your staff understands the issues and supports you.
3. Create a vision of where you want to take your suppliers.
4. Create environmental awareness and communicate the issues.

Perhaps no company has worked harder at outreach to suppliers than S.C. Johnson, a U.S. maker of household cleaning products. After taking up the sustainable development banner in 1990, the company formulated long-range goals to support its green philosophy and began working on spreading it to suppliers as well.[5]

To make the point about the seriousness of its commitment to SD and its suppliers' role in the process, S. C. Johnson convened a conference for nearly 200 managers and suppliers, many from outside the United States. CEO Richard Carpenter pointed out cases in which better environmental performance also meant higher profits and laid out specific, measurable goals for company-supplier performance. Attendees also heard from some of the company's important customers, which left them with a stronger vision of the green interdependence of the various parts of the production process. Follow-up mailings and a newsletter for showcasing successful partnering keep the gains and aims of the conference alive and continuously communicated.

And in true form of the two-way interaction we have talked about that is so important with customer publics, you can *learn from your suppliers* as well.

The utilities industry has perhaps done more than any other from the suppliers' perspective with its demand-side management techniques to influence efficient consumption. These DSM programs range from efficient lighting (such as encouraged in the EPA Green Lights program) to "feebates" for efficient electricity consumption in new buildings, to energy centers where companies like Southern California Edison showcase new technologies in efficiency for their consumers.

Chapter Thirteen

Inspecting and Correcting The Process

The QUALITY Communication Model is a loop, a recirculating system, not a conveyor belt. You can tap into the system at any point. You can apply all or part of the system to any tactic or challenge.

To underscore what we've said earlier, the effective envirocomm process constantly enriches and improves your communication with your core publics. It helps ensure that you are on the public green while you pursue the technical and operational aspects of greening.

"INSPECT, DON'T EXPECT" IS A WORKABLE MOTTO

This is something you can't just delegate and forget about. It's a total quality management approach for communication, accepting the fact that the key to satisfying customer-publics is quality control. The communication tactics used in the envirocomm process must be periodically inspected, just as you would regularly inspect and audit manufacturing processes.

The inspector—the manager qualified to supervise the construction and maintenance of public relationships for the organization—checks the objectives and time frame for reaching them and uses the information constantly generated by the QUALITY system to assess performance.

LOOKING FOR BEST PRACTICES

Tactics that work are nurtured. Let's say you are with a company that has entered into a cooperative arrangement with law enforcement and fire officials, neighbors, and others in your community to make emergency response plans for serious environmental incidents.

Let's further suppose that a meeting of the local environmental-emergency group is conducted with exceptional tactical success. The group reaches a high level of interaction and participation, asks questions not previously raised, allows your company to better understand points of contention, and/or achieves a break-through in understanding the challenges your company and the community need to address together.

This meeting and the events and actions surrounding it may be held up as a "best practices" candidate, a tactic to be bench-marked, to be matched or improved even further in the future.

Tactics that don't seem to be working are examined for faults. Did we listen too little or talk too late? Were we at the right place at the right time with the right people? Did we score with our core group (most important), even though we're not on the same wavelength with individuals who have their own (conflicting) missions? Do we toss out this tactic as unworkable or untimely? Or do we focus on the weaknesses and try to correct them?

Feedback is essential. The QUALITY model says that you are never through with the highly productive exercises of quantifying and refining relationship candidates, asking *what, why,* and *how* questions of customer-publics, and listening intently to both their answers and their questions.

You must inspect, interpret, and initiate the appropriate action to keep the communication system fresh and effective.

INSPECTION FROM TOP MANAGEMENT

Cooperative groups like the one used in this example are catching on. Community committees can encourage partnerships for envi-ronmental achievement. Key executives in some firms participate in as many of these neighborhood groups as possible, and per-sonally read reports from the committees.

This is a good way both to check up on the envirocomm process and to experience firsthand the signals of both warning and opportunity it sends to top management. And when a conflict arises and it is important for the top people to get involved in communication as organization spokespersons, it helps to have had some previous involvement and to have reached some level of comfort and trust in the process.

This is how the envirocomm process works as a quality-management system, as an indicator of need, and as a mechanism for correction.

THAT WILL BRING YOU BACK TO "DO"

That wonderful do-re-mi song in the *Sound of Music* floats in the air when our firm is using the QUALITY model. At the Y in the process, you need to reconnect to the Q at the beginning. On the second and subsequent times around, think of the Q as also standing for "Question the process!" How is it working, how can it be improved? What "old" ideas need to be discarded and replaced by better ideas?

Inspection and correction of the environmental communication process can yield better communication practices and results, with all the attendant benefits.

But you've got to *have* a process, and management has not only to stand behind it; management has to be in the middle of it.

P A R T

III

HOW TO . . .

Chapter Fourteen

Traits of the Greening Executive

If your company is going green, you could find yourself carrying the banner. Walking the talk is critical, as every business executive has discovered, if his or her organization is seriously committed to successful greening. How do the winners do it?

Whether you are the "chief environmental officer," as some CEOs now consider themselves, or the designated manager of the corporate environmental mission, you may find it helpful to examine the five traits I see most often in today's environmental executive.

(1) Transparency. This is the answer to entrenched public skepticism. To overcome doubts that business is really serious about acting positively with regard to the environment, the greening executive needs to invite inspection.

This is simply facing up to facts discussed previously in this book. We cannot relate to publics in the way we used to, and especially not when it involves the sensitive, personalized topic of environmental matters. Greenism forever destroys the acceptability of "competitive secret" or "proprietary information" as explanations for corporate confidentiality. The wall between the company and inquiring publics has been replaced by a magnifying glass.

To get on the green, be the model of openness. Initiate dialogue. Encourage questions.

I've seen openness and dialogue become magic keys for many greening executives in recent years. The keys were identified initially by 70 companies that met in Rotterdam under the International Chamber of Commerce umbrella in 1991; they produced the Business Charter on Sustainable Development, which at this writing has been endorsed by more than 1,000 companies across six continents. So the keys are being duplicated at a rapid pace.

Plug into this model as your organization goes green. *Sustainable development* means working to balance ecology and economics. *Openness* means letting people watch you do it. And *dialogue* means constant conversation with everybody who has a stake in your environmental performance.

This suggests that, for the greening executive, honesty may not be the *best* policy. *Better* is transparency—so people can look into your motives, examine your management data (for example, the results of your environmental audit, or the numbers showing how you've done with waste reduction or pollution abatement) and make up their own minds about your honest efforts.

Some CEOs, like Dow Chemical's Frank Popoff, whose company has set up open, self-examining committees in the communities where the company operates in the U.S. and elsewhere, take a don't-trust-us-track-us stance toward customer-publics. Others go face to face with employees and other customer-publics. An example is Bob Daniell, United Technologies' chief, who, when it was not practical to speak personally with all employees, held a live, open-circuit televised interview with employees at several locations to discuss his plans for greening, and to get feedback.

Do you really have to meet your customer-publics? Can't you learn what you need to know by listening to your staff (or your boss) talk about what the publics want or require? How about reading reports? Some of the good research reports or polling data have actual quotes from people—isn't that helpful? And what about the telephone? Surely, phone conversations with legislators or journalists or suppliers are direct and efficient ways to interact, right?

Bob Crawford, the CEO of Brook Furniture Rental in Arlington Heights, Illinois (a company that grew from $800,000 to more than $50 million in revenues under Crawford's guidance), credited much of his success to being a "road warrior." He made a habit of spending an extraordinary amount of time going to see clients.

"The CEO has got to be able to sense the marketplace in order to have confidence that he's moving in the right direction," he told an *Inc.* magazine reporter. "I need to be able to temper reported facts and trends with my own feeling for the real, current market climate."

The benefits of face-to-face meetings—or of simply being in the room with a customer-client group, for example, during a club meeting or community program—are invaluable.

(2) **Accountability.** This applies on two levels. First, you should be ready to relate to the concern and confusion that can be caused by free-flowing, government-required green data. For example, the Superfund Amendments' Title III emissions data have to be available to government, communities, employees, and the news media. This information, often perplexing and frightening ("1,000 pounds of toxic chemicals emitted last year"), goes also to activist groups that sometimes use the data as long knives with which to attack the company.

Greening executives are becoming accustomed to this requirement for accountability and are even going further. Some, for instance, are cooperating with the U.S. Environmental Protection Agency in its voluntary toxics release inventory reduction program, saying in effect, "Hold our feet to the fire in the future, and we'll give you the coals to get it going."

The second level of accountability involves criminal action against executives. Government enforcers and private litigators have discovered the power of green-collar charges. The federal Clean Air Act specifically makes corporate executives accountable for green-law infractions and some are already facing fines and jail terms. (See Chapter Thirty for more grisly details.)

While aware that the buck can't be bucked, the greening executive is becoming an enthusiast for sharing accountability inside the company. He or she can be expected to support performance reviews that put a premium on environmental stewardship.

(3) **Connectability.** The profile of the loser in the greening game is the executive who is aloof, isolated, and reactive—particularly when that reaction is slow to come.

More than being accessible (which has long been a model executive trait), the successful greening executive will be *interactive*. He or she will find ways to demonstrate that the company and its various publics are connected—i.e., acting more or less in harmony—when it comes to environmental progress.

Partnerships are a good way to get connected. The top executives of McDonald's, for example, sat down with the leader of the Environmental Defense Fund. Some people question whether one result of their move (getting rid of plastic clamshells) actually helps solve solid-waste disposal problems. But it did reconnect the fast-food giant with vital consumers who had picketed against the clamshells, and it did so apparently without compromising the company's mission. (See Chapter Twenty-three for more of these stories.)

Greening executives can't afford to wait for complaints or even for requests for environmental information. They anticipate the emerging interest and unasked questions of employees, stockholders, government, neighbors, and other publics. In a sense these are marketing moves, with the publics recast as the *customers* needed to buy in to the company's green success.

With employees or within the community, look for the good greening executive to be seated on the same side of the table with others whose interests are linked to his or hers—and listening a lot.

(4) Commitment. The environmental executive has to prove he or she means business, starting inside the company.

A Chemical Manufacturers Association survey showed that employees often show less support for their company than for the surrounding community. So the best corporate green policies are those grown *organically,* with top managers helping to develop a company consensus.

It's not all top-down. One executive conducted a survey to find out which conservation groups were supported by employees, and then began helping to align company support with the independent employee participation.

Du Pont—which, like other prominent companies, draws its share of aggressive green critics—evaluates managers for their compliance with a tough corporate policy and the impact of green programs they initiate.

The environmental stewardship program at Du Pont gives close attention to all customer-publics, involving employees, suppliers, customers, citizen groups, and business-partner companies in many countries.

Du Pont is convinced it has started a trend within the company that will not be easily reversed. Meanwhile, as a visible sign of persistence at the top, most of the public speeches given by CEO Ed Woolard are at least in part a greening report.

Likewise, Richard Mahoney, CEO of Monsanto, a few years ago laid out his company's seven-point green manifesto—The Monsanto Pledge—and he and his top managers have been defining the details and reporting the hits and misses ever since.

Incidentally, as we've said, no executive gets green points for a commitment simply to meet regulatory standards. Par won't make it. The specialty of the successful environmental executive is pushing subordinates for goals that come out ahead of the law, and even slightly ahead of the expectations of some publics. Thus, AT&T's executives are committed to the goal of completely eliminating any toxic air emissions by 2000. Du Pont has pledged to reduce hazardous wastes by 35 percent from 1990 levels.

(5) Courage. This is an old-fashioned executive trait, implicit in commitment and needed more than ever when, in the course of company greening, the going gets rough.

Getting onto the green sometimes means going against the grain. It can require the loneliest move of all—when you leave your counselors behind and let your green light shine out.

John Hall, CEO of Ashland Oil Company, showed grace under fire after the Monongahela River oil spill in January 1988. Against legal advice, he went to Pittsburgh and met the press and hostile publics. He showed his personal concern for the contamination and his commitment to a solution, on the scene, immediately, and is credited with minimizing negative reaction.

I think there is food for thought in a column written by Meg Greenfield of *The Washington Post* during the 1992 presidential race. She examined what she called the "gut criteria" on which every candidate is judged. Her comments are just as applicable to the company CEO who is being judged on his or her handling of an environmental mission.

A successful presidential candidate, Greenfield says, must exhibit the qualities of responsibility, a public interest purpose, and strength.

A candidate who is in for the winning run cannot be perceived as ducking a problem by blaming it on someone or something else. Responsibility—the courage to continue on a course to which a commitment has been made—this is truly the defining principle for the job of a candidate running for high office or the head of a company going for the green. There is a lesson in Greenfield's surmise that when a candidate ducks an issue or lies outright "it is less the fact of deliberately speaking an untruth, than the fact of refusing thereby to take responsibility that is regarded as disqualifying."

She suggests that this was the perception when candidate Ross Perot dropped out of the race and asked the public to believe that it wasn't his fault, that he hadn't even been responsible for hiring his campaign manager. This lack of accountability or responsibility or *courage*, said Greenfield, is "the worst attribute a presidential candidate can have on his resume." And business executives know this is true in the Green World of Business as well.

Like the political candidate, the winning greening executive needs to show that he or she is driven by a public purpose, not simply a business purpose, and certainly not merely ego.

The courage to connect to various customer-publics and to face tough questions and rough times on their terms and on their turf, is a winning trait for the greening business executive in the 1990s.

Greenfield says, about presidential candidates, "Following a purpose, taking the heat for it, making it come about—these are the evidences of strength." CEOs and environmental managers are surely tested as much or more on these qualities as presidential candidates!

I hope these insights may help you carry the green banner for your company the way that other winners do—open to inspection, accountable for your record, connected to every customer-public, with a commitment that just gets tougher when the going green gets rough.

Chapter Fifteen

Listening: Be a Hearperson

As a business executive fretting about your role in green communication, you may feel like those bronze statues of the monkeys with their paws over their eyes and ears. Your big concern is what will come out of your mouth.

My advice is to relax. Put your paws over your mouth. Speak later—after you've done some seeing and hearing.

In Chapter Six, I point to the *L* in our QUALITY envirocomm model as a reminder that *listening* comes before the talking (*T* for taking charge) phase.

Listening yields two big benefits: information to process and customer-publics who know you care.

REEDUCATING YOUR LISTENING INSTINCTS

Here's another case where we'll have to break some formerly well-regarded molds to fit into Green World.

First, you need to toss out the simplistic public-relations definition of "doing good and telling about it." This is not the best guide for communicating on sensitive issues like the environment.

That's because "doing good" is so highly objective; it's really in the eye of the beholder. For example, the improvements you made last year may not meet community green standards this year. And "telling about it" puts us back on that mountaintop, handing down the tablets or tooting our own horn. At worst, you can attract critics who claim that you are misstating your green value. (A major company drew serious criticism for ads that were self-congratulatory.) In any event, "telling" can easily come across as an arrogant display of strictly one-way communication.

The correct point was made by Brig. Gen. (USAF, Ret.) Jerry Dalton, the head of public relations for LTV Corporation, when he observed that "there is no substitute for face-to-face, person-to-person communication."[1] And, while I agree with Jerry, I'm sure he wouldn't mind my adding: ". . . provided the persons take turns listening!"

No, you don't get much new information while you're talking (a friend who is a terrific college teacher with great rapport with his students often challenges a voluble youngster to "take the cotton out of your ears and put it in your mouth") and, likewise, you don't collect quite as many answers as you might, if you go into the market already armed with ready-made answers.

Ries & Trout's "bottom-up marketing" approach is just right for green listening.[2] They say a preformed strategy, with supportable messages, leads you to see or hear only the problems that fit your answer.

If you believe you always win by being a hammer, then you will look so hard for nails that you will blind yourself to every other possibility.

Cognitive dissonance—conflicts between what you think you already know and what you hear—tricks you into ignoring questions, concerns, and desires that don't fit what you came to offer. So breaking the "hammer" mind-set is a good first step.

Go into your customer-public market looking openly for the tactic that is needed; you may discover the best tool is a butter knife or a paintbrush or a comb.

The work of first-term Oregon Governor Barbara Roberts on her state's budget deficit is an excellent example of bottom-up marketing—one that, even though it deals with another entirely different issue, is a good model for environmental managers.[3]

In the fall of 1991, Roberts launched "Conversation with Oregon," a series of electronic town meetings on reducing the state's $1 billion budget deficit. Over the four-week series, Roberts met—whether face-to-face, or on an electronic video screen—with more than 10,000 constituents to ask their suggestions for the not-so-easy task of cutting the mammoth deficit. The result was that although no one suggested any one government program for the chopping block, Roberts came away with some creative (some useful, some not) suggestions for slicing the deficit.

But this is far from all. If the governor had really *just* wanted suggestions, she could have employed opinion research of a different and far easier sort: public opinion polling. What Roberts *also* hoped to do—and accomplished—was to let her constituents know how difficult those decisions really are. So, more importantly, Roberts wanted to interact with her customer-publics. By so doing, she created a group of constituents sympathetic to her plight of deficit reduction. She did not hand down a decision to them—a no-win situation—but employed them in the process.

"The people were too cynical and too angry and too frustrated just to accept anything a politician told them about what tax reform was going to do," said Roberts. "The people [feel they are] so much in the dark and so frustrated. The only way to win them over is to make them feel like they are part of the process."

Many of your publics probably feel as distrustful of industry as they do of politicians; they start out feeling cynical, frustrated, in the dark about your operations. Listening to your customer-publics and interacting with them, through town meetings, plant tours, and other creative channels, like the governor's electronic town meetings, is the best way to win them over, or, as I like to say, get them together with you on the green.

WHAT YOUR CUSTOMER-PUBLICS ARE ASKING

The questions you will hear with regard to greening will be different in each customer-public market.

Employees will want to know if they can trust their workplace. Are these chemicals I'm handling every day safe? Has the company taken adequate precautions to protect me from accidents? Is the company releasing all the information about its operations that I'm entitled by law to have?

Stockholders, if given the opportunity, may ask you about potential environmental liabilities to which your operations might expose the company. Some of them will want to know if your company has signed a set of green principles, such as those suggested by CERES, the Coalition for Environmentally Responsible Economies.

Community neighbors may ask what chemicals are used in your plant and what risks they pose, among many other things. (See the list at the end of this chapter for questions posed by highly informed people in communities.)

If you produce products that flow through a distribution chain, there will be questions from wholesalers, retailers, and customers.

Suppliers may tell you of new options for environmentally friendly packaging—what's been tried and successful with some of their other customers. They will wonder if their materials are up to your green standards.

So it goes. The information you need is out there; you just have to be receptive to it. In the interactive, sustainable-development era, when you are trying to establish customer-public relationships, listening is basic.

Ask questions. Know the types of questions people ask or are afraid to ask. Help them ask you questions.

As author Stephen Covey says in *The Seven Habits of Highly Effective People,* if two people want to be understood at the same time, there is no communication. There is only a collective monologue.[4] Covey argues that successful communication requires listening with intent to *understand.* Period.

If we follow the Covey principle, we won't listen in order to make a reply, to control, or to manipulate. We will listen just to understand.

The key test of this is to be able to describe the other person's point of view as well as she or he can. The winning comment during conversation is, "Let me see if I can understand your view (your concern) (your position)." When you do it well, it's a powerful tactic. It puts you in charge. Covey again: "Instead of projecting your own autobiography and assuming thoughts, feelings, motives, and interpretation, you're dealing with the reality inside another person's head and heart."

Through a conscious plan to facilitate the right flow of information from another party, you hear what you need to empower you to talk.

Essential public relationships—those between a company and its encouraging core constituencies—often begin with the company decision to listen.

Behavioral scientists say that communication began as a call for help. In its most basic form, the attempt of one individual to communicate to another begins when he or she asks, "Do you see me? Know me? Understand me?" and "Can you help me?"

Scientists like Dr. Laura Ann Petitto of McGill University in Montreal say the need to communicate begins at birth—babies cry to be fed, changed, and held—and is universal. Dr. Petitto proved that words don't matter. Her research with deaf babies of deaf parents showed how distinctive hand gestures are repeatedly used until the need is understood. Sign language, says Dr. Petitto, starts with the person asking to be recognized and understood. Humans find a way to reach out, regardless of the obstacles placed in their way.

Tom Peters has made the point that every good action plan should include a listening strategy, because it's only by really *hearing* the other person—his or her wants, fears, questions, confusion—that you can learn what to talk about. This then gives you the chance for a horizontal conversation—not talking up, or down, or past each other.

Research conducted to find out why companies lose customers is quite revealing. It shows that two-thirds of customers who abandon a company do so because of the perceived indifference of the organization or one of its representatives. Your customer-publics—with whom you need to create sustainable relationships—likewise, will reject you more often for indifference than anything else.

We know, don't we, that the greatest hunger of human beings is the need to be understood? So why do we starve our publics while we talk?

It's not easy. It requires emotional strength. "Listening involves patience, openness, and the desire to understand—highly developed qualities of character. It's so much easier to operate from a low emotional level and to give high-level advice," says Covey.

THEY'RE ASKING: "DO YOU CARE?"

In our work with business organizations, our surveys of customer-publics consistently reveal that the vital questions are "Do you care about me?" and "Do you care about us?"

FIGURE 15–1
Vital Questions From Vital Publics

Managers:	What are we doing? What do we believe? What is our commitment? What do we tell the employees?
	Also: Managers want to know—How can we say anything if everything is not "perfect"?
Employees:	Do you care about me? What are we doing *together*? What can I tell my family and friends?
Community:	Do you care about us? What are you doing for us (change to "with us")? Is what I hear you say the same as what I see, hear, smell, understand—and hear your employees say?
Customers (& Stockholders):	Do you care about us? Why should I buy your products (stock, viewpoint)? Is what you say consistent with what I think?

Source: E. Bruce Harrison Company

A survey of company managers shows they are asking: What are we doing as a company with regard to the environment? What does our top management believe? What is our commitment? What do we tell the employees?

And these managers frequently want to know: How can we say anything if our environmental record isn't "perfect"?

Down the line, company employees want to know: Does the company protect me? What are we doing together, as company and as employees and families? What can you tell me that I can tell my family and friends who ask me about the company's green policies and practices?

Customers query: Do you care about me and my fears about your products or services? Why should I buy your products? Can you reassure me about use? Is what you say consistent with what I think about your company and its products or services?

Stockholders' questions are similar to customers': Why should I buy your stock, viewpoint, approach? Are your green policies consistent with mine? Will your decisions affect the company's ability to compete and to succeed?

And in the communities of these companies, employees' families and neighbors ask: Do you care about us? What are doing for us? Is what I hear you say the same as what I see, hear, smell, understand—and hear your employees say?

I have spent a lot of time with executives learning how to be good *spokes*persons for organizations and causes. Moving into the Green World, and hoping to succeed in business, we'll do well to spend even more time learning how to be good *hear*persons.

Following are some questions developed by a task force of business, government, academic, and environmental groups, as typifying the concerns of community residents. The subject of this list is the relative risk of airborne emissions—such as might be released by a plant in normal operations, and reported to the government under Title III of the SARA.

Questions community neighbors may ask you about chemicals and airborne emissions:

1. Is anyone in the community at risk?
2. How much of the chemical could have been breathed or ingested by an individual?
3. Are the concentrations safe?
4. What is chemical risk?
5. What is chemical toxicity?
6. What is "exposure"?
7. What were the quantities emitted per day?
8. Were releases continuous, intermittent, or planned?
9. What is the danger of chemicals detected at low concentrations?
10. What is the source of that information?
11. What else is the chemical combined with or in the presence of?
12. How often, when, and how are the releases occurring?
13. At what height are emissions released?
14. At what temperature?
15. Where on the property?
16. What is the prevailing daily wind direction? Are releases restricted during certain wind or weather conditions?
17. What are the potential exposure routes (e.g., drinking water, air, or surface water) for the community? Are the air and water safe?

18. How do the chemical risks compare with other risks in the community?

19. What are the symptoms of adverse chemical exposure?

20. Are people who work outdoors at greater risk?

21. Is it risky to sleep in rooms with open windows?

22. Is eating fish from or swimming in local streams risky?

23. Are older people, pregnant women, and children at greater risk than others?

24. Are chemical risks affected by diet, smoking, and other personal choices?

25. Are government standards the best guide to determine "safety" or "purity" of drinking water or contaminant levels?

26. Are "toxic" and "hazardous" the same thing, in regulatory language?

27. What are "extremely hazardous substances"?

28. Why can't these emissions be stopped entirely?

29. What will the government do about this?

30. Why didn't you tell us this before?

Chapter Sixteen

Speaking on the Green

Coincident with the rise of corporate environmentalism, more business executives are standing up to speak. I believe there are two explanations for this. One is the realization by executives that, on the topic of greening, they not only have to say something; they also have something to say. The push of green laws is toward openness. We have to tell what we use, do, and plan to do. That makes public speaking a management tool.

The second explanation is that for owners, managers, and executives in companies large and small, there are audiences truly interested in the organization's green program and views on green topics. Customer-publics look to the organization for information they can use and to be reassured that the firm cares about them.

• The head of a communications equipment firm realizes that the green policy statement just written for company publications won't mean much unless she personally stands up and talks with employees about it.

• Senior officials at a textiles company decide their relationship with retailers will benefit if each of them starts talking about the company's environmental record and commitment in seminar and trade-show programs.

• The chief financial officer of a chain of six hotels feels the need to report directly to the investment community on how environmental challenges are being handled.

• The Rotary Club needs a speaker on a Monday during Earth Month and asks two local businesspeople to join a panel, along with a state government regulator and a local conservationist.

This chapter is about speaking in public. While my purpose is to help you improve your environmental communication, the advice is generic. The pointers offered here can apply to any speaking opportunity.

POINTER #1: ANYBODY CAN DO IT.

After coaching hundreds of people, most of them in business and industry, one thing I've learned: *anybody can be an effective speaker.* You don't get to where you are in the organization without *knowing* something—your areas of experience and expertise—and without being able to *talk about it.*

That's all there is to effective speaking: knowing what you know and talking about it. If you *don't* know your topic, it's not your topic. Don't agree to talk about it. If you are *assigned* a topic—for example, you have to explain the company's green policy; the boss has assigned you—don't talk about it until *you can make it your own.* Get somebody else to write it—or you write it with help—and then you work on it, ask questions about things you don't understand, leave out what's absolutely not right for you, and make it work for you.

I emphasize this now because the problem with most people who think they can't give a speech is that they are worried about the material, about the questions they may get, about how they will look. These won't matter nearly so much if you come to believe, as I do, that *anybody can be an effective speaker if you know what you are talking about.*

The rest is easy. If you adjust your thinking right here, we can go on to the tips, techniques, and rules that have to do with style. But it is *substance* that will take you to the podium (you accept because you have something to say), and it is *substance* that will shine through any style, good or bad, that shows up at the podium.

There are very few born speakers. I've met a few who seem that way. Mostly, I've worked with ordinary, terrific businesspeople who hate to Make A Speech, but have to, and who turn out to be effective speakers.

POINTER #2: DON'T MAKE A SPEECH, GIVE A TALK.

You write a speech (more on that later), but you give a talk. Just understanding the subtlety of that can make all the difference in the world in how you approach this *opportunity to communicate.*

If you think of yourself as Making A Speech, you put the emphasis in the wrong place. On yourself. You are up there on the mountaintop again—okay, only a platform or a dais!— handing down the Word! You think of preachers, politicians, great orators, sales motivators, People Who Speak! And you begin to get uptight at the prospect of being on display, hoping not to make a mistake, fearful of being judged as having Not Made A Good Speech.

Turn it around, and give a talk. Now this shifts the emphasis off you and into the audience. You know how to talk. You do it every day. You talk to someone or, better, *with* someone. A talk at the podium can be somewhat like a conversation that you start.

An executive we once trained told us: "I like to think of the talk as a dialogue. I do my part, the audience does its part. I talk, and they listen. But it's more than that. I get reactions, I look for eyes and heads and body signals to see if I'm making sense. I have often paused some place in my talk to ask if what I am saying makes sense, or if anyone has a question. I usually don't get much verbal reaction, because people don't like to speak up. *But they know I am paying attention to them and consider them part of the dialogue."*

If you are making a talk—communicating with real people in real time—it is a dialogue, a conversation. You can presume it may be continued, either in the Q&A session or informally, in the room afterwards or, if those are not possible, at some other time. You can consider a letter you get later or a comment from a colleague or customer-public after the talk as just part of the dialogue.

We're still talking attitude, not style. This is the important part; the rest is lubricant.

POINTER #3: GET INTO THEIR SEATS.

Mentally, that is. Put yourself out there in the marketplace where you are offering your ideas and thoughts; that is, look at yourself with the eyes of the audience. More important, imagine how the audience will *listen* to you.

Remember radio station WIIFM? The station that everyone, but *everyone*, listens to every waking moment? You know: "This is WIIFM. What's *In It For Me!"*

You need to think market. Think audience. Think customer-public, in advance. What are they ready to buy? What will make them resist what you have to sell? What are their fears, concerns, desires, hot buttons? How can you plug into their own self-interests? What are the areas of possible mutual benefit?

Do audience research any way you can. Talk with the program chairman, leader, or colleague who knows this group, this industry, this *type of audience*. Anything you do that gets you into *their seats before you write your speech or make your talk* will add 30 to 40 percent to the effectiveness of your talk.

POINTER #4: GET THERE EARLY AND STAY LATE.

Vincent Covello, whose writings on environmental risk communication have helped many speakers to reach audiences, says that too many of us are still fumbling the ball in a very basic way: We don't spend enough time at the place we're speaking.

"Ninety-eight-point-five percent of speaking executives," said Covello, "arrive exactly on time and leave exactly on time. This sends the message to the audience that they don't give a damn." You can help establish trust—which is truly the basis for most of the positive reception a speaker gets—by arriving a little early and leaving late. "This communicates that you're open and accessible," said Covello.[1]

Covello, a professor of public health and communication at Columbia University, reminds us that somewhere between 50 and 75 percent of information content comes from nonverbal communication. You begin the process of building relationships with your customer-public at the speaking engagement the moment you enter the room. You are then and there starting the dynamic situation that will *include* your speech. The medium is the message; the room and your presence in it is your medium; the message starts with you.

Enter confidently and expectantly, with a smile or an open and accessible manner. You know what you know, and this is your speech. Now you must gear your thinking and your externally expressed attitude toward success. You must say or do nothing that will distract from what you will say later from the platform.

Your mental preparation when you arrive at the location, before you see a single soul, should be that which Dorothy Sarnoff taught; you should be silently saying to yourself, *I'm glad I'm here, I'm glad you're here, I know that I know.*[2] This will calm you, give you confidence, open you to the expectation of success, and prepare you to meet the audience and start to construct a relationship that might last for an hour, or for a longer time.

And do as Vince Covello suggests, arrive early and don't rush out as though it didn't matter.

POINTER #5: WRITE A SPEECH THAT'S RIGHT FOR YOU.

Sure, you're going to make a talk, but first let's get a speech in front of you that is right for you, in content and appearance. First, content:

Write about what you know. Pick one main point you're going to make. For example: our company is looking for green partners. Then you can go one of several ways:

• Use the old, tested one-two-three: tell them what you're going to tell them; tell them; and tell them what you told them. Make your point, say why you feel this way, give an example or two, work in the benefits to the audience (or community or other beneficiary). Deal with at least one downside to your commitment or point or position. Summarize the point and benefits again. And ask for something: action, order, reaction, something.

• Or, use the Problem, Downside, Big Idea, Benefit formula. State a problem. For example: our plant for the last two years has wrestled with tough, new clean air rules. Expand on the situation: say what will happen negatively, not to your benefit or the benefit of the public, for example, if the current condition continues. Reveal your good idea: plans, commitment, idea for cooperation, ability to deal with the problem. Show why this big idea is good for the audience, public, or other beneficiary. Summarize the point and benefits. Close by asking for the order, cooperation, understanding, action, reaction.

Put in a lot of examples that people can understand. Little stories (I mean real-life stories, that may or may not be funny, poignant, or moving), quotes, and the *occasional* statistic or number can help you make your points. Keep it simple, speaker.

POINTER #6: WRITE SO YOU CAN TALK IT.

Now we're into style. Get some help here if you need to—a speech-writer or editor, colleague, or family friend. The point is to make the speech into a talk. This should be written for the ear. Are sentences short enough? Are you making one point or expressing one thought in a given sentence? Or are you crowding too much into that sentence? Are the words understandable? Can you pronounce them? If not, use other words. You are not stuck with the words in the first draft. Read it aloud. Get somebody to listen. Tape yourself. If you have a video camera, use it and look at yourself. Listen. Say it aloud and really listen. Get somebody to ask you questions about what you've said—and determine if they're hearing what you're saying.

POINTER #7: WRITE IT SO YOU CAN READ IT.

I've seen it all, over the years of coaching speakers: speeches scribbled on legal pads; speeches on cards; speeches on yellow, blue, white paper; speeches stapled together; speeches in boxes; speeches single-spaced, double-spaced, triple-spaced. I once saw a speech, prepared for an executive whose eyesight was not the greatest, typed in letters nearly two inches high.

Obviously, there's no one way. Pretty speeches don't necessarily produce a wonderful talk. I've heard very effective speakers who use those legal pads with handwriting all over them.

But, the obverse is true: a poor text, not easily readable—or if you're not exactly reading, not easily reference-able—can louse up your talk.

So I'll tell you how I like them. Usually. Sometimes I don't, as I'll explain in a minute.

I like my speeches typed in narrow measure,
just about this wide—seven or eight
words to the line. The left is flush. The
right is ragged. Usually, the copy is
double-spaced. Sometimes, I try triple
space. My point is to have the lines just
wide enough so when I look down at the page

I can see most or all of the line at a
glance. I don't have to read way across a
page. This lets me dip and deliver. By
that I mean, look down and then out to the
audience readily. I DO NOT USE ALL CAPITAL
LETTERS BECAUSE I FIND THESE ARE NOT NEARLY
SO EASY FOR ME TO READ AS upper- and lower-
case letters, such as I'm used to reading
in books and newspapers. Comfort is
everything. My other point is to leave a
lot of white space over to the right of the
copy, so I can make notes to myself later.
These notes or symbols let me add thoughts
later—for example, just before I speak!
—and help to remind myself to pause,
emphasize, smile, gesture, and so forth.

Now here is my trick. After looking this over, I usually take it to a photocopy machine with enlargement capability, and have this text blown up—120 percent or so. This lets me read the copy without my reading glasses. It also tends to darken the type, making it more readable still. Comfort is everything. The bigger type is comfortable—but I still want plenty of room at the right for my notes and reminders, which I usually write with red or green markers.

Whatever works. A high-level government official that I used to coach liked his speeches typed in very wide measure, across a horizontal card. He believed he had a sight problem that made it uncomfortable for him to dip very deeply into a page. He wanted all his speech up high on the page. So he would arrange these horizontal cards right up near the edge of the lectern and glance down and across them. It would not have worked for me; it would have driven me nuts. But it worked for him. He was, and is, a terrific speaker who gives a terrific talk.

POINTER #8: PRACTICE, PRACTICE, PRACTICE.

I know. Now I'm sounding like your tennis coach, golf pro, or your old piano teacher. But you know it helps.

Just consider, every time you read your speech aloud, you improve a little. By the time you get to the scary Make A Speech Moment, this will be as comfortable as an old shoe, or at least an old song that you've hummed a hundred times.

You must go for the comfort. That means practice. Read it aloud in solitude a few times. Never mind the mirror; I find that's disconcerting at first, to be watching myself trying to read while watching myself trying to read. What I usually do is just close the door to my office, stand up behind my desk, and read the thing to the chair in front of my desk. Sometimes, I wait until the rest of the staff has left for the day. Then I can really belt it out.

Then you really need to read it to somebody. You need the experience of *talking with* or *conversing* with a real live audience. You need to look at eyes, see smiles, grimaces, confusion, whatever *now*, before it's *too late*. So get somebody to sit and listen. And don't be discouraged, no matter what reaction you get. That's not the point. The point is to feel a connection with somebody while you read this thing. It *helps* if you get a response, a question, a comment or suggestion. But don't worry about this. Believe me, practice helps. Better here than there. And *then*, THE TALK WILL BE BETTER *THERE* THAN HERE.

Videotaping is incredibly helpful. When I coach, I turn on the videocamera. The playback does the coaching. People look and learn. They get better. "I didn't know I was doing *that*" (pulling at his tie, swaying from side to side, etc.) is a common comment. People usually don't like what they see; if this is your case, again don't worry about it. You will do better than if you didn't see yourself. I am not sure why this is true, but it is. Maybe your subconscious self—the one that helps you do all that natural talking and conversing all day—takes over at the lectern.

POINTER #9: USE YOUR NATURAL ABILITY.

I say to my clients: "I'm not going to make a star out of you. I'm going to help you be the best possible you. This is not Professional Speaking. This is you, talking comfortably, effectively, with audiences you care about."

That's it. And that's my problem now. I don't know who or what you are—your talents, your looks, your voice level, your mannerisms, your willingness to gesture, to laugh, to pause. If we were in a coaching session, I would want you to use the best you've got, to advantage.

I've helped a police officer—who had to Make A Speech to several community groups on the subject of drug abuse—to look like a police officer who knew what he was talking about and who cared about his audience. When he began, he was trying too hard. He had an image of a speaker as a cross between a TV salesman and an evangelist. In time, he relaxed, understood how important, how engaging, how trustworthy he naturally was—and *that was what his audience would be expecting of him.*

Engineers don't have to be entertainers when they get up to talk. They can be engineers. They can actually have fun helping the audience to understand *how things work.* After working with one of our clients, a chemical engineer, he was able to explain how deep a deep-injection well is. He used the image of three Empire State Buildings, one stacked atop the other and buried straight down. "Groundwater, where we get all the water we drink and use, is located at about the depth of the radio antenna on top of the top building," he said. "The waste is injected down to the basement of the bottom building. The safety zone is the depth of those three Empire State Buildings." The company engineer was very comfortable using examples like this. He didn't talk philosophy or vision. His audience got what *they* expected.

My point is to work with your natural intelligence with regard to *content* and your natural ability with regard to *style.* Your comfort level with gestures, stance, moving around and not moving around the lectern, and the rest is what matters most. Try them all—if possible, with an experienced speaker or coach—and see what works for you.

POINTER #10: BEWARE THE UNCARING EXPERT.

Experts from the business community have a hard time communicating. Much of the problem is self-inflicted, by:

Exclusionary language. Experts in their fields flood the communication channel with jargon. Curiously, this happens more often in public than when spokespersons are talking to peers. Is this because peers won't put up with garble, or because the professional is more interested in preserving domain through exclusionary language? Some of both doubtless act as motivators, along with the sheer comfort of hiding behind the jargon.

Professional selfishness and arrogance. When more than 300 people registered for a seminar on risk communication in Washington, one participant was clearly offended by the turnout. "Why are all these people here," she asked. "What do they know about this subject?" This specialist was possessive of her area of specialization and was not eager to let others horn in.

Blow softeners. Carcinogens, shortfalls, revenue enhancements, and other such expressions, designed to reduce listener defenses, have their place in the communication process, but they leave muddy pools on the carpet that we professionals ultimately have to clean up.

What is happening to cheer us? A fair amount. Take the research of Dr. William McGuire at Yale's Department of Psychology. It makes the point that people seem to be less persuaded by poised experts than by earnest or even bumbling speakers.

As to the value of unfamiliar phrases to soften the emotional impact of information, Peter Sandman and his colleagues at Rutgers have shown the overwhelming danger of letting somebody else (including us, the professionals) clean up the expert language. In a study of New Jersey newspapers covering environmental issues, Sandman, et al., found that reporters almost always escalate the danger when they try to translate technical jargon into more familiar—and far more volatile—lay terms.[3]

In sensitive public issues such as those involving environmental hazards, the time seems to be especially right to take research results like these to expert spokespersons.

"Right to know" (or "sunshine") laws require mass volumes of private, technical information to be delivered into public hands and explained. Litigation on product and professional service liability is turning the courtroom (and the media) into increasingly active forums for technical discussion. Technology itself, with unprecedented power for measurement and evaluation, is yielding more and more data that must be explained.

The land on which experts in these issues once stood is rapidly shifting. Maybe the guiding principle for us as spokespersons ought to be, "Everybody knows everything." This is, of course, not quite true, but if we adopted that as the starting point for communication, we might be less worried about giving out information, appearing to be an expert, or trying to be perfect.

People don't really want to hear from experts. They want to hear from somebody who (a) is human, (b) knows what he's talking about, (c) speaks plainly, and (d) seems to care.

TAKE IT FROM ABE LINCOLN

Garry Wills has said that Abraham Lincoln was our only chief executive who got to be president because he could organize his thoughts *as a writer.*

The great address on the burial ground at Gettysburg stands high above all the other lessons about public speaking. It was simply the best. Lincoln in two minutes delivered 272 words that not only blew away the professional speaker who had delivered a two-*hour* peroration on the same platform; he gave new meaning to America's course and the real cause of democracy.

Let's look at how Lincoln did it. First, he wrote a speech, crafted specifically for the occasion and for the audience who would hear it. He had a point—a big idea—and he made it. His point was: We must make sure that we reach the goal that these soldiers died for.

Did he tell 'em what he would tell 'em, then tell 'em, then tell 'em he told them? Yes—and most important, he followed a pattern that I believe is the most appealing:

First, he showed his human, caring side. Second, he made a personal commitment. Third, he asked the people to make a commitment.

Over and over again, we come to realize that audiences want to know how much you care about them, and what you are committed to do in the public interest. This done, they are more ready to accept you as a trustworthy person with whom they can communicate.

To get on the green, to the place where communication about the environment is open and interactive, give a talk that shows caring, commitment, and credibility.

Chapter Seventeen

Communicating About Risk

William Ruckelshaus, during his second tour as head of EPA, was challenged on a TV news show after a nationwide scare involving pesticide residues in baked goods.

"Can you *guarantee* that I won't get cancer from eating this cookie?" asked the TV host. Ruckelshaus wanted to reassure, but of course he couldn't "guarantee" anything. The best he could do was to say that *he* had no fear—that he and his family would "eat the cookie."[1]

How do you explain risk? When people are concerned about the dangers they perceive, is there a good way to reassure them? What can you do to put risk into proper perspective and possibly head off a panic?

Can facts calm fears?

In the landscape of environmental communication, "risk communication" is surely the most slippery slope. You try to get a toehold, but five factors are working against you:

1. **The very science of risk assessment—what lies under the slippery slope—is itself a shifting landscape.**

The popular history of the environmental and health movements of the last few decades has been one of apparently increasing risk. The media drumbeat about what a dangerous world we live in has created a firm public belief in the inevitability of things getting worse—"Tomorrow they'll announce that breathing causes cancer," and so on.

However, the science of risk assessment is actually tending the other way. The methodologies developed to help implement the first wave of green laws in the 1970s were quite conservative, partly in deference to the embryonic state of the science. With new knowledge, many key assumptions of this "better-safe-than-sorry" approach have come under heavy fire. For example, the traditional linear dose-response assumption—that the effect of a substance increases smoothly from small doses to large ones, with no thresholds or "jump" effects—is being sharply questioned.

The implication is that things may not be as bad as we have believed. But that is a tough message to sell, especially when those who most need to tell it could be seen to have a conflict of interest.

2. **People want certainty—guarantees, if they can get them—and you can only speak of probabilities.**

"Risk communicators" talk about odds, the chances of something happening. They point to the list of relative risks, which says, for example, that you are more likely (over the next 50 years) to be killed by a falling meteorite* than you are of dying in an airplane crash.

There is a corollary to the demand for guarantees:

3. **People think of risks in personal terms, while you must deal in aggregate, societal terms.**

People are not reassured by odds. When a concerned mother hears, "The odds are one in a thousand," she is likely to think, "But what if that one is my child?"

4. **News media coverage of environmental stories keeps the slope wet.**

People want to read or hear about the latest danger. We are conditioned to expect it. Reporters look for it. Hints of new risks make the news every time.

Pollution levels—for example, pounds of toxics emitted by a company in a city—are constantly recurring news.

If we're in industry, we cringe while others interpret our own data, while speculations soar about the human health risks involved if all those toxics are pouring out. We know about the numbers. We've been monitoring our operations, and know they

---

*As a very junior journalist on a small-town weekly, I once interviewed a woman who had been hit by a falling meteorite. It happened in Talladega County, Alabama, in 1955. A photographer and I went to the woman's home, saw the hole in the roof where the heavenly missile had ripped through, and took a picture of the bruise on her hip where the thing had struck. Obviously, you wouldn't have tried to reassure people in that town in that year about the odds of being hit by a meteorite!

FIGURE 17–1
Threats: A Comparison (Estimated risk for an American over a 50-year period.)

Risk of death from botulism	1 in 2,000,000
Risk of death from fireworks	1 in 1,000,000
Risk of death from tornados	1 in 50,000
Risk of death from airplane crash	1 in 20,000
Risk of death from asteroid impact	1 in 6,000
Risk of death from electrocution	1 in 5,000
Risk of death from firearms accident	1 in 2,000
Risk of death from homicide	1 in 300
Risk of death from automobile accident	1 in 100

Sources: Clark R. Chapman, Ph.D., and David Morrison, Ph.D.

are in compliance. And if asked about the relative risks, we try to respond. We begin explaining and find ourselves once again on the very thin, slippery ice of defense.

Will reporters and editors help you put releases and risks into perspective? Some will, even though the story is in the threat and not the reassurance. But even if the media try to balance the story, they escalate concern through examination of relative risk, according to media research. Reporters misuse technical terms, or turn to various experts who offer conflicting views.

Research by Rutgers University social scientist Peter Sandman shows that news coverage of risks, even while trying to be balanced, inevitably raises misunderstandings and the fears of readers and viewers.[2] Headlines, sometimes out of sync with the stories underneath, can easily hype the scare further.

5. **And sometimes we shoot ourselves in the foot.**

Paul Slovic, a research associate at Decision Research in Eugene, Oregon, argues that people overestimate the probability of spectacular, vividly imaginable causes of death—like airplane crashes and nuclear explosions—because they are easier to imagine than the far more common but less dramatic causes like lung cancer.[3]

This can cause reasoned explanations to backfire. Slovic tells of engineers trying to explain why nuclear power plants are safe. They described the "fault tree" to show how well equipped the plant was with backup safeguards. But the explanations actually *raised* fears. People thought: "I didn't know so many things *could* go wrong!" Risk became *"more imaginable . . . more likely,"* says Slovic.

Yes, risk communication is risky business. There are no guarantees of success here, either. Fortunately, there are some guidelines.

CARDINAL RULES WHEN TALKING ABOUT RISK

A few years ago, I was part of a working group on risk communication assembled by the American Chemical Society to help both industry and public health spokespersons discuss relative risks of chemical releases (touched off by SARA Title III, Section 313 data requirements.) We examined the risk communication work of Sandman, Slovic, Vincent Covello (Columbia), Frederick Allen (U.S. EPA), and others.

Covello and Allen came up with seven cardinal rules of risk communication, summarized here:[4]

1. *Accept and involve the public* as a legitimate partner. The goal is to produce an informed public that is engaged, interested, reasonable, thoughtful, solution-oriented, collaborative.

2. *Listen to your audience.* If people think you aren't listening to them, they won't listen to you or trust what you say.

3. *Plan carefully before communicating,* and evaluate your performance. Develop clear and explicit objectives consistent with your risk communication goal. Remember that there is no such entity as *the* public; there are many publics, each with its own interest, needs, concerns, priorities, perceptions, and preferences. (As we've seen, it's useful to think of the various publics as customers with whom you are transacting.)

4. *Be honest, frank, and open.* When communicating with the public and the media, state your credentials but don't expect to be trusted. If you don't know the answer to a question, admit your ignorance. Admit mistakes. Get back to people with answers.

5. *Speak clearly and with compassion.* Technical language and jargon can pose substantial barriers. People can grasp many complex scientific subjects if explained in clear, everyday language. It's especially important to acknowledge and respond to emotions people may express, through your speech and actions.

6. *Coordinate and collaborate with other credible sources.* Third-party experts are extremely useful because information is reinforced and the audience does not have to rely on a single source. Try to coordinate with other interested organizations—government agencies, industry, trade associations, unions, academic institutions, and environmental groups.

7. *Meet the needs of the news media.* This, of course, means being open and accessible to reporters, and respecting their time and space constraints. Provide information tailored to the needs of their particular media. Offer background on risk issues that are difficult for nontechnical people to understand. Cultivate media relationships. If you leave it up to the journalists to explain relative risk, the outcome will always be more dire. By intention or not, a journalist seeking to simplify the explanation of risk tends to paint a more horrific picture.

ABOVE ALL: REMAIN CREDIBLE

To these cardinal rules, I'd add and underscore another point: *Assess and nurture your credibility.*

Studies emphasize that the believability of the source is the single most important factor in effective risk communication. Company executives who are distrusted or seen as insincere are unlikely to communicate effectively even though they do everything else well.

Peter Sandman also makes the critical observation that the best you can do is to open a channel for dialogue with concerned people.

That means risk communication, like envirocomm, must facilitate relationship. It must start in the market, where your customer-publics live and work. The process begins by listening to what core publics are saying, asking, and *fearing.*

Sandman says that risk communicators' number one job is telling top management what exactly the "risks" are that people are worried about, what "terms" they understand, and how they would consider management "credible."[5]

The point is to understand the risks of risk communication and not be totally unprepared if the time comes when you are, in effect, asked, "Can you guarantee . . . ?"

MOVE TOWARD A DIALOGUE

Listen with concern for the concerns of your customer-publics. Interpret through inquiry. And continue into dialogue that creates a relationship.

If the dialogue progresses, you might get a chance to ask a few questions of your own, such as:

How would you like us to discuss the relative risks? What would you suggest as an acceptable risk, given the fact that little or nothing in this world is totally risk-free? How can I best reassure you? What commitment would you like to have from me? Could we get on the same side of the table and look at this "risk" question together?

CONFESSING YOUR SINS: WHEN INTERNAL ENVIRONMENTAL AUDIT REPORTS BECOME PUBLIC DOMAIN

I argue that Nimbyism [the "Not-In-My-Backyard" syndrome] is caused not by selfishness or ignorance, although these factors play a role. Rather it is the manifest rage of victims, the desperation of the powerless.

—Charles Piller, *The Fail-Safe Society*

What's the allure of technical assessment documents to a housewife down the street from your facility? What's so fascinating about soil and groundwater reports to a computer programmer who lives a mile away from the front entrance of your plant? What can these people and their neighbors possibly learn from a six-inch-thick report that is so highly technical that it takes a team of doctorates in chemistry, geology, toxicology, and environmental science to write it, and a Nobel laureate in nuclear physics to read and understand it? The more important question may be: What do these people think they are learning?

Legal disclosure requirements will continue to mandate that technical documents and other notifications be made available for public scrutiny by individuals who may not have the technical background to assimilate the information from the same perspective as those who prepared the data. To examine this further, we need to look at the role of communication and the background of those with whom we communicate.

"AS A PRACTICE, WE DON'T COMMUNICATE WITH OUR NEIGHBORS." The fact is: you do. A technical assessment can say more about your facility and your operations than you think. Technical assessments, like Toxic Release Inventories and other reports, are viewed by outsiders as rare opportunities to see the real inner workings of your operation. Unfortunately, assessments are rarely written for this purpose or for interpretation by non-technical activists.

Most of us feel largely confident that when technical assessments, incident reports, or other communications are filed with regulatory agencies the documents will be reviewed by a professional with an engineering or scientific background, and that the data will be evaluated against the most up-to-date risk assessment science available, without preconceived bias against the information. And for the most part, this is so.

But what happens when these documents find their way into the "public" file? The numbers and findings can take on whole new meanings, based on the perspective of the reader. The mere detection of a chemical in the environment surrounding your facility can be easily labeled as a widespread contamination problem, and the science of exposure, dose, and background is disregarded as a picky detail.

The news media have taught the American public to view most every situation in a black-and-white dichotomy: Either something's right or it's wrong. And if something is wrong, was it caused by stupidity or maliciousness? Too often, facility managers unsuccessfully attempt to split hairs in this dichotomy. "Well, the presence of this chemical isn't necessarily 'right,' but it's not 'wrong' either, because. . . ." All too often, this response is perceived by reporters and the watching public as some form of excuse to justify a screwup, and the media and their audience are left to themselves to determine industry's motives of carelessness or contempt.

WIIFM RULES

Every day we see examples of how people are willing to take acceptable risks in their personal lives, whether it's driving a car, flying on an airplane, or eating a char-grilled hamburger. Yet these same people may petition the state legislature and regulatory agencies to shut your plant down because you found 0.2 ppm of triethylmethyl-death in a localized patch of soil six feet behind your facility.

Why? WIIFM—what's in it for me?—the balance of risk versus benefit. If risk outweighs benefit, then the risk is considered too great. If the benefit outweighs the risk, then the situation is forgotten until something reminds us about the risk. Example: Many people are a little more cautious when driving immediately after a family member or friend is involved in a traffic accident. Eventually, they will resume their normal driving habits until another incident triggers their sensitivity to the risks of driving. But as long as the perceived benefits of driving outweigh the perceived risks, they will continue to drive.

An important distinction should be made, however, between our idea of technical risk assessment and risk evaluation by our neighbors. Technical risk assessments are usually made from the point of view of a given population—a 1:1,000,000 cancer risk, for example. For the rest of the world, risk assessment is a personal, individual set of decisions that rarely have any relationship to technical estimations. In an individual layman's mind, perceived risk is just as real as actual risk. And more often than not, decisions about your facility will be based on this perception of risk.

Often to an individual, unless that person or a family member is an employee, your facility offers no perceived benefits, only perceived risks. Here are some concerns when communicating in this environment:

There's no such thing as a "general public."   Many facility managers claim that they make efforts to communicate with the "general public." Truth is, there is no such thing; everyone is someone. That is, each individual is a property owner, or a parent, or a naturalist, etc., or a combination of many. If you and your facility are perceived as being in conflict to these interests, then these individuals *must* oppose you in order to protect their interests. To communicate effectively, you have to understand each person's own self-interests (WIIFM) and prove that you, too, are committed to these same interests. This is often difficult for plant officials because they are surrounded by like-minded colleagues and are often unable to detach themselves personally from the operations.

Every parade needs a drum major. If the perceived risk is great enough, someone will rise to the surface as the leader of your environmental situation. Will it be you and your company? Or a homemaker down the street, a local activist, or the community news media, or a local politician running for reelection? Because of the continued decay of public trust in technology and science, you can no longer assume that your company will be left alone to clean up your own problems. The public needs a watchdog.

In some cases, companies have successfully established leadership positions in an environmental situation, but it takes a lot of work. If your company takes charge in disclosing even unpleasant information, regularly hosts neighborhood meetings, and initiates briefings for the city council and commissioners court, you will help preempt someone else from taking lead of the situation. Otherwise, if you sit back and wait, you will be following someone else's agenda and will be forced to respond to their actions.

Concentric circles: pollution is everywhere, until you prove to me differently. How many times have we seen a facility announce to a state agency that it found a localized patch of soil contamination, and within days property owners in a 15-mile radius want their drinking-water wells tested by week's end?

Technical site assessment filings with a regulatory agency usually announce some form of chemical release into the environment. However, chances are that the actual release occurred many years ago, leaving you—particularly at the early stages of notification—with probably more questions than answers. To address this, engineering studies should try to establish "concentric circles" as soon as possible. That is, define the broadest extent of the contamination so that you can show not only where it is, but where it isn't. This move should put people who are not technically at risk at ease, so that you can focus on those who may have actual exposure risks.

Get real: talk is cheap.   For those people who may actually have a potential exposure—and even for those that you cannot yet prove do not—provide real solutions, such as bottled drinking water, to prove your commitment to their family's health. Then, as additional engineering studies are completed and you prove that there is no actual risk of exposure, you can begin to rescind previous actions.

The idea of risk is risk enough.   Too often, fearing legal ramifications, companies want confirmed proof that they are actually endangering someone before they take action. From a technological and legal perspective, companies may say, exposure and risk are nonexistent until proven. In the public perception, however, exposure and risk are real until you prove differently. As mentioned before, a difficult concept for technically educated professionals to understand is that even the perception of risk (fear) is just as real as actual exposure to most individuals, and needs to be addressed.

You can turn any data into bad news.   If your facility neighbors are predisposed to distrust and combat you—that is, if it is in their self-interest to do so—then even the most insignificant detection of chemicals in the environment can be presented as a plague upon the community, and your attempts to define *minimal risk* are likely to be lost in the roar of the crowd. Work must be done ahead of time—NOW—to align your interests and concerns with those of your neighboring community. If your interests are parallel already, work now to prove this to your neighbors. Doing so will allow you to make disclosures in the future with more assurance that the technical data will retain the perspective that its scientist-authors intended.

Chapter Eighteen

Communicating in Crisis Conditions: Lessons of the *Exxon Valdez*

What can you learn about environmental communication from the tragic incident of the *Exxon Valdez*?[1]

Years ago, back when Dudley Moore was part of a comedy team known as "Beyond the Fringe," there was a very funny skit about a hapless businessman.

In this skit, Moore interviews an unsuccessful entrepreneur who has just made the mistake of opening a restaurant with a very limited menu (two dishes featuring frogs and peaches), in a very unlikely location (the middle of a peat bog).

"Have you learned from your mistakes?" says Moore.

"Yes," replies the businessman. "I have learned from my mistakes, and I can repeat them exactly."

Unfortunately, some managers and executives seem to keep making the same mistakes when a crisis or environmental episode occurs and the news heats up.

The most common mistake is saying too little, too late. And that's what this chapter is about.

YOU DON'T HAVE TO BE EXXON TO HAVE A *VALDEZ*

Let me emphasize that you don't have to have a supertanker or be in the oil business to apply the lessons of the *Valdez* to your situation.

Whether you're in manufacturing, retail, tourism, hospitality, or other services—in fact whether you're in industry or in another kind of organization—a bank, an association, a professional group—the principles of communication that should have worked, and didn't, in the case of the Alaskan oil spill, can apply to you.

Mistakes in environmental communication, at the time of severe conflict or crisis, can, in effect, sink your boat.

Not long after that incident on Bligh Reef in Alaska's Prince William Sound in 1989, my associates and I placed calls to dozens of people, most of them public relations professionals, to ask their opinion of the communication handling. We wanted to know: What were the envirocomm lessons from the *Valdez*?

These observers saw a classic case of what can go wrong when tested public relations strategies and good common sense take a back seat in an environmental crisis.

I've worked those observations into the following lessons and suggestions:

1. IT CAN HIT *YOUR* FAN AT ANY TIME

Our sources reminded us that you can *always* rely on Murphy's Law #33: *Bad things will happen at the worst possible time.*

The *Valdez* oil spill occurred when green was becoming a very hot topic. In March 1989, the environment was on everybody's agenda. A summit in Paris would have world leaders looking at environmental as well as economic conditions. Around the world, green action groups were looking for focus. The media were ready, with many new reporters signed on to the environmental beat.

Exxon was moving cautiously with its Alaskan shipments. The Alaskan pipeline, so far, was reassuringly without incident. The oil companies were hopeful that they could build on their good record and commitment, extending into the production of oil in other Alaskan territories.

It was a very good time for a bad environmental story.

Let's see how this applies to you, wherever you may be:

• You are a manufacturing operation with tough competition and marginal profits. You are in negotiations with a deep-pocket investor who can pull you into the black. And a major spill occurs at your plant.

• You are a bank trying to restore your stability after a series of real-estate loan defaults. And you—as well as the media—discover big environmental problems with the property you've just taken over.

• Your trucking firm has finally gotten its chin above the waves of new, tough regulations on chemical transportation. You're in compliance and your drivers have terrific safety records. Then one of your trucks is involved in a huge traffic accident on an interstate highway in the center of a metro area.

• You are a retail business in a medium-size city. You've made some tough decisions in the last year, including layoffs and salary freezes, to keep your head above water in the toughest year for retail businesses in recent memory. And you are picketed outside your business by animal rights activists with gruesome posters of trapped animals to protest the sale of your leather goods.

• You're a hospital that has tried to differentiate yourself through environmental, health, and safety awareness in a competitive marketplace. You've spent a huge sum over the past year for an environmental audit that includes the analysis of your waste disposal from beginning to end. You've made important changes based on the audit, which requires your waste disposal facilities (landfills and incinerators) to make full accounting of waste treatment and disposal; you have heavily promoted those actions in your marketing campaign. Then a sudden outburst of news articles reports that lots of medical waste has washed up on the nearby shore, closing the beaches to vacationers. The waste is determined to be five years old . . . and is tracked back to your facility.

2. YOU'VE GOT TO HAVE A PLAN

You hope and pray, and no doubt you take steps every day to prevent negative environmental incidents, such as a spill or a leak, or a contamination involving your product.

But since there are no guarantees, and since you obviously can't control the *timing* of an environmental incident (or, for that matter, the discovery of the *news* of an old environmental problem to which you may now be connected), you need to be combat-ready at all times.

The combat analogy is appropriate. You may indeed find yourself in battle conditions—under seige from the media and concerned customer-publics, while you try to bring the physical situation under control.

Before addressing the communication aspects—dealing with the media and customer-publics—I will assume that your organization has an emergency plan, dealing with the technical, physical, and operational aspects of an incident.

This emergency plan is your battle plan—admittedly, for a battle you hope you'll never have to fight. It contains strategy and tactical moves to deploy your people, protect your territory, and confine the action so it has little or no negative effect on those outside.

If you're a manufacturing operation, your readiness plan tells everyone what to do, in what order, according to circumstances, and by whom, when an incident occurs. What processes must be shut down, diverted, or contained? What equipment must be utilized? Who notifies authorities? The plan contains quick-access numbers and references. In short, it prepares your organization with everything needed to focus your reaction to an incident and minimize (if not prevent) a potential crisis or disaster.

If you did it right, the creation of your plan was a group effort, crafted with input from all the supervisors in your operation. Taking a page from the Japanese management textbooks, you have involved in the decisions those who will have the responsibility for carrying them out.

Your employees know about it. Local authorities probably know about it, too. And you may have had a dry run or two, just to make sure it works.

That's the ideal situation. However, I realize, based on experience with a lot of companies over the years, that I would make a major mistake if I were to assume that each of our clients had this overall plan in place, and that my job was to focus solely on the envirocomm, or communication, part of preparedness. The fact is, sadly and dangerously, many organizations—especially those not in sensitive manufacturing operations—don't have emergency preparedness plans.

The reasons I hear are many: "I don't think we need one. We're a small company and most of us here would know what to do." Or: "I know we need one, but we haven't gotten around to it." Or: "We have one, sort of. At least we've talked about it with our key people, and we put together a list of names and numbers some time back. It's probably out of date . . ."

If people put off making a will, thinking they won't need it *this* year, it shouldn't be too surprising that they would put off making a company preparedness plan. But isn't it foolish for an otherwise careful and successful manager or top executive not to take the moves now that one day could keep him or her from having to explain why there was no plan, when it all hit the fan?

So, just in case you haven't gotten "a round tuit," I'll use the next chapter to help you get started.

My point here is this:

Your best bet in a bad situation is advance preparation.

Since you can't control so many things—you can't predict when a situation might develop, or who will be available to deal with it, or if they will remember everything that must be done—it's important to make sure that your organization has in place your environmental emergency plan, including the communication part, and especially the designated spokesperson.

3. THE PLAN MUST BE ACCESSIBLE

An important local plant of ABC Company (I know the name but I refuse to disclose it!) went to a lot of trouble to prepare an emergency plan. It had a very detailed list of assignments, names and numbers to call, all the tactics needed to take charge of a crisis. All the key people in the plant helped write the plan. It was put together neatly in thick red binders, and everybody received a copy.

One summer Sunday afternoon, when everyone was home, there was an explosion at the plant. Some of the officials, out mowing their lawns, looked up to see the smoke billowing from the plant. The company people jumped into their cars and raced to the plant.

Unfortunately, the conditions were such that it was unsafe to reach the offices where all the copies of the emergency plan were safely locked up.

I mention this, not because you would ever do such a thing, but because I thought you'd be interested.

You, of course, would take a copy of the plan home with you and make sure others did likewise. You'd even stash a copy in the trunk of your car, or carry a card with key numbers in your pocket. You may have even thought it a good idea to establish an off-site emergency communication center for your organization—for example, a local hotel or the chamber of commerce office—where you kept a copy or two of the plan, along with a box of supplies you might need, just in case.

These are what ABC Company did, in fact, *after* the fact.

4. PEOPLE WANT TO HEAR FROM THE TOP

As the decade of the 90s began, the editorial director of the *Harvard Business Review* made an interesting observation. "We are witnessing," he said, "the rise of the ego-less corporation."[2]

His point was that as America moved out of the wild and wooly M&A, real-estate-boom, S&L climate of the 1980s, a certain change came about in the attitudes of publics and of business itself.

Those who had worshiped at the altar of the high-flying CEO (or perhaps more accurately, the CEO's *ego*) were standing up and walking away. They would no longer abide the over-leveraged egos of some corporate leaders, displayed in the 1980s not only in self-praising pseudobiographies but also in the brash and unrestricted decisions to buy, sell, and otherwise manipulate corporate assets.

"Ego is out and humble is in," said Alan Webber, writing in *The Wall Street Journal.* "Lavish is out and genuine economy is in. Go-it-alone is out and getting close to suppliers and customers is in."

I agree with that. This is what I see happening with regard to the environment. CEOs of leading companies are putting the concerns of customer-publics first. They are not saying, "I've got all the answers, get out of my way." Instead they're asking for input from those both inside and outside the organization. They are saying, "Let's approach environmental problems, and the options for action, together." This is what I refer to as the mental greening of corporate America, and I believe it is rapidly spreading to all forms of business, large and small.

And as we move into the Green World of Business, where sustainable development is the dominant agenda, our spokespersons will rely more on interactive publics than on self-advancing ego to communicate.

But I want to underscore that while the new, greening organization may be ego-less, it can't be faceless. People outside and inside still need to put a face with the organization's message—and this is particularly true when there is a negative environmental incident or crisis.

I go back to the Exxon *Valdez* for instruction. Our conversations with public relations people after that environmental incident kept returning to one point: Environmental incidents put the focus of public opinion directly on the executive who personifies the company and will communicate for it. When there's trouble, people want to hear from the person who can promise action toward a solution.

Television ads and the rise of a great many public-speaking executives have conditioned the public to expect the CEO to speak directly in good times.

From Iacocca to Victor Kiam and Frank Purdue, we've come to expect the head of the company to look us in the eye and say, in effect, "I'm personally involved. I'll see that you get a good product (service)." And, if there is a problem: "I will be on your side."

When trouble brews, there is no more powerful medicine than that of the top guy stepping forward and saying, "I am concerned about this situation. A mistake has occurred—and here's what we're prepared to do about it."

Exxon's chief executive drew heavy fire for failing to inject himself directly, forcefully, and helpfully into the news coverage immediately after the *Valdez* accident.

Immediately is a key word.

5. THE LONGER YOU WAIT, THE LESS YOUR OPPORTUNITY

When an environmental incident hits an organization, the potential positive effect of the CEO's appearance is directly related to the time that elapses after the first break of news.

This is an opportunity that melts faster than ice in Phoenix in August. And the greater, more sudden the news impact, the quicker the opportunity disappears, because the hungry news machine must be fed and it will be fed by others, if not by you.

In the *Valdez* situation there was a damaging hesitation. When top management failed to speak quickly, positively, and caringly, a vacuum was created. Into this vacuum were sucked confusion, mistrust, the credibility that the company otherwise had the right to enjoy, and a field day for detractors who were ready to speak up.

Not that I don't understand. I do. I was an executive in a corporate environment. I know how many different pieces of advice there are, how easy it is to make a mistake by speaking too soon, how dangerously long-term the wrong thing can be if it is said under pressure today.

So it's natural to paw the ground, avoid the phones, and hold one more strategy meeting with advisers, secretly wondering, *Do I have to do this now? Should we wait awhile? Isn't it better to let the authorities outside tell about the situation first? Can this wait until after the quarterly meeting?*

If you want a voice of experience, listen to what the CEO of Hooker Chemical Company had to say years later, after his company had gone through the devastating aftermath of the Love Canal toxic contamination episode.

When asked why he or another top spokesperson didn't speak up to address concerns of the public and to express the company's commitment to at least investigate the situation, Hooker's president told a reporter:

"I wish I had. I wanted to. But instead I listened to the lawyers. They were concerned about the legal ramifications. By the time they cleared our statement, it was all over. We never caught up."

Compare this with the experience of John Hall, the chief executive of Ashland Oil, who overrode the advice of some of his people following a spill near Pittsburgh.

Taking charge of the situation, and putting himself at the risk of having questions asked that he could not answer, Hall flew straight to the scene of the environmental incident and met the press.

His forthright involvement, timely and caring, was the main factor in preserving the company's credibility and its long-standing relationships with core publics.

No matter the size of your organization or whether the impact of the incident is large or small, plan *now* to be the spokesperson, for at least part of the time.

6. YOUR SHORT-TERM HESITATION CAN HAVE LONG-TERM IMPACT

"The oil industry inexplicably misjudged the rising public apprehension about environmental damage," said Robert Irvine, a member of a think tank set up by an Anchorage public relations firm to help Alyeska Pipeline Service Company reexamine its communication strategy following the spill.

"Politicians and the media are always ready to fill the void," he told us, "and they are always on the side of injured or threatened parties or interests."

Within weeks of the spill, the Alaska state legislature enacted a tax increase on oil from the North Slope fields. "The spill made the political atmosphere different from what it was before," said Governor Steve Cowper. "It became a matter of competing credibility: the credibility of the state versus the credibility of the industry."

Congressional committees moved just as quickly. Senate bills were introduced to dramatically increase liability limits and potential compensation for oil-spill damage, and to increase the money available through the industry-financed Offshore Oil Pollution Compensation fund. In the House, GOP members joined in a proposal to set up a group of 10 regional response teams, certified by the Coast Guard but paid for by the oil industry.

And the House voted (374 to 49) to extend an existing moratorium on oil and gas leasing off Alaskan and other coastal waters, despite its irrelevancy to tanker accidents.

Ripple effects reverberated. "They [Exxon] killed ANWR," lamented a lobbyist who had worked with other oil industry representatives for months to advance the Arctic National Wildlife Refuge oil exploration option for consideration on Capitol Hill.

No company can stop public scrutiny and legislative opportunism, but Exxon—a company with tremendous resources and public affairs experience—was seen by public relations observers as late and lax in public positioning. *Valdez* teaches that delay in attending to positive communication can result in an irresistible political force.

The *Exxon Valdez* story illustrates the high stakes involved in communicating over the environment. "Five years from now, *'Exxon Valdez'* will be the answer to a trivia question," said Irvine. "However, a lot of the laws and regulations and controls put in place as a result of the *Valdez* will be anything but trivial. They'll be with us for as long as oil is being shipped and delivered."

Chapter Nineteen

Dos and Don'ts of Crisis Communication

IF YOU'RE IN CHARGE, HERE ARE SUGGESTED STEPS

Public relations professionals see in the *Exxon Valdez* environmental incident a neglect of critical basics, centering on Disaster Communication Rule #1: Quickly take charge of the news flow and give the public, by way of the news media, a credible, concerned, and wholly committed spokesperson.

If you are a key executive in an operation of any size, you can learn from the unfortunate circumstances of the *Valdez* what you must do, if you are to stay on the green, in an emergency. Here are my general suggestions:

- Get in on the story fast and *personally.* Take charge, both as an example to your troops and as a messenger through the media to key customer-publics. Show your concern in personal terms. If there's a focal scene of tragedy, go there immediately.

- Make sure your communication plan is implemented, along with the rest of the emergency-response plan.

- If a product is involved, immediately consider the pros and cons of pulling it—and err on the side of caution rather than "evidence." Remember that perception is reality, and that your best chance of sustaining customer-public relationships is to take away—temporarily, at best—the object of concern. (Remember how Johnson & Johnson pulled Tylenol after a poisoning incident.)

- Make sure somebody personally sees or calls key opinion leaders in each of your defined customer-public markets— and make some calls yourself.

- Become the visible, concerned, and active corporate persona or, if you absolutely can't handle it, delegate all of this to your second-in-command and don't second-guess his or her public performance.

These moves are not easy. Some won't be natural, but the survival of your organization, its public relationships, and your own future success may depend on your making them.

You build your reputation and your success an inch at a time. Why blow it by the acre because of a reticent and reactive role taken during an unexpected negative situation?

It may be helpful, by comparison here, to heed the words of a highly successful political consultant about waging a campaign:

> *We have a compressed period of time in which we will make our case that our candidate is decent, honest, qualified, intelligent, and fair. The opposition will try to make the case that he is . . . unqualified and a little strange. Our job is to block their message or at least dilute it, and get ours out.*

And, continuing in the political vein, here is what *The Washington Post* said in analyzing why Judge Bork didn't make it to the Supreme Court:

"Bork's opponents seized the momentum . . . and by the time the White House geared itself up to go to bat for its nominee, the damage could not be undone."[1]

When an environmental crisis occurs, the executive's position is not much different from that of the political candidate. Both need to reach and win the understanding of customer-publics. Both have detractors. And both have to race the clock.

Emphasizing what's been said in the previous chapter, the most important thing to do is: Take charge of the news about you before the news does you more damage than the incident.

COMMUNICATION BASICS

There are many lists of specific dos and don'ts about crisis communication.

I have boiled them down to five, drawing on the experience of numerous industrial public relations professionals, who have tested them under fire.

1. Inform the employees and their families. Be prepared to convey any information about employee injuries to the appropriate relatives.

2. Refrain from speculation. Don't guess about unverified causes, damage, costs. Label rumors as such. Tell what you know. Don't minimize impact or raise emotions. If you don't know, say "I don't have that information."

3. Express your concern and commitment. Your presence and attitude mean a lot. Get to the positives—control of the situation, intentions to stay with it. Be cool (confident) and warm (caring).

4. Expect everything to be on the record. Help the reporter do a good job of reporting. Don't argue about news values or the validity of questions, and don't ask to see the story before it runs.

5. Have someone keep up with what you've said to whom; a list at least. Better, a list plus a tape recorder. The list is for follow-up, which allows you to check up on facts and deliver more information later. The tape is for you to review later what you've said and how you've said it. This can be helpful (a) in remaining consistent in your interviews, and (b) in self-analysis of how you are coming across.

CRISIS FIRST-AID KIT

The best crisis insurance is preparation, says friend and fellow PR counselor Bill Corbett,[2] who learned this very early in his career as a communicator. As a 22-year-old second lieutenant in the Air Force, he found himself in charge of handling the communication aspects of the first of six aircraft crashes.

Bill was ready for the challenge because of a quirk of events. Eager to get started as an Air Force officer, he reported for duty at his assigned post several days ahead of schedule. "What are you doing here?" asked his superior officer. When he explained that he wanted to be prepared for his assignment, so he could start at full tilt, he was admonished. "No one ever reports early for military service," he was told. "Go home and come back on the correct date." Bill left, but he took with him a copy of a red looseleaf booklet entitled, "Crash Manual," which he happened to see on a shelf.

Since he was a stranger in town with little to do, Bill dedicated most of his waiting time to reading and rereading the "Crash Manual." He found it fascinating, full of short case descriptions of various plane crashes and clear, helpful guidance on how to communicate with families, military personnel, the news media, and other publics if you are in charge of communication at the site of a crash.

Three days after Bill reported for duty, on the *correct* date, a crash occurred and Bill was rushed to the scene. His superiors were very impressed with the young officer's grasp of the situation and complimented him on his steady handling of communication at a tense time.

"My career as a crisis officer was launched," says Bill, who went on to become the communication officer for companies and national organizations, such as the American Institute of Certified Public Accountants and Avon Products, Inc., and as a public relations advisor to the U.S. Information Agency.

"Be prepared," is Bill's advice. I asked him to tell me specifically what he would put into a preparedness package for a company executive or communication officer.

Here is Bill Corbett's "first-aid kit" for use in an emergency. Much of what he suggests here would be applicable if an environmental incident or crisis occurred.

1. Be prepared to operate from your home or a remote site since crises often occur during off-hours. At home and the office, have at your fingertips an annual report, prepared statements covering hot topics, biographies and photos of senior management and board of directors.

2. Keep copies of the most recent proxy statement, quarterly report, and a list of home and weekend phone numbers of senior management and communications staff members, key media, and wire services.

3. Have an up-to-date fact sheet and economic-impact statement on each facility, along with home phone numbers of local management.

4. Have a fax machine at home for normal and emergency use. Needless to say, a typewriter or word processor and portable phone are also essential. And know how to use them!

5. Keep updated safety statistics at your fingertips. There will be no time to gather them when everything hits the fan and you're besieged by the media, government officials, and your own employees and management.

6. Again, presuming that you might not be able to reach your office, make arrangements now—and carry the numbers— for a heavy-duty copying service, where you can get 24-hour access. Likewise, know the number of a reliable round-the-clock messenger service.

7. Have written procedures in place that ensure there is only one source of information so the press cannot whipsaw you by getting seemingly conflicting information from others in your organization.

You may want to copy and keep Corbett's Crisis First-Aid Kit handy, just in case. One or more of these seven helpful hints can get you back onto the green faster, if an environmental incident jars you and your organization.

PREPARE YOUR OWN CRISIS COMMUNICATION PROFILE

I've provided you with some general suggestions and some more-specific tips to apply in most crisis situations, no matter who you are.

But to have a successful response plan that is best suited to your needs, it is most helpful to draw up a crisis communication profile for your particular facility(ies). To have such an *updated* profile on hand maximizes your efficient, successful response when a crisis occurs.

Even the most forward-looking company may be surprised at the findings of such a crisis communication audit.

One client, a successful chemical production company, asked our Public Policy Research Group to conduct an assessment of their crisis management and response plan. Here are some surprising weaknesses we turned up after a number of lengthy interviews with senior management and tours of each of a dozen facilities, as well as their surrounding communities:

• Lack of trained backup spokespersons: Necessary backup spokespersons and communication contacts had not been adequately identified or trained at several facilities.

- Lack of communication hardware: Most of the facilities relied upon a singular or limited communication resource, and lacked adequate supplemental hardware—cellular telephones, outside emergency phone lines, fax machines, etc.—to maintain communication if primary resources became disabled or unavailable during a crisis. This included the absence of alliances with neighboring facilities through which access to those resources could be gained.

- Lack of crisis communication drills: Crisis drill procedures did not appropriately address communication aspects or test communication capabilities of facility personnel.

- Lack of community alliances: Alliances with, and support from, local civic and business communities had not been cultivated by several facilities. In time of crisis, tremendous logistical assistance and public advocacy could be obtained from these communities.

- Lack of monetary resources for local contributions: Funding for contributions to local ad hoc efforts was perceived as largely unavailable to plant management, yet this is one means to cultivate the business and civic alliances outlined above.

- Variation in corporate notification contacts: The initial notification contacts at corporate headquarters and the subsequent secondary communication were highly varied and lacked consistency.

- Variation of management levels among spokespersons: The primary spokespersons identified at each facility were drawn from a variety of management levels, ranging from personnel administrators to senior plant managers. This variation could lead to inconsistencies and contradictions in crisis statements.

- Variation of facility attitudes toward corporate assistance: At the plant level, there existed great variation in the expectations of, and desire to rely upon, corporate resources for expertise in public affairs, environmental, engineering, legal, and other fields.

As I said, these were surprising results to this very progressive company. But it's important to note that identifying these weaknesses allowed company management to build a stronger crisis response plan.

FIGURE 19–1
Crisis Management and Response Assessment: Workforce and Community

	Plant #1	#2	#3	#4	#5	#6	#7	#8	#9	#10	#11
Unionized Workforce	X	X	X				X	X			X
Local Community Chief Environmental Concern	Groundwater Contamination	Desert Preservation	Air Emissions	Landfills	Air Emissions	Marine Life	Air Emissions	Air Emissions	Marine Life	Landfills	Air Emissions
Local Media Is Sensitized to Environmental Concerns	X		X	X	X	X	X	X	X	X	X

FIGURE 19–2
Crisis Management and Response Assessment: Facility Location and Operations

	Plant #1	#2	#3	#4	#5	#6	#7	#8	#9	#10	#11
Close Proximity to Residential Areas		X			X			X		X	X
Location Is near/on Body of Water		X		X			X	X	X		X
Likelihood of Transportation Incident				X		X	X	X	X		X
Likelihood of Weather-Related Incident	X Hurricane/ Tornado	X Earthquake				X Hurricane/ Tornado			X Hurricane/ Tornado		
Threat of Incident from Neighboring Facilities		X			X	X	X	X	X		X
Most Likely Crisis Scenario	Spill Migrating Off Site	Earthquake	Reactor Incident	Ammonia Leak	Odor	Fire/ Explosion	Fire	Butane Incident	Vapor Cloud/ Explosion	Fire	Barge Incident
Last Major Crisis	1985 Weather-Related Power Outage	—	1982 Explosion	1978 Fire	1991 Odor Release	1985 Explosion	1979 Fire	1986 Explosion/ Fire	—	—	Early 80s Truck Explosion

FIGURE 19–3

Crisis Management and Response Assessment: Crisis Communication

	Plant #1	#2	#3	#4	#5	#6	#7	#8	#9	#10	#11
Designated Primary Spokesperson	Plant Manager	Plant Manager	Human Resources	Plant Manager	Plant Manager	Human Resources	Plant Manager	Plant Manager	Human Resources	Director	Plant & Operations Manager
Designated Backup Spokesperson	Quality Manager	Plant Manager	Unclear	Director Admin.	Production Supervisor		Production Manager	Environ. Manager		Division Manager	Mfg. Supervisor
Primary Spokesperson Trained/Experienced	X/X	X/X	X/–	X/–	X/X	X/X	X/–	X/–	–/–	X/–	X/–
Secondary Spokesperson Trained/Experienced	X/–			X/X	–/–		–/–	–/–		–/–	X/–
Designated to Call Corporate	Plant Manager	Plant Manager	Management Team	Plant Manager	Plant Manager	Plant Manager	Plant Manager	Plant Manager	Plant Manager	Director	Plant & Operations Manager
No. of Calls to Corporate	Single	Single	Numerous	Single	Numerous	Single	Numerous	Single	Single	Numerous	Numerous
Immediate On-site PR Help Expected				X		X	X	X	X	X	X
Most Likely Crisis Scenario	Spill Migrating Off Site	Earthquake	Reactor Incident	Ammonia Leak	Odor	Fire/Explosion	Fire	Butane Incident	Vapor Cloud/Explosion	Fire	Barge Incident

Here's a sample of what may be relevant characteristics to serve as a guide in preparing your profile:

1. *Facility and Operations*

Location: Get down on paper the geographic location and terrain of each facility. How old is it? How near are the nearest towns? Is it on a river or waterway? Identify other area industries.

Plant Management: Identify management hierarchy, titles of top personnel, and how long they have served the facility (an institutional memory can be "golden" in a crisis situation). Include home and work phone numbers.

Work Force: Quantify and qualify your personnel. How many are located at this particular facility? Do they belong to a union? What is the turnover rate? Identify areas of strength (support) and weaknesses (disgruntlement) within your work force. Are jobs within your company valued within this particular economic community?

Products/Raw Materials: Identify number and quantities of raw materials used and products produced. Review toxicity or potential toxicity of materials in anticipated situations.

Material Transportation Routes: By what method of transportation do raw materials and products arrive at your facility? By what method do they leave? What is the frequency of shipments for products and materials? Are the modes of transportation safe?

Regulations: Characterize compliance with relevant regulations, as well as relationships with regulatory officials. Have you contacted appropriate emergency response officials about any past incidents? What was the result? If not, do you have contacts and phone numbers of regulatory officials handy?

2. *Local Community*

General Community: What is the economic condition of the locale? Is it chronic? Temporary? What is the employment rate? What is the generally expressed view about your industry? Are there any particular accidents, incidents, protests that have colored the view of your facility or business, either favorably or unfavorably?

Government: Are state and/or local governments generally lenient, stringent, or moderate with respect to regulating your industry? Characterize your relationship with relevant officials.

News Media: What are the state and local newspapers, television and radio stations? How many are there? What has been the nature of previous news reports, editorials? Under what circumstances have the media sought your comments? You theirs? Are the reporters generally knowledgeable about your industry, your facility, the science?

Community Leaders: Who are the key opinion leaders in your area? In the past have they been allies? Foes? Are any of your employees leaders in the community?

3. *Crisis Preparation*

Who is currently responsible for communicating in a crisis? Have they been trained as spokespersons? What are your recent operational improvements? What are your shortcomings? Are responsibilities adequate? Do you have specific contacts responsible for lines of communication between departments? What are the crisis resources you can expect from corporate? Your facility? Your community? Do you regularly conduct drills? Include past incidents and plausible future scenarios. What are the facility management's response-capability estimates? Where is your emergency plan kept? Who has copies?

We'll close our discussion of crisis communication with a look at a sample employee questionnaire (see page 179) that is just the right kind of model with which to prepare your particular profile.

CRISIS PLANNING QUESTIONNAIRE

1. What are your general areas of responsibility within the company?
2. What types of crisis situations have arisen in the past relative to your area of responsibility?
3. How were they handled operationally and from a communications perspective, both internally and externally?
4. What types of additional crisis situations are possible/likely to arise relative to your area of responsibility? (Please rank these in order of likelihood of occurrence.)
5. What has been/would be your role in the event of any of these potential crisis situations?
6. How well do you believe you are prepared to deal with any of these crisis situations (i.e., Are there operational plans in place to use as a guide to action? Are responsibilities clear and understood, etc.?)
7. Are internal/external communications currently a part of your crisis preparation and planning? Please describe.
8. In your view, who would (or who should) communicate for the company if an emergency or crisis situation hit today?
9. Is there a clear understanding of communication roles in the event of a crisis? Are lines of communication authority and responsibility established and understood? Please describe.
10. Do you engage in any crisis drills? Please describe.
11. Is communication a part of the crisis drill process? Please describe.
12. Do you currently have an external community relations program in operation? Please describe.
13. Please describe your relationships with the following: local community; local political leaders; news media; environmental groups; local business leaders; employees; state and federal regulatory officials; state and federal elected officials; community groups (police, fire, schools, etc.).
14. Are you involved in the Local Emergency Planning Committee under SARA Title III? Please describe.
15. Overall, how do you believe your company is regarded in your community?
16. How is your industry, taken as a whole, regarded in your community?

Chapter Twenty

What To Do When You're Attacked by an Activist Group

There is no absolutely certain way to protect yourself from a storm. This I learned in the oil and sulphur mining business, operating off the coast of Louisiana in the Gulf of Mexico. You can build a stout platform, engineered for hurricane conditions; you can take precautions; you can routinely train personnel and review emergency plans; you can improve your odds, no question. But if you're going to hang out where hurricanes happen, you can still get hit, and hurt.

It's also true of a business attacked by an environmental action group.

The emphasis of this book is to get you and your organization on the green, where you are communicating with others who share an interest in environmental responsibility. I'm hoping this will help you build a stout platform and improve your odds in environmental positioning.

But what happens if—despite everything you do, or before you have time to do it—you are publicly targeted, picketed, put on notice through angry media play, or otherwise singled out for hostile, stormy action by green activists?

For one thing, you'll probably get less warning than we used to get from the hurricane watchers.

Your antagonists will probably want to catch you off guard and put you on the defensive.

You *might* get a phone call from the head of the environmental group, saying they plan to attack and asking for a meeting with you or a tour of your facilities.

That's the best-case scenario, but don't count on it.

Since part of the reason for singling you out may well be the publicity value, the activists' most effective opening gambit is a news conference or public event that can be covered by the media.

You'll read about yourself in the papers, or you'll get a call from a reporter asking for a comment to put into a story that's already in the works, or you'll look out the window to see picketers arriving, or there will come a nervous call from your front desk, saying, "There are some people out here, asking for you . . ."

Of course, your best defense is a well-formed emergency or crisis-avoidance communication plan. If this is in place, as we've discussed earlier, roll it out, play your positives to advantage, and stay on the "green."

But real-world—real Green World—conditions are not always that neat.

So let's go through some of the steps that can help you minimize damage if storm clouds suddenly burst on your organization.

KNOW YOUR ATTACKER'S MOTIVES

Who is this group? What do they want? Why are they picking on *us* (instead of somebody else)?

Your instinctive first questions are exactly the right questions. Our envirocomm model, in Chapter Six, emphasizes the need to question, quantify, and understand, before you seek to be understood.

Now you've got to question, quantify, and understand *fast*, taking advantage of shortcuts. This is true even if activists are already at your door or the gates of your plant. You may need to scramble, but you can and should get some calls going, so you know something about your challengers.

Fortunately, it's not hard to get basic information on who the group is and what they say they want. More than likely, this will be in the newspaper or on TV, depending on where the news breaks. The reporter who calls you may know.

Also, research a little. If you have literature from the group, look it over. See what their agenda is, what they stand for, what they've done. You may learn, for instance, which industries or individual companies they've singled out in the past.

Call the local library. Ask someone to consult a computer data base. For example, if your organization or one of your consultants subscribes to a service such as Nexis (Mead Data Corporation), you can quickly call up news stories that mention the group.

A phone call to a trade association, chamber of commerce, or local business organization can be helpful. If you're able to identify a company that has *been there*—has survived a bout with your attacker—you may want to consider placing a call to an executive in that company.

There are other more elaborate—and maybe unnecessary— ways. A private investigator in Buffalo, New York, admitted he had been hired to investigate the local activist group, Concerned Citizens of Cattaraugus County, which had opposed a proposed 423-acre landfill in a rural town 40 miles to the southeast. The investigator characterized his investigation as good homework, "basically what any corporation would do when they're trying to find out what the enemy is all about." The activists responded that the investigation was an invasion, that "they [the corporation] look for garbage and then circulate it."[1]

Doing good research, even to the point of an investigation, is "good homework," although I don't think I would agree with characterizing the activist group as the "enemy." The point is to get to know your attacker so you can find potential common points that could bring you to the table together, not to go in with preconceived, negative notions of who they are. Such an attitude is also likely to dispel any increased negative reactions from the activists.

Let me emphasize that the point of this quick research is *not* to dig up "dirt" on the activist group. That's a loser move, any way you cut it. Quite the contrary. Your biggest need is to stay on the green, if you've been there, or to get on the green. You and your organization need to find footing on the public-interest turf—a place where there is the possibility of positive action.

So you are looking primarily for areas of emphasis, areas where there are misunderstandings and contentions, and areas of possible agreement. You don't want to fight or flee; you want to see where you can agree, where you and the public share a commitment.

But even if agreement is not immediately practicable, you need the advantage of research to deflect the attack. You need to know the true nature of the attack, of the essential energy behind it.

In Oriental martial arts, such as jujitsu, the target of attack *uses* the energy of the attacker. The physical thrust is turned or channeled so that the attack is averted. This requires knowledge about movement and energy as well as calmness under attack.

In effect, instead of responding, we are, at this stage, trying to look past the attack and into the heart and mind of the attacker.

Ted Williams was a great hitter because he thought like the *pitcher.* He understood why and how each pitcher would throw to him.

So if someone is chunking rocks at you, let's understand why and how.

WHY ME?

It is not necessarily because you have done anything "wrong"—or, if you have made an environmental mistake, it is not because you couldn't explain it, if you had the chance.

Remember that your organization and the green action group are quite similar when it comes to management goals. You're both trying to create customers. Without customer-publics, nothing else matters for either of you.

The customer of the green action group is a member—a contributor, voter, or supporter—who must be attracted to the group. That attraction requires publicity. The group must be publicly observed in action, in behalf of a case or cause that has appeal to potential customer-publics.

If you have been singled out for attack, chances are it is because this basic motivation of the attacking organization—to create customers through publicity—attaches to some characteristics of you and your organization, such as . . .

You have a well-known name. This depends on whether the assault is from a national or a local green group. The national news value of attacking IBM or General Motors is obviously greater than that of attacking Main Street Dry Cleaners. Locally, however, Main Street Dry Cleaners may be a familiar name. (In the famous flap over clam-shell hamburger boxes, the McDonald's name happened to satisfy both local and national news values.)

You are in a business that has built-in risks. The chemical industry has always been easy to attack because of the public's conditioned fear of chemicals.

You are located in an area convenient to the attacking group. One company came under attack mainly because it was headquartered near a college campus where an activist group needed a summer project.

Your name has not been in the paper too much. "Villains" can wear out their news value, so fresh targets are needed.

Your company can be connected to a hot topic. When the news curve is rising on toxics or dioxin or food scares, local news media can be aroused by a charge against a local company that suggests a connection.

Or any of a hundred other "reasons"! Companies are put under fire *ostensibly* because they have not signed a particular pledge, because they have not made a particular commitment, because they have not gone public with cleanup plans, or whatever.

By now you are anticipating the point: You can be attacked despite all your preparations and all your good works. The attacking group needs conflict and publicity to build support and membership—and you are in the right place. You are presumed to have at least one chink in your armor.

KNOW YOURSELF: ORGANIZE YOUR INFORMATION

The attacker's weapons are a public barrage of innuendo, questions, and facts out of context, which can make for heavy going. But if it's true that information is power, *you've got the real power.*

If you're going to take charge, you've got to organize your information. Focus first on the object of the attacker's fire, since that is what reporters will ask you about. Anticipate their questions. See if actual *facts* can set the record straight.

For example, if the subject is your Toxic Release Inventory data: What were the conditions under which these data were gathered? Are these conditions the same today? How do these compare with other data? What steps have you taken to correct, remediate, reduce, eliminate, *clean up*? Is there something you can give or show to reporters or to the activist group?

Similarly, if it's about an alleged leak of materials underground: What are the facts? What have you told the government? What is the indicated technical solution? What are you committed to doing? What are your show-and-tell possibilities now?

You may not have been ready to talk about some of these things, but that was before the storm broke. Now you need information—truthful, reasonable, and as much of it as practicable—to help you get onto good, green, dry ground.

So get your information lined up—fast—and have it ready.

TALK TO THEM IF YOU CAN

Explore options. Depolarize. Personalize and listen. Get them on the phone. Offer to meet with them. Invite them in.

Your office is best, but if they won't come to see you, offer to meet at some neutral place—a setting you feel comfortable with, not a place where you are vulnerable to a media sneak attack—maybe a hotel you choose or a business conference center.

Your task is to try and deflate their balloon *and* to get direct information about what's motivating them, how serious they are, who they are, what they will consider "success."

How? Ask friendly questions. Listen. Be friendly. Politely put off giving more direct information. Offer to meet with them again. As long as you are talking, you may not be fighting. Maybe you can come up with multiple options for mutual benefit that will satisfy their needs. What can you "give" on—but not agree to yet?

GET THIRD PARTIES INVOLVED

This will help depolarize the incident. Encourage several allies—from business, politics, academics, sciences, whatever makes sense—to say something to the press and to the group about your track record and intentions.

At the same time, arm your friends. And make new friends, and arm them. Put them onto a mailing list and service them aggressively.

The critical point is to immediately reduce or remove the "us vs. them" element, the polarity of the one-on-one relationship. You'll lose if it's like this, because press and politicians will get into the act unless they see others take your side.

TAKE CONTROL OF NEWS

In an attack mode, the activist group will put news handling first, because everything is done for the publicity impact. You've got to get out of the response or defense mode and begin managing this critical publicity.

There are several things you can do to get on the green—where you've got at least some control over the news handling.

Whatever you say to the group, put it into a news release. Even if you don't actually give the release to the media, you'll have your comments prepared so there's no slipup or misstatement by you later. And, assume that everything you say will appear in your antagonists' news release.

Be prepared at all times for media calls or sneak attacks. Keep your news statement on your desk. Keep a card in your pocket with your two or three key points.

Have spokespersons ready and strategically placed. Line up credible third parties—for example, a physician who is qualified to speak on a health issue or an expert on a scientific question—who can be additional news sources.

Erase "no comment" from your vocabulary. It doesn't work. I know this may be hard to swallow, but your best response to a question from the press would start with the words, "I'm glad you asked that." And then, in a direct and friendly manner, you make your points.

INFORM YOUR CRITICAL 20 PERCENT PUBLICS

Your core customer-public relationships are never more important than in times like these. If you shut down on the transactions with those who are close to you, you are not only disarming friends, you run the risk of alienating them.

One simple step is essential. Fairly early in the confrontation with an outside group, send a letter or memo (and maybe copies of news items and your news release) to employees, key stockholders, political friends, suppliers, major customers, and others who have a stake in your well-being.

Here's where you are most efficient in using your envirocomm system. You can manage the information flow. You know what these customer-publics are interested in—your continuous interactions have already told you this—and you have the pipelines in place to reach them for two-way communication.

Invite dialogue. Offer to provide more information. Maintain your good relationships. This can help you head off defections, uninformed and damaging comments to the news media, or one of those awful public circumstances, such as an attack on your chairman at a community event or the company annual meeting.

Your attitude of openness and your commitment to good public-interest principles will go a long way with your friends, followers, and objective observers.

Union Carbide CEO Bob Kennedy says that the company regularly meets with activists—though it's not *always* anticipated.[2]

There's the more regular annual meeting when a variety of activists on a wide range of issues come to present resolutions, asking for time. Kennedy says that this has been going on more than several years and that they've "all kind of gotten used to each other." He says experience has been a great teacher in the most effective ways to handle such meetings. For instance, Kennedy says he likes to meet with activists in advance, to make sure the company understands the agenda.

Then there are the periodic meetings with a variety of coalitions. Kennedy says that a number of widely known environmental groups have gotten together and sponsor local grassroots coalitions, known as "Citizens Concerned About (fill in the blank)," which can be marketed virtually anywhere, on virtually any issue.

Again, Carbide (and Kennedy, when requested) agrees to meet, but sets ground rules: no press, no tape recorders, no post-meeting statements to the media. The format generally consists of prepared statements and about two hours of dialogue.

At one such meeting, a "Concerned Citizens . . ." group asked about their involvement in the company's policy making. Carbide pointed to their Community Advisory Panels (CAPs), composed of community teachers, fire chiefs, etc., but the group still felt left out. Carbide agreed to let the group draft a protocol for organizing a CAP.

Tactics for setting ground rules are not always successful. One group was critical of a Carbide operating plant in Texas. The company and group discussed demands and a time when the activists could come to the plant to present them. When the two couldn't agree on a mutually convenient time, the group came to the plant and staged a mass demonstration. The company was forced to turn them away at the gate, and explained to the media that their suggested date had been turned down. That message was strengthened when Carbide pointed out that the demonstrators weren't even locals, but were out-of-towners who had flown in to stage the protest for the media.

Carbide's message was clear and credible: "We don't respond well to demands. We are ready for dialogue."

PRINCIPLES OF CONFRONTATION

Here are my observations on the general principles of confrontation, regarding the environment, from the business perspective:

1. Attack can come despite good works and preparation.
2. The goal of some attacking groups is the conflict itself, not amicable resolution.
3. Avoid at all costs the zero-sum game, where one side wins only at the expense of the other.
4. When conflict resolution is not possible, reposition the opposition.
5. The polarity of us-vs.-them invites additional attackers against us.
6. Involving third parties depolarizes.
7. Response to high-profile attack should usually also be high-profile; that is to say, with publicity.
8. To minimize the coopting and alienation of stakeholders, they must be aggressively informed.
9. Key disarming traits are openness to dialogue and commitment to public-interest principles.

10. Resolution means the sorting of multiple options to satisfy mutual interests.

A NOTE ON WHERE ACTIVISM IS HEADED

Though there's been an increasing tendency for some of the more moderate environmental activist organizations to move toward cooperation with business—the McDonald's/Environmental Defense Fund partnership described elsewhere in this volume is probably the most celebrated example to date—don't get too comfortable.

As we've said, environmental groups are organizations that have a business agenda too (increasing memberships). As a number of activists move toward the center, competition for those members will become more keen and the extremists will insist on marketing strategies which rule out business coopting environmentalism.

The expected trend is that, after the Earth Summit, more and more environmentalists will move to differentiate themselves to their members. As "Critical Trends in Environment" editor Tony Leighton says, "Expect them to be less polite."[3]

Greenpeace is proving this trend true with recent attacks on Canadian pulp producers with its antidioxin campaign, and on Du Pont's manufacture of CFCs, despite its continued phase-out plan.

Chapter Twenty-One

Choose Your Green Partners

There is no way to hide from the green spotlight. Wherever you operate, your business will be under constant scrutiny by community citizens and officials who are by now well aware of their rights in Green World.

An environmental episode of even the most routine or technically manageable nature is likely to touch off negative community reaction. Even if you think you're "doing good" you can get into trouble.

Companies are sometimes surprised to find that even a proactive, pro-green move, such as installing waste-treatment facilities, or government-mandated activities, such as cleaning up old dump sites, can raise inquiry, resistance, and contention among community neighbors.

More than one company has learned the hard way that one-way communication—making green decisions behind closed doors and delivering them via terse and technical news releases—is an invitation to a public barbecue. *Yours.*

As more and more information flows into the public domain from business, directly and indirectly (for example, data reported to government), and from other sources (such as green action groups), community leaders and activists are primed to apply heat to any organization that makes a green move without community consent.

PARTNERING IS REQUIRED AND DESIRABLE

Choosing green partners at the community level is without doubt the best strategy to improve your standing. It's smart on two levels: It avoids some legal problems, and it widens your options.

190

(1) The force of law

The law requires you to do some partnering. Your emergency plans—spelled out in the federal law, the Emergency Planning and Community Right-to-Know-Act (EPCRA)—are an example. You can't make a move without calling in local law enforcement people and community representatives.

Other laws and regulations encourage you to inform workers about hazards—leading you into discussions that have the effect of binding the company and its people into a cooperative arrangement.

(2) Room for options

Community decision making can easily proceed without the input of every business organization. Consequently, green decisions that affect your operations can very well be made without you, reducing your options.

To keep your options open, it's in your interest to plan, act, and speak with others in the community, even when the law doesn't require it.

Roger Fisher and William Ury, directors of the Harvard Negotiation Project in the early 1980s, made the point that it's in my interest to keep the system open, if I expect to have it deliver benefits to me.[1] They counseled the successful negotiator—the one who "gets to yes without giving in"—to invent multiple options that might yield mutual benefits.

If the system is kept open, and I am in the game, my "yes" and the other person's "no" might fit together. Or at worst, I'll be aware when the "no" is coming.

Both to gain consent and to be empowered by community decisions, you need to increase your Green-World options. You can, with systematic effort, create better community relationships and keep them alive.

EXAMINE YOUR RELATIONSHIPS

Look around you. Environmental partnerships—or coalitions, task forces, or local committees working together toward green goals— are happening already. Examples are schools, clubs, churches, and companies working with each other and with local government and green action groups.

If you are already involved in some of these joint efforts, you should take some time to examine the relationships, to see if they are right for you.

- Do they cover your key customer-publics?
- Do they put you into the best possible light?
- Did you choose these relationships, or did you simply respond, much as you would to the request for a charitable contribution?
- Are there any pitfalls, gaps, and possible inconsistencies with your corporate mission?

You and your business or organization can't afford to be involved in any relationships that will backfire or that will lack the support of your core publics, such as your own employees.

The key idea is to involve important customer-publics in your decision-making *process* before you make any environment-related move and to set up interactive relationships that will give you a forum to discuss green issues and options for a long time to come.

IDENTIFYING PARTNER CANDIDATES

You don't have to work with everybody. It might seem like a good idea to be best friends with all the players in your community, but it's usually impractical and it's simply not necessary. You may recall in our QUALITY model that we suggest zeroing in with laser-like specificity on key individuals as you quantify your customer-publics. Community leaders are the place to start to find representatives and influencers of your specific customer-publics.

Community leaders are not just the politicians. These may be the most high-profile influentials, but you'll need to go beyond elected officials. Your success or failure in your local community of Green World may well mean looking at some familiar faces a little differently; your list may well include your own employees and even some of your competitors!

We're in the sustainable development era, where sharply competing companies are buying and selling each other's pollution credits. So you're able to look upon competitors as providing opportunities, not just challenges.

At the same time, your employees, whom you generally view as providing you with opportunities for success, may provide challenges as well—and you may not even know about it. A company we worked with discovered through a survey that its employees were making significant contributions to a green action group that the company considered a hostile adversary.

My point is, you'll need to have all kinds of allies to be successful in envirocomm. You'll be looking at employees, competitors, and action groups differently when you consider that you need these relationships, and you can't afford to be left out as they team up on the green.

WHO ARE THE "LEADERS"?

By "community leader," I mean *opinion* leader, an individual whose point of view is respected in the community and who has the ability to lead or to persuade others.

Community leaders can help you succeed in very practical ways. You might think of the community leadership structure as a kind of focus group—a cross-section of influencers to whom you can introduce your idea, message, or problem, for reaction and guidance.

Procter & Gamble, some time ago, decided that the best way for the company to make more friends at the community level among its many manufacturing plants was to conduct local open houses.

It began with a plant in Quincy, Massachusetts, where relations were already good with local government leaders. The plant manager met with these leaders, explained the company's desire to "expand the 'right to know' to the 'right to inspect' our operations."

The response was encouraging—but cautious—until the plant manager arranged for a special preview visit of the officials to the plant. A tour was followed by a shirtsleeves session, in which the manager and the officials together ironed out details for the community open house.

The keys to the successful program that followed were (1) political awareness, (2) strategic flexibility, and (3) aggressive media relations. P&G was able to demonstrate leadership by clearly communicating and soliciting feedback from the community—which it actually used in planning its program (again, a bottom-up approach).

P&G, in the process, developed a model for a community relations program that it duplicated in plants around the country with accompanying editorial board meetings. Successful partnering was well under way for the company.

QUANTIFYING THE LEADERSHIP STRUCTURE

Using our QUALITY envirocomm model, the first step is to *quantify*—that is, to identify and catalogue or list—the community leaders.

Research to determine the individuals needed for partnering in the community need not be extensive. It may be as informal as a plant manager simply coming up with a list based on his or her knowledge of the community and how it works.

If the community is larger, or the organization's manager wishes to expand or validate his or her knowledge, the research can be more sophisticated.

You, or someone you appoint, can call on several people in the community (they may or may not themselves be opinion leaders) and ask them: "Who do you consider to be the opinion leaders in this area?" Your survey participants might be a local labor leader, the head of the chamber of commerce, or a public official who has been in the community for some time (especially if the official has been elected and reelected to office, an experience that exposes opinion leaders rather effectively). The answers will produce names for you to consider as you shape your contact list.

Quantifying your customer-public leaders will lead you to a list of individuals from categories such as these:

- Elected officials
- Community experts
- Community managers or administrative leaders
- Regulatory or appointed officials (such as public health officers, for instance)
- University professors
- Club leaders

- School officials
- Ministers
- Union leaders
- Newspaper publishers (or, in some cases, editor/publishers)
- Television and radio station owners (if they are local residents)

As you consider partnerships, I suggest you start with the most compatible community leaders and move out from there.

RELATING TO THE "ACTIVE OPPOSITION"

What about activist-group leaders, including those who oppose your point of view?

Certainly consider them as another potential partner for environmental awareness and improvement in the community. You need to take every opportunity to learn about concerns and to spread your base of support just as far as you practically can.

In the next chapter, we look at some good examples of partnering—some in which green activists and business found ways to work together.

But keep in mind that partnering won't always be easy. The *customer-creation* goal of a green activist organization can handicap the process of partnering. In the extreme, you can encounter such barriers as the necessity for a group such as this to play to their customer-publics, to avoid the appearance of compromise, and to meet the news media's need for conflict.

FIGURE 21–1
Comparison of Factors Affecting Environmental Communication

Industry	Environmental Groups
Purpose of the Organization	
To create customers for goods and services. This requires management of wide range of concerns, personnel, and capital not directly related to environmental issues.	To create members and funding to support action on environmental issues. Involves management of concerns, personnel, and capital compatible with environmental action.

FIGURE 21–1 *(continued)*
Comparison of Factors Affecting Environmental Communication

Industry	Environmental Group
• Generally favors industrial growth, which in current society may require "self-serving" defense.	• Generally opposes industrial growth, siding with public fears about presumed pollution.

Internal Support

Industry	Environmental Group
• Generally varied, divided, sometimes hostile.	• Generally united.
• Inconsistent (competitive) perspectives on environmental issues within the company and among companies within an industry.	• Intergroup rivalries generally sublimated in interest of united impact.
• Accountability to stockholders who may have little, no, or conflicting interest in the environmental issue.	• Positions worked out in private: messages delivered are timely, usually hardhitting.
• Relationships with employees and employee families with varying stakes in issue.	
Such factors cause difficulty in gaining company (or in the case of coalitions or associations, inter-company) approvals for taking or delivering positions. Result: delays, missed opportunities, softened messages.	

External Support

Industry	Environmental Group
• Perceived as generally unfavorable regarding environmental aims and actions.	• Varies, most often by geographic area, but generally enjoys public support for pro-environment aims, actions.
• General public mistrust of industry, particularly big industry; low credibility, according to polls.	• High credibility, according to polls.
• Relationships to customers and others who may be affected by company statements on the issue.	• "Customers" are members or potential members who "buy" viewpoint and are reinforcement—not a distraction.
• Community relationships created by the location of plant.	• Grass roots stimulation creates perception of strong community relations.
These can handicap or help in formation, delivery, and acceptance of messages, depending on compatibilities of the particular group, company, or plant with relevant publics.	These are nurtured by group leaders and made part of overall formation, delivery, and acceptance of messages involving various publics.

Relationships to Government

Industry	Environmental Group
• Regulated at many levels.	• Not regulated. Subject to some tax, lobbying laws.

FIGURE 21–1 *(concluded)*
Comparison of Factors Affecting Environmental Communication

Industry	Environmental Group
• Regarding current environmental regulations, position generally is to seek legislative relief from current or additional regulatory control and cost burdens.	• Advocates maintenance and strengthening of environmental laws and regulations, with little concern for industrial cost and control burdens.
• Believed to have self-interest in legislative positions.	• Perceived as representing public interest.

Relationship to News Media

• Varies widely, reflecting factors about plant, location, company reputation in other aspects, predisposition of media.	• Varies (geographic locations, economic, other interests, predispositions) but is often symbiotic: delivers what media needs.
• Generally responsive, not aggressive on environmental issues.	• Aggressive on environmental issues.
• Seeks thoughtful, interpretive coverage of issues.	• Seeks dramatic, people- and fear-oriented coverage of issues, as well as thoughtful, interpretive coverage.
• Often does not provide simple messages and good spokesperson, or "wrong" person is found by media for response.	• Usually provides simple message, willing and articulate spokesmen. Ready to initiate media contact and respond with "right" person.

Source: E. Bruce Harrison Company

"INSPECT, DON'T EXPECT" IS THE GUIDELINE

The company that takes the initiative in envirocomm gives itself leverage onto the public-interest green. Partnering and openness are the levers.

When the desired company-community partnership is achieved, it will be because at least three characteristics are in place: open doors, open dialogue, and open options.

We've already mentioned open houses as an ideal way to show openness.

An advertising campaign by the chemical industry (for the Chemical Manufacturers Association's Responsible Care Program) made the point that people mistrust, dislike, or fear a company or a facility on the basis of what they know or hear or observe. The copy in the bright yellow ad said: "You're driving by that chemical plant, just like you do every day, when one of your kids asks you what they make in there and you answer that you're not really sure and it occurs to you that you probably should be." CMA offered more information through a toll-free phone call.

When the subject is environmental risk, the thing most feared is that which is unfamiliar—and presumably dangerous and uncontrollable.

Plant tours, open houses, and toll-free numbers, with the right kind of preparation and implementation, like those promoted by the Responsible Care Program (see more in Chapter Twenty-Six) can build up community acceptance and good will—and can provide you with valuable "market" information, as your customer-publics come to you, with their interests, concerns, and questions.

You are saying to community neighbors: "We want to be your partner for environmental progress and we are willing to take the initiative. We can make promises and commitments, but we'll do a better job if you know us and we know you. Start by looking us over. Inspect us—before you expect some action or attitude that you dislike or distrust."

OPEN DIALOGUE, WITH MEDIA COVERAGE

The industrial environmental communicator must be squarely on the side of the public interest. The goal must be a public-interest goal. The message must be clear, positive, and nondefensive. The community must be convinced that its interests come first. The key is open dialogue with the community and an attitude of helpful honesty in which issues of mutual concern can be discussed. Open houses, participation in community clubs and events, and, especially, taking the lead in relating to the community's news media can promote open exchange with the community.

A good example of what can be done is provided by the plant in Ohio that requested roundtable discussions with the editorial boards of area newspapers.

Three people from the Aristech Chemical plant (a spinoff of U.S. Steel) gave the editors and reporters full details on environmental matters and offered to be news sources (on the record) at any time. They left behind a package of company information, along with their work and home phone numbers.

Open dialogue is also achieved by giving the community a menu of options for solving environmental problems. For example, the company wishing to locate a waste facility or to enlarge a plant would be foolish, in a potentially contentious community situation, to wait to unveil or to routinely announce its well-considered and essentially completed plans.

Instead, if you understand the dynamics of doing business in an environmentally sensitive community, you'll present the community leaders with a range of alternatives—location possibilities, building design options, provisions for monitoring environmental change, financial factors—that can be openly discussed.

While this "a la carte" approach may lack the efficiency or control that experienced business planners or industrial decision makers prefer, it is a rational response to a citizen climate that questions and rejects decisions that are presented in finished form.

The *presentation* becomes as important as the *intention*. The community must perceive that it has some control over, or useful input regarding, its own destiny.

In the sustainable-development era, where the equities are shared, you will do well to take charge of the envirocomm process in a way that empowers others in the community.

I am certainly not suggesting that any company give up responsibility for its destiny. No business will, or should, placidly follow community decisions that are poorly formed or totally inimical to its operations.

I am underscoring two facts of life in the new Green World of sustainable development:

1. Logic alone, presented to a community as an accomplished fact, is unlikely to persuade in our skeptical citizen climate.

2. If communication is open and objective, and partnership decisions are made involving community leaders, the business and engineering logic employed by the company may prevail.

Community health and safety—not just the safety in your plant—is the goal that will pull your business onto the green. This public-interest goal will harmonize your interests with those of community leaders and can lead to a partnership that is winning for all concerned.

MODELS OF SUCCESS

Chapter Twenty-Two

Policy Statements: Put It in Writing

A recent study by the Conference Board showed that the number of corporate codes of ethics doubled from 1987 to 1991. The study also showed increasing sophistication, distribution to lower levels of management involved in decision making, and institutionalization of such codes. The codes were taking shape in three distinct categories: (1) compliance, (2) accountability, and (3) philosophy.[1]

A good corporate environmental policy statement should cover all of the above, and the leading ones do.

What can a green policy statement do for you? Let's look at the plusses:

- It can add up your good works and make them understandable.
- It can give you an answer to the question, "Have you signed (whatever the green pledge happens to be)?"
- It can be part of the agenda-setting process.
- It can put your organizational mission in harmony with the green goals of activists, regulators, and other challenging publics.
- It can energize workers, impress neighbors, needle suppliers, reassure customers, neutralize critics, and give the media something good to say about you.
- It can put you and your employees on the green with your publics.

A good policy statement can go a long way to achieve these goals, persuading suppliers of the competitive edge in environmental responsibility and winning new business.

FIGURE 22–1
Policy Statement: Objectives

---

1. Top management commitment; a pledge consistent with a mission
2. Goals that operating units, divisions can use as guide
3. Document for external publics
4. Alternative to "theirs"

Those are the positives. On the downside:

It can be an empty gesture. Another framed certificate. Or worse: a bomb created by you that can explode in your face.

What makes the difference? Three factors: why you're doing it, what you say in it, and how you make it come alive.

Intent, content, and how you implement.

INTENT: STATEMENT WITH AN ATTITUDE

By your published statement, you display your green *attitude* and commitment.

Arrogance and isolation are losing attitudes in the sustainable-development era. Cooperation, willingness to listen and learn, and a solid pledge to do your part are the winning attitudes.

An environmental policy statement, published for anyone to see, posts your availability to participate in greening. You say to customer-publics, inside and outside, "We're committed. Here it is in writing. Read it and judge us by it."

Ciba-Geigy's green credo is a good example. Entitled "Science Serving Mankind," it expresses four intentions:

1. To take environment protection measures as a positive challenge, not a hindrance to operations.
2. To stress solving environmental problems at the source, through application of innovative production processes.
3. To promote a fully informed public on matters concerning the environment.
4. To seek a cooperative relationship with public regulatory agencies.

FIGURE 22-2
Policy Statement: Caveats

---

1. Don't copy; create
2. Involve all levels in process
3. Leave latitude for implementation
4. Make public interest #1
5. Communicate; inspect

Ciba-Geigy brings its policy statement alive. One of the things it has done is to invite residents around its Toms River (New Jersey) plant to monitor its treated wastewater. Neighbors know firsthand if the company is meeting the "positive challenge" of complying with regulations.

The principles drive the reorientation for the entire organization, signaling your pursuit of environmental quality as a competitive priority and incorporating attention to environmental factors at all levels of the organization. It asks the questions:
—Is this realistic to achieve?
—Does it fit into our mission?
—How does it compare with our past?
—Does this imply arrogance ("we know it all")?
—Do we acknowledge shortcomings?

CONTENT

You may be proud that your organization's environmental policy statement reads: "Our company will comply with all environmental laws and regulations relevant to our operations." But people outside your company—or, in fact, employees inside your company—may shake their heads and read this as saying: "Our company will operate legally." You will get no green points simply for not breaking the law. You need to go beyond compliance in Green World. And don't *always* expect to get points even when you do!

The policy statement is part of a process. It should flow logically from what has gone before. But it should build on the past and

FIGURE 22–3
"Compliance Plus" Goals

AT&T:	"Eliminate CFC emissions by '94"
Monsanto:	"Cut toxic air emissions 90% by '92" (achieved)
	"Reduce *all* chemical releases 70% by '95"
Textile Industry:	"Zero Waste"
3M:	"90% reduction in manufacturing emissions by the year 2000"

present a new commitment. I've provided a few good examples at the end of this chapter.

IMPLEMENT: TAKE IT TO YOUR CUSTOMER-PUBLICS

The goal of the policy statement should be to raise the odds on your ability to reach the public-interest green and to stay there with respect from others.

Just as it has a role in validating your past performance (compliance, as well as beyond-compliance green moves) and tying this to your future expectations, the publicly stated policy has a critical role in the continuous process of building relationships.

By your policy, you state the terms on which you are willing to make friends or allies for environmental protection.

A good policy statement gets rid of blockage in the communication channel. If you say it, if you show it and live it, you can break down bias against you.

Polls show that people think business is the problem. Your customer-publics may be skeptical. But when they read your policy, they may lower their suspicions just enough for a productive relationship.

If you go on record with a goal of zero pollution (or more likely, a goal of moving in that direction), you will get the attention of some skeptics. They may say, "Wait a minute. That's my goal, too. Maybe I should take a closer look at this outfit."

FIGURE 22–4
Whom They Blame

Q.   Whom do you think is most to blame for endangering the
         nation's environment: political leaders who do little to
         protect the environment, companies that pollute, or
         citizens who don't seem to care?

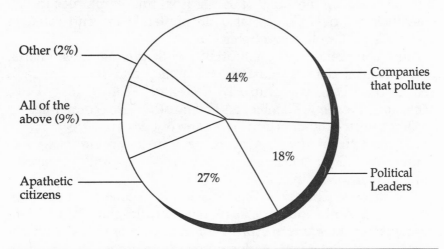

If this occurs, it will be your chance to invite them to learn
more, through inspection and dialogue, while you listen to their
concerns and questions and learn. Rather than a document written under duress and filed for emergency use, the policy statement becomes a tactical tool.

It is easy to see that if you think of the statement in this way—as
a sort of enabling certificate for new friendships among your
customer-publics—you will benefit from wide distribution of it.

The managers and employees of the organization, whom I hope
will have been co-authors with you of the document, will need to
receive it and fully understand what it means. In addition to
publication in magazines and newsletters distributed within the
organization, and posting on walls and bulletin boards, you will
need to try fresh ways of delivering the policy and its supporting
evidence.

Robert Daniell, the chief executive of United Technologies, held an interactive TV session with the company's various facilities. He and his vice president for environmental affairs Frank McAbee, answered questions about the new green policy, after it had been well distributed through the usual employee information channels.

A number of companies, including Colgate-Palmolive, have held small-group meetings of supervisors and employees to discuss their policies. Colgate also distributed flyers and cafeteria tent-cards with policy highlights.

More comprehensive publications, with photographs, charts, and statistical data to illustrate the policy and the company's record, have been useful to AT&T, General Motors, IBM, Dow, Monsanto, Procter & Gamble, and many other large companies, in mailings to stockholders and other key publics.

Prepared kits of materials for the news media would, of course, feature the policy statement, as well as stories and fact sheets supporting it.

The Business Charter on Sustainable Development, launched at the Second World Industry Conference on Environmental Management in Rotterdam in April 1991, is a kind of global environmental policy statement, endorsed by the International Chamber of Commerce. At the time of publication, more than 1,000 businesses worldwide had signed on to these 16 principles of environmental management, which address such issues as education, technology transfer, and auditing.

Your written policy statement is a practical tactical move. If you do it right, and if you use it right, it can improve your odds for making friends on the green.

HIGHLIGHTS OF ENVIRONMENTAL POLICY STATEMENTS BY LEADING CORPORATIONS

AT&T

AT&T is pursuing "continuous improvement" in environmental excellence, using three fundamental approaches: (1) applying quality principles to all operations; (2) applying technology to environmental problems; and (3) accelerating existing programs, such as recycling and innovative packaging. The company has set a number of specific environmental and safety goals:

- Phase out CFC emissions from manufacturing operations 50 percent by year end 1991 and 100 percent by year end 1994.
- Eliminate total toxic air emissions 50 percent by year end 1991 and 95 percent by year end 1995; strive for 100 percent elimination by year end 2000.
- Decrease total manufacturing process waste disposal 25 percent by year end 1994.
- Recycle 35 percent of paper by year end 1994.
- Reduce paper use 15 percent by year end 1994.
- Improve safety by ensuring that 100 percent of eligible facilities gain acceptance into the OSHA Voluntary Protection Program or an AT&T Equivalent Program by year end 1995, and ensure that 50 percent gain "Star" status (the highest category of achievement in OSHA's program).

Colgate-Palmolive Company

Colgate-Palmolive Company has made it a worldwide policy to "manufacture our products and operate our facilities so that we comply with or exceed applicable environmental rules and regulations." This concern has been translated into specific programs:

- **Products**
  —apply high standards to formulation, manufacture, labeling, and marketing of products
  —continuously evaluate impacts of products and residues on the environment
  —minimize environmental risks
  —communicate with consumers concerning product environmental impact
  —reduce product volume through the use of concentrated formulas

- **Packaging**
  —examine and quantify environmental impact of packaging
  —eliminate those heavy metals in inks and colorants that may leave hazardous residues
  —reduce the volume and weight of packaging
  —use recycled and recyclable materials whenever practicable

—code plastic packaging with appropriate recycling symbols
—support efforts to educate consumers to become part of
the recycling solution
—contribute to solid waste research

- **Facilities**
    —conduct periodic reviews of operations' environmental
    impact
    —continuously evaluate potential environmental impacts
    of operations in the design, construction, and improve-
    ment of facilities and processes
    —seek to minimize environmental health and safety risks
    to employees and the communities in which we operate
    —maintain open communication with local communities
    —dispose of all hazardous wastes through safe and so-
    cially responsible methods
    —strive to use environmentally safe and sustainable en-
    ergy sources
    —strive to improve our processes to use fewer raw materi-
    als and produce less waste
    —encourage employees to identify potentially hazardous
    environmental, health, or safety conditions

- **Business decisions**
    —review potential environmental issues and liabilities
    prior to any acquisition, divestiture, discontinuance of
    operations, leasing, or entry into joint venture
    —evaluate owned and operated property to identify sig-
    nificant environmental issues
    —participate in the voluntary identification and cleanup of
    environmentally contaminated locations as appropriate
    —where past C-P practices may have resulted in significant
    risks to public health or the environment, act responsibly
    to address those risks and cooperate with regulatory agen-
    cies and other interested groups in achieving acceptable
    solutions

DowBrands

This subsidiary of the Dow Chemical Company has reaffirmed its
commitment to environmental protection to its external audiences
through its "Green Goals," a company-wide program promoting environmental responsibility and excellence in all aspects of its business.

The Green Goals represent the formal consolidation of more than 25 specific environmental initiatives that have been in use at DowBrands for a number of years. They provide guidance on environmental improvements in six categories:
—Product formulations
—Innovations in packaging
—Source reduction and recycling
—Recycled content in packaging
—Overall manufacturing waste reduction
—Marketing and education efforts
The Green Goals are managed by an internal environmental steering team chaired by DowBrand's vice president of corporate affairs.

Duke Power Company

Duke Power established an environmental oversight committee in 1989, which then drew up a series of Environmental Principles, summarized in the following pledges:

- To maintain a corporate environment that is open and sensitive to environmental matters and to cooperate and comply with all regulations according to the letter and spirit of the law.
- To use fuels and other energy sources that increase energy efficiency with minimal impact to the environment and to dispose of wastes and other emissions responsibly and safely.
- To provide products and services that are safe to human beings and to support research and development aimed at improving the environment.
- To assign environmental activity oversight responsibility to a senior company executive and perform periodic reviews and audits to ensure that company programs and practices are consistent with these principles.

Du Pont

Shortly after assuming the chairmanship of Du Pont in 1989, Ed Woolard recognized the need, in his role as chief environmental officer, for a series of goals that addressed the corporation's environmental concerns, to be achieved by the end of the 1990s. They include:

- reducing hazardous wastes by 35 percent compared with 1990 levels;
- reducing toxic air emissions by 60 percent (by 1993, over 1987 levels);
- reducing carcinogenic air emissions by 90 percent;
- eliminating or rendering nonhazardous all toxic discharges to the ground or surface waters;
- eliminating the use of heavy metal pigments in polymers;
- taking greater responsibility for plastic wastes disposal;
- including local communities in safety and environmental planning at all sites;
- providing for the management of 2,590 square kilometers of wildlife habitat, with a special emphasis on wetlands;
- phasing out the manufacture of chlorofluorocarbons by 2000 at the latest, and replacing them with safe alternatives; and
- procuring double-hulled tankers and double-walled storage tanks at all gasoline stations.

General Motors

GM's dedication to "protecting human health, natural resources, and the global environment" includes integrating sound environmental practices into business decisions. GM personnel are guided by the following six principles:

- "We are committed to actions to restore and preserve the environment.
- We are committed to reducing waste and pollutants, conserving resources, and recycling materials at every stage of the product life cycle.
- We will continue to participate actively in educating the public regarding environmental conservation.
- We will continue to pursue vigorously the development and implementation of technologies for minimizing pollutant emissions.

- We will continue to work with all governmental entities for the development of technically sound and financially responsible environmental laws and regulations.
- We will continually assess the impact of our plants and products on the environment and the communities in which we live and operate with a goal of continuous improvement."

IBM

IBM formulated a set of principles for environmental protection in 1971. They state that "IBM will:

- meet or exceed governmental regulations and, where they do not exist, establish its own stringent standards;
- use nonpolluting technologies wherever possible and minimize energy and materials consumption;
- minimize our dependence on waste treatment through recycling; and
- help government and other industries develop solutions to environmental problems."

The company has also pledged to discontinue the use of chlorofluorocarbons in products and processes by the end of 1993, four years ahead of the internationally accepted timetable to reduce their use by one-half.

Monsanto

Monsanto has pledged to:

- "reduce all toxic and hazardous releases and emissions, working toward an ultimate goal of zero effect;
- ensure no Monsanto operation poses any undue risk to our employees and our communities;
- work to achieve sustainable agriculture through new technology and practices;
- ensure groundwater safety;
- keep our plants open to our communities and involve the community in plant operations;

- manage all corporate real estate, including plant sites, to benefit nature; and
- search worldwide for technology to reduce and eliminate waste from our operations, with the top priority being not making it in the first place."

Procter & Gamble

To fulfill its commitment to "improve the environmental quality of its products, packaging, and operations around the world," P&G has established policies to do the following:

- "Ensure our products, packaging, and operations are safe for our employees, consumers, and the environment.
- Reduce or prevent the environmental impact of our products and packaging in their design, manufacture, distribution, use, and disposal whenever possible.
- Meet or exceed the requirements of all environmental laws and regulations.
- Continually assess our environmental technology and programs and monitor progress toward environmental goals.
- Provide our consumers, customers, employees, communities, public interest groups, and others with relevant and appropriate factual information about the environmental quality of P&G products, packaging, and operations.
- Ensure every employee understands and is responsible and accountable for incorporating environmental quality considerations in daily business activities.
- Have operating policies, programs, and resources in place to implement our environmental quality policy."

Union Carbide Chemicals and Plastics

For Union Carbide Chemicals and Plastics (C&P), its commitment to the protection of the environment and to the health and safety of employees and the community is manifested by:

- "Worldwide compliance with all applicable governmental and internal health, safety, and environmental requirements.

- Air emissions of potentially harmful chemicals are controlled so that potential exposure levels in the community are at least 1,000 times lower than workplace standards.
- Discharges of potentially harmful chemicals to surface water are controlled so that concentrations in the receiving stream are substantially lower than any level known to cause adverse health or environmental effects.
- Technology and operating practices are continuously upgraded with the ultimate goal of eliminating process emissions to the environment of known and suspect carcinogenic chemicals.
- Minimization of process emissions and wastes is a high priority in the design and operation of facilities.
- C&P incineration capacity exists to manage burnable chemical process waste internally.
- The use of land disposal for process waste is eliminated to the maximum degree practicable.
- The C&P mindset and way of life, for research, development, design, and operation of all facilities, is that all episodic incidents and spills must be eliminated.
- Precautions are taken so that even major accidents will not result in serious adverse effects on our employees, neighbors, or the environment.
- All C&P employees understand their roles in achieving C&P's environmental vision and are committed to its success.
- All C&P businesses and functions have programs in place that result in continuing reductions in process emissions and episodic incidents and spills.
- Measurement systems are in place to track progress.
- Results are communicated so that the community, customers, employees, governmental agencies, and the media recognize C&P's environmental accomplishments and leadership."

Chapter Twenty-Three

Best Practices of Partnering

Now that we've discussed the importance and benefits of partnering, let's examine some examples that are good candidates for green-progress benchmarking.

We'll start with perhaps the most widely publicized case of environmental partnering, the waste reduction program created jointly by McDonald's and the Environmental Defense Fund; we'll follow with First Brands Corporation's Glad Bag-Based System, which tapped market needs; the hazardous-waste cleanup partnership known as Clean Sites, Inc.; and the "bio-reserve" concept put forward by The Nature Conservancy.

McDONALD'S AND EDF

It's a strange marriage when the partners are a hamburger institution epitomizing fast-food convenience and a liberal green activist group whose motto used to be "Sue the bastards."[1] But that's what makes this such an unusual story, of such far-reaching impact.

It starts in 1989, when the Environmental Defense Fund targeted McDonald's as a high-profile place to advance the war for environmental reform.

Not that McDonald's was a particularly bad actor. In fact, McDonald's had pursued a relatively aggressive environmental policy. Long before it became trendy, McDonald's voluntarily committed to spend $100 million a year on recycled products and to encourage polystyrene recycling.

But because of its popularity and many great locations, and because it generated lots of waste—including the famous clamshell package for Big Macs and other food, earlier regarded as a miracle innovation because of its ability to keep food hot—McDonald's was an attractive target for pro-green reform.

EDF and local action groups they stirred up began to organize protests. Schoolchildren—McDonald's primary customer-public—were led to see clamshells as undesirable. Letters from kids, posters, and protests staged for the news cameras proliferated. The company's popular mascot became known as "Ronald Mc-Toxic," and consumers began mailing sandwich packaging back to the company.

In the late 1980s, the company slipped into its worst sales slump ever—and the anti-McDonald's drive of the green activists was at least partly blamed.

Shelby Yastrow, the company's general counsel, began to take up the theme that McDonald's had to change its packaging, that it couldn't afford the perception of being anti-green.

When Yastrow found himself on the same TV show with EDFs Executive Director Fred Krupp, he took the initiative and invited Krupp to come to Oak Brook, Illinois (McDonald's headquarters) for a talk. Krupp said yes.

The Situation at EDF

Krupp was ready for a link-up with business, if the terms were right. He had become convinced that the business-bashing of the 1960s and 1970s was not right for his group in the 80s and 90s. The way for EDF to distinguish itself now was to ease attacks and to spur business greening by transforming markets through economic incentives.

Krupp saw the golden arches of McDonald's, the nation's fast-food marketing king, as a sign of opportunity. After all, was it not McDonald's who, by insisting on rectangular containers to save space, had forced the entire dairy industry to convert from packaging its product in bottles and cans to plastic and paper containers?

Other green groups had been after McDonald's and at least one of them had met with the company, but antipathies got in the way of discussion and there was no possibility of partnering.

Krupp was ready to deal, and so was McDonald's.

The Marriage

The meeting between Krupp and Yastrow was the start of a new green partnership. EDF and McDonald's, their goals having converged, entered into union on August 1, 1990.

A joint Waste Reduction Task Force, including packaging and solid-waste specialists from the two groups, put together a cautious prenuptial agreement.

McDonald's would not be allowed to publicize the task force. EDF could (and would). The company was not bound to adopt any of the task force recommendations and required that EDF's members work in one of its restaurants. Either side could terminate the agreement at any time.

The Results

First task was to deal with the clamshell. The highly publicized decision to stop using it met boos and applause.

Competing environmental groups, such as Audubon, said the decision was not based on total-life-cycle analysis of the package. Plastics makers said the impact of clamshells on the solid-waste stream was tiny, and that great strides were being made in polystyrene recycling.

Even EDF admitted that the plastic-coated paper burger wrappers used instead of the clamshell were not recyclable.

But the death of the clamshell was final, a move that met EDF's need to show progress and McDonald's need to show response to concerned customers, especially kids who had been motivated by the green activists to boycott.

Behind this high-visibility move were less-noted initiatives, 42 in all.

They covered source reduction, reuse, recycling, and composting, with the potential to reduce the company's total waste stream by 75 percent.

McDonald's moved quietly into the use of unbleached paper bags, smaller napkins (folded to look the same size as before), and larger ketchup packages to reduce the number of discarded containers. It pledged to recycle all corrugated cardboard and to experiment with the composting of organic wastes such as eggshells and coffee grounds.

And all initiatives were implemented with no inconvenience to the consumer—a key aspect for the company.

The Detractors

I hold this account up as a historic example of green-growth partnering and not as an absolutely ideal move. The partnership definitely has had its share of critics.

Besides the environmentalists and industrialists who felt the agreement was not based on sound scientific evidence, there were others. McDonald's peers said the company had caved in before it found out the real environmental benefits, and would set precedents that would create pressure on industry. More extreme environmental groups felt that EDF was consorting with the enemy. As writer Bill Gifford put it, "Many environmentalists seem to have difficulty condoning the *existence* of McDonald's." And then there was the competition factor—the drive to compete for customer-publics. Citizen's Clearinghouse for Hazardous Wastes claimed that EDF had seized ownership of years of grassroots work on the clamshell. But CCHW had already tried to meet with McD's and the result was total disaster.

Important Milestones of the Agreement

Nevertheless, the agreement set important precedents. The Task Force:

- brought together two seemingly opposing interests that overcame traditional biases and demonstrated real achievements, while maintaining the independence of both parties;
- demonstrated the forces that environmental groups could marshall for change; and
- established a landmark precedent that may alter the way environmental protection is achieved, moving away from regulation and command-and-control toward partnering (even with environmental activists).

In the current climate of knee-jerk reactions to environmental issues, the Task Force proved that there are creative ways to achieve environmental improvement and increase your customer-public base that can keep both industry and activists happy.

Instead of just throwing money at an environmental problem to demonstrate care, the Task Force developed a real change in operations and in attitudes.

McDonald's went even further and required its suppliers to use materials with 35 percent recycled content. And because McDonald's large customer base is also the customer base for other businesses that have begun to feel pressure from green consumers, McDonald's has become a mentor to other businesses. Thus, the company is encouraging environmental protection by taking care of its own.

And though no money changed hands between EDF and McD's, new members and customers abound. The satisfaction of economic and environmental needs for the business, the environmentalist, and the consumer exemplifies sustainable development and was the keystone of this successful case. It was a win-win-win situation.

EDF's Krupp says, "We're not ideologues on environmental issues. The myth blocking progress is the notion that all environmentalists should be trapped in one narrow set of tactics." Krupp says enviros need to maximize the "tools in our tool kit . . . and should be able to problem-solve with corporations."

As Gifford put it, "Krupp loves to talk about harnessing market forces, but . . . Krupp and his movement *have become a market force*. McDonald's already was one . . . and is still the American consumer's 'kind of place.'"

FIRST BRANDS CORPORATION'S GLAD BAG-BASED SYSTEM

Troubled by research that revealed mounting local and municipal solid waste problems, and wondering how its Glad brand trash bags might provide a solution instead of contributing to the problem, First Brands Corporation began research on its "Bag-Based System" for recycling.[2] The system is now working in more than 30 cities in the United States and Canada.

Let's take a look at how First Brands developed a creative approach to better handling solid waste—and turned it into a market advantage.

Data collected from the Environmental Protection Agency and First Brands' research department revealed dramatic trends toward federal and state officials handing off responsibility and funding for environmental protection to struggling municipalities. Statistics predicted an increase in this buck-passing as federal budget woes continued amid heightened demand for environmental protection.

First Brands was convinced that it could build on its record of environmental health and safety by working with municipalities toward a workable solution. Since 1969, plastic bag trash pickup had provided a cleaner, safer, and quieter collection method than the old metal trash can system.

Despite the notorious publicity about the "degradability" of plastic trash bags in landfills, First Brands was adamant, based on its historical success in environmental protection, that it could use its product to advantage. The company's determination resulted in development of the Glad "Blue Bag" system for recycling. Here's its success story:

First Brands started out with some bottom-up marketing. It went to the source to find out how it might best get consumers to actually participate in a recycling scheme of municipal solid waste.

With some help from survey research by the U.S. Testing Company, the company was able to determine that many consumers did not participate in their local recycling plan because the process was inconvenient. Most plans depended on the consumer to go out and buy recycling bins and keep the recyclables sorted by material. Surveyors discovered that storage space, carry out, and retrieval were problems for the consumers. They also learned that collectors found the retrieval and return of bins to the curbside time-consuming and cumbersome. Therefore, the system—the process—just wasn't working.

First Brands now believes it has developed the ideal bag for recycling: a blue recycling bag that is available alongside its regular trash bags in grocery, hardware, and mass merchandising stores in participating regions.

Because separation of recyclables from regular trash is done in the kitchen, the company started with the traditional 13-gallon bag. Consumers can simply place all recyclables they dispose of in the blue bag, instead of their standard trash bag.

Through extensive product development and consumer research, the company was able to confirm that its resulting blue bag product was identified by customers as the most distinctive of colors tested (there was a strong preference for a colored vs. clear bag due to privacy issues).

This critical piece of research gave rise to a product that is transparent enough so that a hauler can determine it contains recyclables from four feet away and ensure they have been correctly disposed of, but its contents cannot be identified by neighbors from 40 feet away. This is the First Brands "4/40 rule."

The bag-based system works whether a community has a collection system for commingled recyclables (collected separately from regular refuse, for instance, on different trash pickup days) or not, so it is flexible enough to fit within the existing trash collection infrastructure.

Once the refuse is picked up by the collector, it is taken to the existing materials recovery facility where it may be sorted by traditional manual debagging and sorting methods or by specially designed debagging equipment provided by First Brands to participating municipalities. This equipment uses a weighing and magnetizing process to automatically separate aluminum, paper, and plastic, which cuts down on time and manpower. (The company is now developing a system to recycle the blue bags themselves and for including recycled materials in the new bag.)

But perhaps the biggest selling point for municiple managers is that there is a built-in distribution network for the recycling bags already established, i.e., through retail outlets. The Blue Bag complements residents' normal shopping and purchasing habits, causing little perception of burden, and the municipality is not required to enter into the "bin business," diverting its attention from greater concerns to ordering, distributing, and replacing the bins.

The three big plusses:

• The municipality can make use of readily available private sector resources and existing infrastructure with great cost and time efficiency, in a day when this is vital due to budget constraints.

• The consumer can participate in the recycling and environmental protection process with little or no extra effort.

- First Brands increases market share of its trash bags, simultaneously assisting municipalities in resolving pressing waste problems and becoming an environmental protector.

This is what it's all about—what they mean when they say, "Protecting the environment is not only good business, *it is business.*"

CLEAN SITES, INC.

Another excellent example of teaming up is Clean Sites, Inc. Unlike McDonald's and First Brands, however, Clean Sites didn't exist as a business; *it became a business* through the process of partnering. The nonprofit corporation has helped communities solve hazardous waste site problems for more than seven years, through technical cleanup, management analysis, and public policy formation—with the greatest emphasis on speeding up the process and weighing benefits together with costs.[3]

It allies industries with the Environmental Protection Agency and the communities affected by hazardous waste contamination in a kind of triumvirate where it serves as court diplomat.

The Plan

CSI is the brainchild of William Reilly and the Chemical Manufacturers Association. (The innovative spirit of compromise embodied in CSI's founding was a source of great distinction and credibility for Reilly—with industry, government, and environmentalists—when he was later nominated by President Bush as head of EPA.)

Back when Reilly was an environmentalist attorney and president of the World Wildlife Fund and Conservation Foundation, he became increasingly frustrated with the pace of toxic waste site cleanup, which was bogged down in excessive litigation. As *The New York Times* put it, the "crusade against polluters [had] turned into a diversion which siphons off money and technical expertise from more pressing environmental concerns."

What Reilly had in mind was an organization that would foster cooperation among the parties with the goal of effecting settlements that avoided costly court actions—costly for industries *and* EPA.

In May 1984, a coalition of current and former industrialists, environmentalists, and government officials officially founded Clean Sites. The founders were depending on an "ironclad promise from EPA" that it would use its settlement and enforcement powers to provide incentives for companies to come forward.

CMA agreed to fund the organization to get it off the ground, a three-year commitment that initially accounted for 95 percent of the funding.

The Results

It's important to note here what we discussed in the previous chapter: that partnering is not always easy. CSI was slow to start and concedes some failures.

Basically, it was a great idea that took a little while to heat up. Reilly and others were depending on EPA to force incentives. They set out to specialize in hazardous waste cleanup based on the mammoth Superfund program. And they set an ambitious goal for cleaning up 60 non-National Priority Sites (where the federal government was not already heavily involved) in a year.

But it took longer for EPA to come around at that time. As current CSI President Thomas Grumbly says, "While I don't want to cast blame . . . when you're in a situation where the government seems to shoot the people who raise their hands to cooperate, an incentive is created for the private sector to say, 'Hey, let's not do anything.' And when you have as bad a record of cost recovery as the agency did for a while, all these things taken together create an environment in which it wasn't possible to do as much as was promised."

CSI has since downsized its goal to a more reasonable, but still ambitious, 25 to 40 sites. Still ambitious, says Grumbly, when you consider that EPA hasn't delisted anywhere near 60 sites since Superfund began. And even Bill Reilly now is painfully aware of the time, energy, and money it takes to deal with Superfund.

Another disappointment in CSI's early history was when it was about 25 days old. The group had been called in to mediate a cleanup at a well-known site in Colorado. Midway through the project, the regional EPA administrator called in CSI and lambasted their handling of the project. The community was not responding. They feared an outside party coming in and giving all the orders. CSI concedes it spent a lot of time, money, and effort on the project only to find that it should have begun with their now-traditional "bottom-up" approach to community relations.

Christopher Daggett, former head of the New Jersey Department of Environmental Protection, says "nothing focuses convictions like a nearby waste site. Try telling people that the leaking drums across the street aren't a hazard." So perception became reality in myriad Clean Sites cases, just like the McDonald's clamshell issue. Which is why the openness and dialogue we've mentioned throughout this book are now cornerstones of the Clean Sites strategy.

Says Daggett, "The public often blames the 'greedy and thoughtless' corporations for the waste peril and is thus little inclined to weigh the benefits of cleanups against the costs."

And both corporations and governments "take their cues from angry publics" often beyond unreasonable means which leads to goals of returning sites to their preindustrial condition, even when all health and environmental risks have been eliminated.

Now, a much-used tactic, pioneered by CSI, is the Community-Industry Forum, developed because of the gap between citizen and company needs and wants at cleanup sites. CSI drafts a forum agenda and distributes it to all participants, who can review and modify the agenda in advance of their meeting. The regional forums aim to open discussion, not reach agreement. Forum results are then used on a national level to build consensus and develop communication guidelines for a particular project.

Another early, and sometimes current, criticism of CSI is its source of funding. When asked about chemical industry funding, Grumbly says, "I think it's totally predictable when you start a new organization and it doesn't look like any others, people will be suspect about your motives." In fact, he says CSI intentionally picked some people to serve on the governing board and balance the industrialists. Though funded 95 percent by the chemical industry in its first year, at last accounting the industry share was down to 33 percent. Now CSI bills the companies they work for.

But after all, the mistakes have been worth it. "My view," says Grumbly, "is that if you're not having some failures, you're not trying enough."

All the trials and errors have paid off in many achievements, perhaps the proudest of which is the former site of Rose Chemicals in Holden, Missouri. The 11-acre site of Rose Chemicals Company was used to store and process PCBs, the toxic liquid chemical essential to makers of electrical transmission equipment because of its great insulating properties and stability at high temperatures. Though the materials had been labeled hazardous and removed long before, residues remained in the structures, soil, and streambed.

In the late 80s, CSI was called in to tackle the site, considered one of the largest deserted PCB sites in the country. The site was a particular embarrassment because it was created *after* the Super-fund law was passed.

Clean Sites discovered community citizens skeptical and afraid. Finding 750 parties involved, CSI went in and helped PRPs (potentially responsible parties) handle technical, managerial, and community aspects of solving the problem in cooperation with a steering com-mittee consisting of Fortune 500 companies *and* the municipalities.

All health risks could have been eliminated for $71,000. But federal and state laws mandated a cleanup costing up to $41.5 million to return the site to a pristine, pre-industrial condition. Said Grumbly, "The last couple turns of the screw [could] not be justified on economic criteria."

So CSI helped fashion a compromise costing $13.6 million to remove all suspect soil and materials and incinerate the debris of greatest risk for burial in a specially designed landfill.

CSI asked the community their fears, wants, and needs and the cleanup was accomplished with great success. As a *Holden Review* editorial expressed, "most important was the open-door policy" established by CSI.

This is important for government involvement as well. Grumbly says that the "credibility of government runs on the transparency of its decision-making. One key to a rational public debate is to let the public in on the game."

Clean Sites is achieving its dual goals to speed the cleanup of hazardous waste and weigh cleanup benefits against costs, through technical and public policy assistance.

It pioneered the allocation of responsibility: taking a tally of total waste costs at a site and divvying up the "numbers" among parties to reach agreement on particular responsibilities and enter into a consent decree with the government.

Says Grumbly, "Now there are other people doing it and they do it just as well as we do. So it's not something we do exclusively anymore. We have more competitors, more people trying to imitate us than when we began in 1984, but I consider that success, not failure."

What of the future? "We're not in it for the business." As current chairman and former EPA Administrator Russell Train put it, "If we're not making a contribution, we should go out of business cause we're sure not making money." But at its current rate of success, it doesn't look as if Clean Sites will be going out of business anytime soon.

THE NATURE CONSERVANCY'S "LAST GREAT PLACES"

Along with the McDonald's and EDF Waste Reduction Task Force, The Nature Conservancy's Virginia Coast Reserve (one in the series of its "Last Great Places" program) was also a winner of the first President's Environmental and Conservation Challenge Awards in 1991 for outstanding environmental partnership projects.[4]

The Situation

While we've discussed the fact that the local community is a strong customer-public and can be an effective motivator toward increased environmental protection, it can also weigh just as heavily on the other side of the argument—especially when economics (jobs) are at stake.

As in the case of the celebrated spotted owl controversy in the Pacific Northwest, we've seen that environmental protection initiatives, while well-meaning, can be at odds with local communities by disrupting small industries and jeopardizing jobs.

Loggers have marched on the nation's capital to protest environmental initiatives that have halted the felling of trees with little or no regard for the economic implications for the industry, its workers, and their families.

In response, to further environmental protection in light of this kind of opposition, conservation groups (those with large memberships and lots of funds) have resorted to what has been dubbed the "museum/fortress" approach: buying up and hoarding as much environmentally sensitive land as possible.

Thus, environmental land management has proceeded on a tactical, not strategic, basis. Managers participate in fire drills to save particular species but fail to see that the overall ecosystem of an area is falling apart—not seeing the forest for the trees, so to speak.

I agree with *Washington Post* environmental reporter John Lancaster, who says that unfortunately the "spate of high-profile endangered-species cases, such as the spotted owl fight in the Pacific Northwest," has led to more of precisely that kind of shortsighted fight.

But the museum/fortress tactic won't work without the cooperation of *people*. Says Conservancy President John C. Sawhill, "*People* are already in the last of our great remaining ecosystems. They've burst through the 'museum' door into the main galleries of the natural world."

The Concept

Thus was born "ecosystem management"—what Dennis Glick, director of Greater Yellowstone Tomorrow Project calls, "after creation of the national park concept, . . . the second great leap of conservation in human history."

Many conservationists call it the "bioreserve" model—perpetuation of biodiversity that "seeks to integrate human activities with natural ecosystems in hopes of protecting all the fauna and flora within them." The model may include all of the following elements: a natural core, possibly an existing park or nature preserve, surrounded by ecologically sustainable development—everything from oil drilling to logging to carefully zoned housing subdivisions that coexist peacefully.

The idea is to manage public and private lands, not as isolated fragments but as integrated parts of a much larger whole, whether it is the California desert or the Florida Everglades. It depends on more networking, community and interagency relations, and law.

Although the bioreserve idea is gaining popularity in Latin America, Africa, and Asia, and among organizations like the

World Conservation Strategy, it is still not universally embraced. There is the expected opposition from some Florida sugar growers, miners, loggers, and cattlemen. There are also environmentalists who are skeptical of the idea that industries *can* conduct business in an environmentally sound way.

But these skeptics are the very target of the concept, and increasing good examples have served to make proponents out of these former opponents.

Along with biodiversity, says The *Christian Science Monitor*, the "concept embraces compromise with the economic, recreational, and residential needs of the creatures once kept mostly at length: humans."

The Best Example

The Virginia Coast Reserve may be the best example of the dozen fragile zones in the U.S. that are part of The Nature Conservancy's "Last Great Places" program. Others include California's Nipomo Dunes, Vandenburg Air Force Base, oil reserves, a sand mine, an off-road vehicle playground, Texas cattle ranches, Block Island (Rhode Island) housing developments, and broccoli farms (diversified, to say the least).

TNC has also identified international sites, including Darien National Park in Panama, a condor reserve in Ecuador, a forest in Paraguay, and a waterfowl reserve in Mexico.

But the best example, and the one that serves as its Last Great Places model, is the Virginia Coast Reserve.

The Conservancy recognized more than 20 years ago that the development of the Virginia shoreline for hotels, condominiums, resorts, and accompanying merchants threatened what was the last chain of pristine barrier islands on the Atlantic Coast. Development also threatened the farming and fishing industries in the area. So the Conservancy—the largest owner of environmental land sites in the world—began buying what has amounted to 40,000 acres of environmentally sensitive coastal property, now set aside as the Virginia Coast Reserve.

But the Conservancy knew that it could not effectively develop its project without the partnership and support of local community members, who might feel apprehensive about the new landowner and its effects on their jobs and industries, particularly the farmers and fishermen.

Consequently, the Conservancy has gathered a broad array of partners in the local communities where it has purchased sites: state and local government agencies, local citizens' groups, the University of Virginia, the U.S. Fish and Wildlife Service, a local chapter of the N.A.A.C.P., and a local housing trust.

The Conservancy starts with a bottom-up approach (as we've discussed elsewhere in this volume) to marketing its project. It works with its local partners to target opportunities for compatible economic development, address aspirations of the community's lower-income citizens, and increase their farming and fishing yields most effectively without environmental damage.

One experiment in the Virginia Coast Reserve is the establishment of buffer zones of trees and shrubs, which filter fertilizer runoff from croplands into estuaries. The Reserve managers are attempting to teach development to imitate nature.

While meeting local community needs, the Conservancy is able to meet its primary objectives of conserving rare and endangered animals, plants, and ecosystems. The project has succeeded in protecting 250 species of birds in the affected 70-mile stretch of land.

The Virginia Coast Reserve is an enviable example of local partnerships of diverse groups, each donating its individual talents in pursuit of environmental protection. It proves that what at the outset looked impossible is indeed doable.

The lesson is, once again, think globally, act locally. "Large-scale environmental protection can succeed only through active, mutually beneficial partnerships with local residents."

Chapter Twenty-Four

More Good News Stories

In journalism, no news is *not* good news. In fact, good news is no news, most of the time.

Following the lead of the more senior reporters, and responding to the obvious interest of editors, young reporters come to understand that the news they are supposed to sniff out is the *bad* news.

Sure, it's okay to file the routine stories of projects approved, council meetings held, contracts awarded. But the stories that get editors' attention, and move the placement in the paper from the second section to the front section—and sometimes onto that glory land for journalists, page one, above the fold!—are those about *conflict*.

Editors know that readers love to learn about disagreements between officials, charges of foul play, challenges to authority, and burdens about to be imposed on taxpayers. Conflicts, villains v. victims, worsening conditions—headline news.

There is certainly bad news on the environmental beat. Reporters go for it. Pick up a paper or turn on the six o'clock news and see their placements: charges of green crime, threats of pollution, food scares, fines, victims, villains. These are news—and people are interested.

In another chapter, we talk about ways to plug into the continuing, absolutely natural interest of reporters in "bad" news—news where there is the element of conflict. And I suggest ways you can help the reporter succeed with his editor—and you can win at the same time.

But I'm going to assume you've had enough bad news for the moment and you're interested in some good news.

After all, if you are going to feel like you're one of the good guys—part of the answer, not of the problem—you will need to have a minable lore of good-news examples.

That's what the rest of this chapter provides—news that didn't always make the headlines, but just might make your day*:[1]

For more than a decade, the **Anheuser-Busch Companies** made water conservation a priority at their many brewing facilities, employing more than a dozen technological innovations in these efforts. The technology resulted in reducing water consumption by 18 percent/barrel of beer. In both 1984 and 1986, the Los Angeles Department of Water and Power presented Anheuser-Busch with special awards for water conservation. The company continues to pursue better ways to conserve and preserve the water supply.

Ashland Chemical, Inc. established a companywide program for continuous improvement in environmental, health, and safety areas under the title The Responsible Care Management System. Ashland management provided the necessary training equipment and systems to ensure a safe operating environment, then employed Responsible Care committees at all levels, from frontline workers through senior management, to identify areas needing improvement and to recommend approaches. Each employee accepted responsibilities for the prevention of injuries, occupational illnesses, and protection of the environment, working in a true partnership with company management.

AT&T committed to eliminating the destruction of the ozone layer by CFCs within its own factories through support of similar efforts across the United States, and by fostering cooperation to help other businesses around the globe to follow suit. AT&T promised to halve its CFC emissions by 1991 and to eliminate them by 1994—and they are meeting those goals. The company was among the first to substitute water-based cleaning systems and, through its Bell Labs, developed environmentally sound

*I am grateful to Dick Siebert of the National Association of Manufacturers and George Eliades and Steve Hellem (formerly) of the National Environmental Development Association for providing many of these good-news examples from their extensive files.

manufacturing processes that eliminate the need for CFCs during some manufacturing applications. AT&T also founded and organized the tremendously effective Industry Cooperative for Ozone Layer Protection, which employs a database information sharing system on CFC substitutes with manufacturers worldwide, especially in Third World countries that lack R&D resources to develop their own alternatives.

Borden Inc. developed an alternative to landfill disposal of excess potato starch, which is a by-product of its potato chip manufacturing process. The process allowed the company to separate the starch from the waste stream and sell it for the manufacturing of other products, such as the binding in paper or for making glue.

Since developing an Environmental Compliance Program in 1980, **Chevron Corporation** has made significant contributions to many environmental efforts, including The Nature Conservancy. Chevron estimated it spent nearly $750 million since 1981 on environmental, safety, fire, and health related capital projects in the United States. The company's most recent effort was a $10,000 donation to the International Bird Rescue Research Center that made possible the development of an instructional videotape on how to properly treat birds contaminated in an oil spill.

In the fall of 1991, **The Clorox Company** introduced a new container for its liquid bleach that is made from 20 percent recycled plastic, the first in a series of Clorox products planned to be packaged in this manner. Although recycling was not new to Clorox products, the use of recycled material in the containers *was* new. The new bottle makes a significant contribution to reducing the number of plastic containers that contribute to landfill waste. Clorox estimated a reduction in waste on a nationwide basis of 50 million containers, or 8 million pounds of plastic.

Colgate-Palmolive has made numerous efforts to render its product packaging better for the environment. The company invested $10 million to convert its 22- and 32-ounce bottles from PVC to PET plastic. PET is both stronger and more easily recycled, with 16 percent less plastic, making it more desirable and more frequently used then PVC. Colgate-Palmolive also introduced bottles made from 20 percent recycled material. Bottles were redesigned so that inner paperboard case packaging was no longer necessary, and the number of bottles per case was increased so as to reduce the amount of packaging necessary. This is only a sampling of Colgate-Palmolive's extensive environmental programs, signifying them as one of the leaders in the corporate world's environmental efforts.

In response to the nation's shrinking wetlands, **Consolidation Coal** constructed five wetland wildlife habitat areas in Southern Illinois on more than 650 acres of surface-mined land. The surface-mine spoils and waste ponds were transformed into productive wetlands, designed and constructed to duplicate natural wetland conditions with significant water depths for thriving aquatic vegetation, as well as to prevent winter-kill of the fish population. Islands and ridges provide safe waterfowl nesting sites and sloping shorelines prevent erosion, enhancing plant life and providing greater utilization by ducks and geese, which tend to shy away from water with high, steep banks. Consol also worked with a local Boy Scout troop that constructed wood duck nesting boxes for the region as a fund-raising project.

Cosmair, Inc., the licensee for L'Oreal cosmetic products in the United States, implemented an environmentally conscious employee program called A.W.A.R.E. (Avoid Waste and Recycle Everything) that has been very successful. Through a number of steps, this large company managed to reduce the solid waste in its model plant facility by 50 percent in the first year of the program. Such steps included eliminating polystyrene or paper coffee cups, using silverware instead of plastic utensils in the cafeteria, and recycling office and computer paper as well as aluminum cans. In the factory, program steps included reusing corrugated cardboard and even old machinery. Wood pallets were taken home by employees and used as firewood. Steel drums were washed out and sold and plastic ones were recycled. Cosmair, Inc. managed to save $500,000 a year in costs for hauling paper and other general waste.

Through its WRAP program (Waste Reduction Always Pays), **Dow Chemical** developed a policy that consistently reduces waste through the education of its employees. With its top-level management team guiding the corporation through waste management decisions, Dow follows a policy that is consistent in its efforts to reduce waste and recycle. In the past two years the company has funded 42 waste reduction projects nationally.

Dow Corning's plant in Elizabethtown, Kentucky, reduced its monthly waste by 600,000 pounds, a 59 percent decrease since 1988. Through a series of steps that identified and corrected three problem areas in the plant, from simple leaks to reusing material that was previously disposed of, Dow Corning not only reduced waste but saved $350,000 annually. The plant received the 1989 Governor's Award for Wastewater Management for reducing emissions of silicone into the Elizabethtown sewer.

Florida Power Corporation found a marketable use for the fly ash that it had previously been unsuccessful in disposing of. The company established a long-term ash management plan that includes selling the ash to manufacturers of concrete building blocks, building an artificial reef made of fly ash in the Gulf of Mexico, and possible ventures constructing sea walls and oyster beds. The success of this plan eliminated the need for FPC to license additional permanent ash disposal sites.

General Motors has made educational programs and market-based pollution technologies the centerpieces of its environmental successes.

GM has introduced GREEN (Global Rivers Environmental Education Network) into schools, grades K–12, to benefit the environment and hometown rivers in its plant cities. This program was helpful in showing local students how their ideas and efforts can make a difference. In Saginaw, Michigan, for example, a local chemistry class discovered that the Saginaw River had unacceptable levels of fecal coliform. The student government petitioned the city government to remedy the situation, and they did. GM's goal is to eventually establish GREEN in all GM plant cities.

In 1992, GM began dialogue with the Environmental Defense Fund to consider market-based incentives for pollution control technologies. Citing common aims with EDF of wanting to protect the environment without harming the economy, GM is looking for ways to take the emissions trading credits system established in the Clean Air Act a step further to allow different industries to swap credits with one another so that the maximum amount of air pollution can be reduced at the minimum price.

Guest Services Inc. initiated a program with the National Park Service to collect separated plastic foam from special receptacles at three Washington, DC, area park sites as a separation-collection pilot program that could be expanded to the National Mall and the other national park sites throughout the country. As a symbol of this new national program, Guest Services developed a successful program to reduce the proliferation of disposable cups. A thermal mug emblazoned with the slogan "Have a Refill, Save a Landfill" was offered to participating government and corporate accounts, compliments of Guest Services.

The **H. B. Fuller Co.** bought a decaying lake in 1979 and restored the area as a headquarters for the worldwide chemical company's research laboratory, as well as the site of a major nature preserve. A program of resource management restored seven zones within the preserve: lake, wetland, bottomland woods, prairie, upland hardwoods, southwest management pool, and upper pond. Fuller received the 1989 Award for Excellence in Ethics from the periodical *Business Ethics* for adopting the highest global environmental standards in its Willow Lake project.

H. J. Heinz Company promoted environmental protection, both internally and externally, through employee awareness programs and aggressive recycling programs. Heinz reduced its packaging and increased and encouraged the recycling of its product packages, as well as enforced internal recycling initiatives. Heinz ketchup is packaged in the new ENVIROPET plastic bottle, the first recyclable container of its kind, which is the result of a multiyear, multimillion-dollar effort to develop an environmentally compatible container for ketchup that is fully recyclable.

Heinz conducted a companywide environmental program to create awareness among all employees of the need for environmentally responsible activity in the workplace and at home. It rewarded employee participation in identifying areas of environmental opportunity in the workplace.

The **Huntsman Chemical Corporation** designed and implemented CORE, an industrial waste recycling/waste minimization program, which reduces, conserves, and recycles waste through the involvement and recognition of its employees. The CORE program diverted 57 million pounds of waste from landfills in 1990 alone. Huntsman Chemical Corporation recycles white computer and mixed paper, aluminum cans, printer ribbons, polystyrene lumps, cardboard, wood pallets, glass, scrap metal, and metal drums. Several Huntsman plants became so proficient in recycling that other businesses, the U.S. Navy, and schools asked for assistance in starting their own recycling programs, modeled after the Huntsman plan.

The **John Deere Company** developed an alternative material to replace the foam used in the manufacturing process of certain products, such as engine cylinder heads. Originally, a toxic solvent was used to dissolve this foam after use, and then the solvent was burned out of the manufacturing core and vented into the air. Deere worked with the supplier of the foam to develop a new material that does not need to be burned off, but merely dissolves in the manufacturing process, eliminating all presence of toxins. In Waterloo, Iowa, where the Deere foundry is located, emissions dropped from 700,000 pounds annually to zero, and the new process saved John Deere more than $300,000.

The **Mennen Company,** one of New Jersey's oldest corporations, protected a 1,100-acre tract of land known as Pyramid Mountain from development. Using a new concept, a "land-swap deal," Mennen-owned land on Pyramid Mountain was traded for 17 acres of land adjacent to Mennen's headquarters, and $2.5 million in seed money was provided to gain a foothold on the mountain. Preserving this land will ensure a habitat for endangered species and a quality water supply.

In 1988, **Monsanto** initiated a program to reduce toxic air emissions by 90 percent from its manufacturing facilities worldwide by the end of 1992—the nation's first industrial program to commit to a stringent numerical waste reduction goal. In 1990, the company expanded its emission reduction goals by formalizing the "Monsanto Pledge," the company's environmental vision for the future. In the two years after Monsanto announced its ambitious plan, the company achieved a reduction of 39 percent for all of its U.S. operations. Its ultimate goal is zero emissions. Monsanto committed to researching technologies that will reduce or eliminate waste, with top priority to those that generate no waste in the first place.

The **New England Power Company** became the first electric utility in the country to sign an agreement with The Nature Conservancy to save critical natural areas. The agreement called for the protection of 11 ecologically significant sites the company owns along the Connecticut River. The goal of the program is to save 100 critical natural areas along the river, and calls for long-term management and protection of the sites. This agreement provided protection for more than 10 percent of the river at no cost to the public or the Conservancy.

Occidental Chemical, which mines phosphate rock in north central Florida, instituted a program to reclaim mined lands and restore them to natural habitats. Federal and state agencies and environmental groups worked with the company on a list of measurable criteria to track the success of the program.

Ohio Edison received two important awards for its effort to reduce emissions of sulfur dioxide and oxides of nitrogen from coal-burning power plants in a project at its Edgewater Power Plant. The LIMB (Limestone Injection Multi-Stage Burner) project received the Governor's Award for Outstanding Achievement in Waste Management and Pollution Control, 1989, and the Environmental Award of *Power* magazine, 1989.

Pacific Gas & Electric Co., the company that put into operation the first commercial geothermal power plant in the U.S., introduced the development of technology that reduces hydrogen sulfide ("rotten egg") emissions from its steam power plants. Without this new technology, geothermal research would most likely have been reduced or stopped.

Six companies—**Shell Oil, Continental Pipeline Co., Dow Chemical, Citgo, Phillips Petroleum,** and **Crown Rancho Pipeline**—donated 8,500 acres of ecologically important wetlands. This gift ensured that the Peach Point Marsh in Texas will remain intact as a Gulf Coast wildlife refuge. Originally intended for onshore facilities to support SEADOCK, a deepwater port that was never constructed, this site provides a habitat for more than 300 species of birds and holds at least 800 species of plants. The value of the land is estimated at more than $5 million.

Simpson Paper bought a pulp and paper mill, only to discover it was an environmental hot spot, fouled by more than 30 years' dumped wastes. The company formed a coalition with local government, business, union, and environmental organizations to restore 17.5 acres of tidal area, to support the company's facilities and a native habitat.

Texaco Chemical, working with the U.S. Fish and Wildlife Service, established nesting sites that increased the populations of the mottled duck. Predators that threaten these unusual and secretive water fowl are captured in a "catch and release" program that protects the duck population.

Rooting for America, a national tree planting program, is a 10-year commitment of **The Linde Division of Union Carbide Industrial Gases Inc.,** to plant trees in all communities hosting Linde facilities. In 1990, its first year, the program was implemented in 13 states and Puerto Rico. Community Tree Planting Councils were established by each Linde facility to serve as the vehicle for involving community leaders and Linde employees in the planning and implementation of all tree planting activities and the establishment and maintenance of "care grounds," a system to ensure long-term nurturing of the planted trees. Out of 5,711 people who were contacted to become involved with the program,

5,312 agreed to become active volunteers and participants. Half a million trees are expected to be planted over the course of 10 years.

As part of the Chemical Manufacturers Association's (CMA) Responsible Care program, **The Uniroyal Chemical Company** has been successful in implementing many changes in its facilities. One example of this is the activity of the research and development group at Uniroyal. In addition to meeting or surpassing environmental and safety regulations in the development of their technology, the R&D team at Uniroyal has completed such projects as a removable plastic drum liner for Adiprene/Vibrathane. This liner keeps the drum clean, which allows it to be recycled, and the liner is easily and safely discarded. The R&D Safety Council has also developed a complete laboratory safety manual, which it has published and circulated.

Unocal Corporation, a petroleum company based in Los Angeles, initiated a program to scrap and recycle 7,000 pre-1971 automobiles in the Los Angeles area. Unocal paid $700 for each car, which emits 15 to 80 times the exhaust of modern automobiles. The program, called SCRAP (South Coast Recycled Auto Program), turned over old cars to a scrap yard for dismantling and recycling, and was an investment of $5 million for the company. Unocal believes eliminating these cars will help reduce air pollution in the Los Angeles area.

Valvoline's Used Oil Bank, launched in December 1989, was the first effort by a major quick-lube chain to actively solicit used motor oil. To help inform motorists in each Used Oil Bank area about the availability of the program, the company staged a series of hard-hitting public service announcements showing oil from a crankcase being drained into the mouth of an actor, dramatizing the threat to water purity posed by improper used-oil disposal. Valvoline worked closely with municipalities to help them recycle locally generated used oil. In its first year of collection, the Used Oil Bank accepted 240,000 quarts of used motor oil. Most of the used oil has been reprocessed for various industrial uses. If burned for electricity, for example, it could heat 225 homes for one year.

Zoecon Corporation, a member of the Sandoz Group, has practiced a respect for ecosystems since the company's establishment in 1968. Recognizing that conventional insect control harmed beneficial insect populations, Zoecon developed the insect growth regulator (IGR) technology, using harmful insects' own biochemistries to eliminate threats to human and animal health—with no effect on life forms other than the target insect. Zoecon researches, develops, and markets IGRs to control pests like fleas, roaches, flies, and ants. The World Health Organization has approved the use of IGRs in drinking water to control disease-carrying mosquitoes. Zoecon has established an environmental review committee, representative of all areas within the company, which works to enhance the environmental sensitivity of products, packaging, and office systems. Recently honored by the National Environmental Development Association for its environmentally sound products, Zoecon continues to lead its industry with innovations that guard human and animal health—and respect our ecosystems.

Each one of these success stories—and so many, many more that only limited room here prevents us from including—are promising signs for business stewardship of the environment, and set examples to be emulated and improved upon in the years to come.

Chapter Twenty-Five

Environmental Awards: More Than Just "Good PR"

Well-respected Washington-based columnist William Raspberry is known for his fairness and his consistently refreshing editorials on, among other public interest issues, how to improve race relations.

His thesis, applied to many different topics, is simple and direct: To overcome problems, you must shun victimization and instead see yourself as part of the solution. He argues that anyone else who is dedicated to solving the same problem that you are is necessarily your ally.

When Raspberry applied his theme to the environment, he used the example of awards programs.[1] He challenged the notion that participating in awards programs is simply "doing good PR."

As I've said elsewhere in this volume, that notion is dying in the corporate world, and anywhere else for that matter, where a person or organization is interested in communication that is sustainable with its customer-publics. We're moving beyond "doing public relations" to "creating public relationships," and there are a number of environmental awards programs that exemplify this change.

Raspberry focused on Renew America's annual competition, the "Searching for Success" awards, a distinctly positive, upbeat, and unapologetic search for good news about the environment. Run by Executive Director Tina Hobson (a former social activist and peace protestor), covering 20 program areas from clean air to recycling to education, and qualifying entrants from all sectors—business and industry, private non-profit, and government—the program creates a gamut of strange bedfellows.

At a "time of dire warnings of impending doom," when environmental rhetoric around the world seems largely bent on naming enemies, is the "sponsor's clear-eyed understanding of the difference between problems and enemies."

Hobson herself has even been surprised at the positive results that come from "what works rather than who's guilty."

Raspberry makes a keen point: "If Renew America had focused on environmental enemies, it might have [as others have done] come up with a list of the 20 Worst Polluters of the Year . . . [but the program] proceeds from a different pair of assumptions: (1) that no one really wants to foul the environment, and many of those who do so might be persuaded to stop if they could be shown an economically feasible way of stopping [see Chapter Thirty-Two]; and (2) that sharing information on what works can make more effective activists of those who care about the environment."

Former peace activist Hobson cites a good example in, of all places, the military. The Marine recruits manual stresses that good training is dependent upon a healthy environment, and troops routinely engage in efforts to protect endangered plants and animals on their bases.

She also applauds unlikely allies in the utility industry's efforts toward energy efficiency and the battered EPA on its "Green Lights" program to encourage voluntary energy-efficient lighting among industries.

Summing up "what works" in an environmental award application is a good exercise for you. It reminds you of the positive aspects of your environmental protection program and gives you ideas about how to emulate them in other areas. It reminds your organization that there are solutions, not just problems.

And revealing your success story, its elements, and the process in a public forum is an important form of technology sharing (even if a new idea is low-tech). This is a key responsibility for parties reaching for global sustainable development, which was so emphasized at the recent UN Conference on Environment and Development.

Following is an incomplete (they're multiplying by leaps and bounds!) but handy listing of environmental awards programs you and your company may want to use as a reference.

FIGURE 25–1
Environmental Awards

Name/Sponsor	Location/Date	Eligibility	Criteria	Nomination	Contact
Alexander Calder Award sponsored by the Conservation Fund	Awards are presented in December in Washington, DC.	Open to individuals through groups or businesses.	Must show protection of wildlife habitat through a cooperative effort that involves business and conservation.	Deadline is February 1 of each year.	Jack Lynn Conservation Fund Suite 1120 1800 North Kent Street Arlington, VA 22209 (703) 683-2996
America's Corporate Conscience Award sponsored by the Council on Economic Priorities	Award presented in New York City in late March of each year.	U.S. corporations.	Categories: packaging; recycling; energy efficiency; transportation; waste disposal; pollution control; reforestation; compliance; development of products & support of special environmental programs.	Nominations for 1993 must be submitted by October 1992.	Ben Hollister Council on Economic Priorities 30 Irving Place New York, NY 10003-2386 (212) 420-1133
Best and Brightest Awards sponsored by the National Recycling Coalition	Awards presented at the coalition's annual congress held in October, 1992 in Nashville, Tennessee.	Individuals and corporations involved in recycling efforts.	Award based on recycling efforts in the following categories: rural; regional; urban; education; corporate; government or community leadership; recycler of the year.	Applications are due at the beginning of August each year.	National Recycling Coalition 1101 30th Street, NW #305 Washington, DC 20007 (202) 625-6406

FIGURE 25–1 (continued)
Environmental Awards

Name/Sponsor	Location/Date	Eligibility	Criteria	Nomination	Contact
Business Enterprise Awards for Courage, Integrity and Social Vision in Business sponsored by The Business Enterprise Trust	Awards ceremony in early 1993.	Any individual/group of individuals associated with business enterprise. Person or entity must have been associated with normal business activity; acts of philanthropy or volunteerism are not eligible.	Not specifically environmental. Judging categories include: "Pathfinders; Investors with a Long-Term Perspective; Entrepreneurs with Vision; Value-Driven Decisions; Profiles in Courage."	Nominations for 1993 must be submitted by June 1, 1992. Nominations must honor a specific action, decision, program or initiative.	Kirk Hanson President The Business Enterprise Awards The Business Enterprise Trust 204 Junipero Serra Blvd. Stanford, CA 94305 (415) 321-5100
Canada Awards for Business Excellence sponsored by Industry, Science and Technology Canada	Presentation on October 29, 1992, in Ottawa, Ontario.	Companies that do business in Canada.	Honors corporate achievement in 10 areas, one being the environment.	Deadline is April 1 of each year.	Dominique Veilleux 235 Queen Street 1st floor Ottawa, Ontario K1AOH5 Canada (613) 954-4079
Chevron Conservation Awards sponsored by Chevron Corporation	Presentation in May in Washington, DC.	Open to corporations and individuals.	Recognizes determination and initiative in improving the environment. Categories include: 1. citizens, 2. professionals, 3. organizations.	Deadline is November 15, 1992.	Ken Walters Ketchum Public Relations 6 PPG Place Pittsburg, PA 15222 (412) 456-3816

FIGURE 25-1 (continued)
Environmental Awards

Name/Sponsor	Location/Date	Eligibility	Criteria	Nomination	Contact
Conservation Award for Respecting the Environment (CARE) sponsored by the Interior Department's Minerals Management Service	Presentation is held at the Western Gulf Oil and Gas Lease Sale at the beginning of August each year.	Federal outer continental shelf leaseholders and offshore operators, as well as private companies engaged in offshore energy development.	Recognizes environmental accomplishments involved in offshore drilling in the Gulf of Mexico.	Deadline is the first week in June of each year.	Vierir Reggio Mineral Management Service 1201 Elmwood Park Boulevard New Orleans, LA 70123 (504) 736-2759
Du Pont/Conoco Environmental Leadership Award	Bronze plaque presented at company mine site. Winner is announced in October during the American Mining Congress Mine Expo.	Any North American mining company. Nominations only accepted from customers of DuPont & Conoco, but nominees can be noncustomers.	Awards based on corporate philosophy, mining reclamation, environmental leadership at sites and in community, wildife, land-use and water quality protection.	Nominations due on February 1 each year. Prize: $50,000 grant to non-profit organization of winner's choosing.	Jennifer Barnes Du Pont/Conoco Mining Services 6855 South Havana Street Suite 510 Englewood, CO 80112 (303) 649-4100
Du Pont Awards sponsored by Du Pont	Award presented at the National Food Processers Association's annual conference in March 1993.	Open to companies involved in food processing and packaging.	Award recognizes new products or technology using an innovative approach to encourage or provide for the reuse of plastic food packaging to help decrease the amount of waste.	Deadline is November 15, 1992.	Carol Marie Citra Nemours Building 11th and Market Street Wilmington, DE 19898 (302) 774-0821

FIGURE 25–1 *(continued)*
Environmental Awards

Name/Sponsor	Location/Date	Eligibility	Criteria	Nomination	Contact
Edison Award for Environmental Achievement sponsored by the American Marketing Association	Award presented in April 1993.	American corporations that manufacture products.	Honors new products with national distribution and demonstrated commercial appeal which contribute significantly to source reduction.	Entry deadline is September 1, 1992.	Jacqueline Ottman American Marketing Association 250 S. Wacker Drive, Suite 200 Chicago, Illinois 60606 (312) 255-3800
Edison Electric Institute's Common Goals Awards	1993 presentation date and location currently being determined.	Only Institute member companies may apply.	Award categories include: public participation; electrical safety; community responsibility; energy management; and special audiences.	Deadlines are to be determined.	Mary Ann Bernald Customer Services & Marketing Edison Electric Institute 701 Pennsylvania Ave, NW Washington, DC 20004 (202) 508-5559
Edison Electric Institute's Eagle Award	First ever Eagle Award will be presented on October 12 in Orlando.	Open to utility companies.	Award recognizes utility representatives for successful customer service efforts and new outstanding company-innovative technological applications.	Exact deadline to be determined. Next award will be in 1994.	Edward Thomas Customer Services & Marketing Edison Electric Institute 701 Pennsylvania Ave, NW Washington, DC 20004 (202) 508-5563

FIGURE 25–1 (continued)
Environmental Awards

Name/Sponsor	Location/Date	Eligibility	Criteria	Nomination	Contact
Edison Electric Institute's Economic Development Excellence Awards	Award will be presented mid-summer (date has not yet been determined) at the Economic Development Workshop.	Open to communications professionals at utility companies.	Award recognizes communication efforts in print and video advertising, direct mail, fact and statistics packages for local decision makers.	Applications are due in early spring—approximately April 1 each year.	Sally Hooks Customer Services & Marketing Edison Electric Institute 701 Pennsylvania Ave, NW Washington, DC 20004 (202) 508-5553
Edison Electric Institute's Edison Award	Award presented at the spring annual meeting in May 1993.	Open to Edison Electric Institute's member companies.	Awarded to a company that is "making a distinguished contribution to the development of the electric light & power industry for the convenience of the public and the benefit of all."	Deadline for applications is January 31 of each year.	Carol Ann Linder Corporate Affairs & Member Relations Edison Electric Institute 701 Pennsylvania Ave, NW Washington, DC 20004 (202) 508-5651
Edison Electric Institute's Land Management Awards	Awards presented on December 18 in Atlanta.	Open to Edison Electric Institute member companies.	Award recognizes a significant contribution to land management activities.	Deadline is October 1 of each year.	Joel Mazelis Environmental Activities Edison Electric Institute 701 Pennsylvania Ave, NW Washington, DC 20004 (202) 508-5461

FIGURE 25–1 *(continued)*
Environmental Awards

Name/Sponsor	Location/Date	Eligibility	Criteria	Nomination	Contact
Environmental Achievement Award sponsored by the National Wildlife Federation's Corporate Conservation Council	Presented in January each year.	Any US-based business. Project must exceed regulatory requirements, show systematic change within company, show evidence of endorsement from environmental group, comply with nomination form.	Innovative and creative corporate environmental accomplishments with proven environmental and economic benefits.	Nominations must be postmarked by April 30, 1992, for 1993 award.	Barbara Haas National Wildlife Federation Corporate Conservation Council Award 1400 16th Street, NW Washington, DC 20036-2266 (202) 797-6870
Environmental Communicator's Award sponsored by National Association of Professional Environmental Communicators	Winners notified: 8/31/92 Awards Ceremony: 10/8/92 at NAPEC Annual Conference, Chicago, Illinois	Enviro. communication programs must have been started, carried out, or ongoing between 1/91 & 6/92. Categories: govt. agencies; local enviro. activists; natl. enviro organizations; corps.; media; associations.	Outstanding programs for the promotion of public understanding and public dialogue on environmental protection.	Nomination deadline: 7/15/92 Fee: $30 (NAPEC members) $60 (nonmembers)	Helen Burnett NAPEC Publicity Committee Ketchum Communications 1201 Connecticut Ave, NW Suite 300 Washington, DC 20036 Questions? (202) 661-1721
EPA's Administrator's Awards sponsored by the Environmental Protection Agency	Post-Earth Day each year. Location to be determined.	Open to: 1. individual citizens; 2. not-for-profits; 3. businesses; 4. educational institutions; 5. governments.	Recognizes outstanding performance in a different enviro. category each year, for example: 1990: Solid waste; 1991: Pollution prevention and 1992: to be determined—will be similar to pollution prev.	Deadline is Feb. 13, 1993	Carol Singer Regional EPA Offices 401 M Street, SW Washington, DC 20460 (202) 260-2090

249

FIGURE 25–1 *(continued)*
Environmental Awards

Name/Sponsor	Location/Date	Eligibility	Criteria	Nomination	Contact
"Global 500—The Role of Honour for Environmental Achievement" sponsored by the United Nations Environment Programme (UNEP)	Prizes are awarded on World Environment Day (June 5) each year.	Individuals or organizations involved in environmental protection.	Awards based on environmental policy, application, and leadership.	Nominations are due on November 15 each year.	UNEP 1889 F Street, NW Ground Floor Washington, DC 20006 (202) 289-8456 (Send nominations to UNEP-Kenya, see Sasakawa Award.)
Gold Medal for International Corporate Achievement sponsored by the World Environment Center	CEO of accepting company must be present at formal awards dinner on 4/30/93 in Washington, DC.	Worldwide corporations with industrial and/or processing functions, having a substantial part of their operations outside the headquarters country.	Award honors outstanding, sustained and well-implemented environmental management policies of industrial operations worldwide.	Nominations are due on August 3, 1992, and must include a most recent annual report. Notification in December 1992.	Ann Vernados World Environment Center 419 Park Avenue South Suite 1800 New York, NY 10016 (212) 683-4700
Good Earthkeeping Seal sponsored by the Environmental Institute	Awarded quarterly.	Any business.	Awarded for environmental projects and initiatives considered worthy of special recognition.	No deadline.	Laura Radford-Rodrigues The Environmental Institute 3520 Northwest 13th Street Gainsville, FL 32601 (904) 375-2221

FIGURE 25–1 *(continued)*
Environmental Awards

Name/Sponsor	Location/Date	Eligibility	Criteria	Nomination	Contact
"Keep America Beautiful" 1992 National Awards	Keep America Beautiful's 39th Annual Meeting Washington, DC December 9–12, 1992	Categories include: state/fed. agencies; civic & youth groups; schools; businesses; communications; government; military.	Program must: 1. Have goal of improving waste handling and environmental stewardship. 2. Be continuing effort. 3. Include community waste handling activities. 4. Educate the community about solid waste.	Deadline: August 21, 1992 Notification: October 30, 1992	Keep America Beautiful Mill River Plaza, 9 W. Broad St. Stamford, CT 06902 (203) 323-8987
"Keep America Beautiful" National Recycling Awards	Keep America Beautiful's 39th Annual Meeting Washington, DC December 9–12, 1992	Categories include: individual; nonprofit organization; government agencies; business/industry.	Outstanding recycling programs that show examples of ongoing public/private partnerships.	Deadline: August 21, 1992 Notification: October 30, 1992	Keep America Beautiful Mill River Plaza, 9 W. Broad St. Stamford, CT 06902 (203) 323-8987
"Keep America Beautiful" Lifetime Achievement Awards	Keep America Beautiful's 39th Annual Meeting Washington, DC December 9–12, 1992	Awarded to individuals. Categories include: "Iron Eyes Cody Award" (outstanding volunteer men) & The Mrs. L. B. Johnson Award (women).	Demonstration of lifelong leadership in public awareness of recycling issues, litter prevention, preservation of natural resources and beautification activities.	Deadline: August 21, 1992 Notification: October 30, 1992	Keep America Beautiful Mill River Plaza, 9 W. Broad St. Stamford, CT 06902 (203) 323-8987

FIGURE 25–1 (continued)
Environmental Awards

Name/Sponsor	Location/Date	Eligibility	Criteria	Nomination	Contact
IPRA Golden World Award sponsored by the International Public Relations Association	Awards are announced in November 1992. Presentation ceremony is in May 1993.	Business corporations, associations, institutions and governments anywhere in the world. Public relations firms and consultancies can enter on behalf of clients.	Environmental category is one of 17. Demonstration of an excellent public relations project concerning a real or alleged threat to the environment. Judging is on the quality of the project's research, planning, execution, and evaluation.	Deadline for nomination is August 31, 1992.	IPRA Golden World Awards Canadian Imperial Bank of Commerce Corporate Communications Conference Room 425 Lexington Avenue, 9th fl. New York, NY 10017 (212) 856-4026
Malcolm Baldrige National Quality Award sponsored by the National Institute of Standards and Technology	Award Ceremony—Fall 1993	Businesses located in the US. Categories include: manufacturing companies or subsidiaries; service companies or subsidiaries; small businesses (fewer than 500 employees).	Areas examined: leadership; information and analysis; human resource development & management; management of process quality; quality & operational results; customer focus & satisfaction.	Eligibility forms due: March 1, 1993 Applications due: April 1, 1993 Application review/site visits: April–October, 1993	National Institute of Standards and Technology Administration Building, Room A537 Gaithersburg, MD 20899 (301) 975-2000
National Environmental Education Awards Program's Theodore Roosevelt Award sponsored by the EPA Office of Environmental Education	First awards ceremony ever will be held in Washington, DC, in spring 1993.	Awards individuals whose work has improved environmental education within the US and its territories.	Recognizes an outstanding career in environmental education, teaching or administration.	Applications due in February, 1993. Recipients must be nominated by a member of the Natl. Enviro. Ed.'s Advisory Council and must have at least two recommendations.	Nancy Lawton Natl. Enviro. Ed. Award Program EPA Office of Enviro. Ed. 401 M Street, SW Washington, DC 20460 (202) 260-5533

FIGURE 25–1 (continued)
Environmental Awards

Name/Sponsor	Location/Date	Eligibility	Criteria	Nomination	Contact
National Environmental Education Awards Program's Henry David Thoreau Award sponsored by the EPA Office of Environmental Education	First awards ceremony ever will be held in Washington, DC, in spring 1993.	Awards individuals whose work has improved environmental education within the US and its territories.	Recognizes an outstanding contribution to literature on the natural environment and environmental pollution problems.	Applications due in February 1993. Recipients must be nominated by a member of the Natl. Enviro. Ed.'s Advisory Council and must have at least two recommendations.	Nancy Lawton Natl. Enviro. Ed. Award Program EPA Office of Enviro. Ed. 401 M Street, SW Washington, DC 20460 (202) 260-5533
National Environmental Education Awards Program's Rachel Carson Award sponsored by the EPA Office of Environmental Education	First awards ceremony ever will be held in Washington, DC, in spring 1993.	Awards individuals whose work has improved environmental education within the US and its territories.	Recognizes an outstanding contribution in print, film or broadcast media to public education and information on environmental issues or problems.	Applications due in February 1993. Recipients must be nominated by a member of the Natl. Enviro. Ed.'s Advisory Council and must have at least two recommendations.	Nancy Lawton Natl. Enviro. Ed. Award Program EPA Office of Enviro. Ed. 401 M Street, SW Washington, DC 20460 (202) 260-5533
National Environmental Education Awards Program's Gifford Pinchot Award sponsored by the EPA Office of Environmental Education	First awards ceremony ever will be held in Washington, DC, in spring 1993.	Awards individuals whose work has improved environmental education within the US and its territories.	Recognizes an outstanding contribution to education and training concerning forestry and natural resource management, including multiple use and sustained yield management.	Applications due in February 1993. Recipients must be nominated by a member of the Natl. Enviro. Ed.'s Advisory Council and must have at least two recommendations.	Nancy Lawton Natl. Enviro. Ed. Award Program EPA Office of Enviro. Ed. 401 M Street, SW Washington, DC 20460 (202) 260-5533

FIGURE 25-1 *(continued)*
Environmental Awards

Name/Sponsor	Location/Date	Eligibility	Criteria	Nomination	Contact
NAEM Environmental Excellence Awards sponsored by the National Association of Environmental Managers	NAEM's Annual Fall Meeting in October 1992.	All corporations regardless of size or revenues. A corporation or an environmental manager can apply.	Corporate category: sophistication of company's environmental program. Manager category: Incorporates leadership & commitment to the greater common interest of an integrated environmental consciousness into the company.	Nominations must be submitted by September 1992.	Gail Stanton Executive Director NAEM 3830 Gateway Terrace Burtonsville, MD 20866 (202) 638-1200
National Wetlands Protection Award sponsored by the Environmental Law Institute and the US Environmental Protection Agency	Date and location pending.	Open to all individuals—not organizations or groups of individuals—whose programs or projects are operative at the state, regional, or local level.	Judgment is made on innovation or excellence in wetlands conservation in state and local government, the nonprofit sector, or a business effort.	Nominations must be submitted by September 30, 1992 for 1993 award.	Steve Meddick or Nicole Veilleux Environmental Law Institute 1616 P Street, NW Washington, DC 20036 (202) 208-3983
NEDA Honor Role sponsored by the National Environmental Development Association	Awards Dinner: June 23 Four Seasons Hotel Washington, DC	Any company or organization with operations in the US	Must demonstrate achievement in one or more of the following areas: Environmental quality management; resource enhancement and protection; environmental communication and outreach.	Nominations must be submitted by March 1, 1993 Nomination fee: $100	Jeff Abboud NEDA 1440 New York Avenue, NW Suite 300 Washington, DC 20005 (202) 638-1230

FIGURE 25–1 (continued)
Environmental Awards

Name/Sponsor	Location/Date	Eligibility	Criteria	Nomination	Contact
President's Environment and Conservation Challenge Awards sponsored by the President's Council on Environmental Quality	White House Awards ceremony. Date pending.	All U.S. residents, businesses, nonprofit organizations, trade and professional associations and state and local governments. Federal government not included.	Four categories: quality environmental management; partnership; innovation; education and communication.	1992 applications must be submitted by May 22, 1992 Must include four copies of application plus up to 10 pages of supporting materials & three letters of recommendation.	Council on Environmental Quality The White House 722 Jackson Place, NW Washington, DC 20503 (202) 395-1154
Robert Rodale Achievement Award sponsored by Direct Marketing Association	October 25-28, 1992	Direct marketing organizations, companies and nonprofits.	Recognizes significant contributions to the development and execution of an effective corporate environmental strategy.	Entry deadline for 1993 is late summer.	Chet Dalzell Direct Marketing Association 11 West 42nd Street New York, NY 10036 (212) 768-7277 ext. 425
Safety Award For Excellence (SAFE) sponsored by the Minerals Management Service of the Department of the Interior	1993 location and date to be determined.	Oil companies.	Recognizes companies that achieve the highest level of safety and environmental compliance in US off-shore operations.	1993 deadline to be determined.	Minerals Management Service Department of the Interior 1849 C Street, NW Washington, DC 20240 (202) 208-3983

FIGURE 25-1 (concluded)
Environmental Awards

Name/Sponsor	Location/Date	Eligibility	Criteria	Nomination	Contact
Sasakawa International Environment Prize sponsored by the United Nations Environment Programme	Date and location pending.	Individuals or institutions of any nation. Nominees can be associated with any field of the environment.	Prize awarded for achievement in: Environmental health, resource management, food & agriculture, population, wildlife, pollution & hazardous materials control, education, information and legislation.	Nominations are due in November each year. Nominees will be considered for two years. Prize is $200,000	Tore Brenik Chief Information Service UNEP P.O. Box 30552 Nairobi, Kenya Tel: (25) 42-230-800
Searching for Success Awards National Environmental Achievement Award sponsored by RENEW America	Presentation in June of each year.	Any individual, community group, school, business or government department.	Judging in 20 environmental categories. Awards given to outstanding environmental programs.	Nomination deadline is January 15 each year.	RENEW America 1400 16th Street, NW Suite 710 Washington, DC 20036 (202) 232-2252
Take Pride in America National Awards Program sponsored by the US Department of the Interior	Presentation is in July of each year in Washington, DC	Any individual or public or private organization.	Award not specifically environmental but recognizes stewardship of natural resources.	No nomination fee. Deadline dates are different for each state, call Take Pride in America for specific dates.	Take Pride in America 1849 C Street, NW Room 5123 Washington, DC 20240 (202) 208-3726

Prepared by the E. Bruce Harrison Company (as of September 1992)

Chapter Twenty-Six

CMA's Responsible Care Program

A program that rose from one industry's need to communicate with its neighbors now is providing both energy to America's greening and a model to private and public interests of the value of good community relations.

Responsible Care (the term is now trademarked) was born out of a negative public image of the chemical industry.[1] The Chemical Manufacturers Association created the program to reassure worried publics—especially neighbors of chemical plants—that nearby facilities are being operated safely, and that the company that owns the facilities cares about their employees and the community.

Operating for several years now, Responsible Care has come to provide a means to exchange information among companies and to bring all participants up to the highest standards of safety and manufacturing practice. Its success has spread steadily, first from Canada to the U.S. and now internationally.

REASON FOR THIS PROGRAM

North America's chemical-process industry has been on the front line of environmental confrontation since the dawn of the modern green age. Since it was first singled out for attack by environmental activists in the 1960s (by the likes of Rachel Carson and her book, *Silent Spring*), public perception has put it high on the list of presumed villains. While its health and safety performance records are excellent, the industry has suffered disproportionately in terms of positive public acceptance.

Historically, some plant neighbors have been afraid they are at risk because of industry operations. The general public has sus-

257

pected risk from industry products, chemical transportation, and chemical disposal.

In the 1980s, when more information about chemicals used in manufacturing operations became available, the industry was in the news. Reporting of emissions, effluents, and other releases to the environment under Title III of the Superfund Amendments and Reauthorization Act (SARA), the Toxics Release Inventory (TRI) tended to reinforce a view that the processes and products of the industry posed public risk.

Remember that when people get more information about a scary subject, their fears are not necessarily relieved. At least for a time—until you can help them *understand* what the data mean—public fears tend to climb. Reported releases raise concerns among people downwind and downstream of industrial facilities—and virtually everyone is downwind or downstream of something.

In the mid-1980s, the cooperative partnership program was put together by chemical industry executives of the Canadian Chemical Producers' Association (CCPA). It has since spread to the U.S. and overseas, and has adopted the Total Quality Management (TQM) ideal. It says to the public: "Don't trust us, track us. Look in on us. Get involved with us in solving problems and planning to avoid disasters."

CCPA President Jean Belanger began the Responsible Care program as a model for the Canadian companies to make a commitment, in writing, to be good corporate citizens on environmental, health, and safety matters. By December 1984, 95 percent of CCPA members had signed on voluntarily.

The timing was historic. Only a few days later, the tragic incident at Bhopal, India, occurred. The methyl isocyanate gas leak at Union Carbide's Indian facility killed 3,000 and wounded 25,000. The world was shocked. Negative news about chemicals, questions like "could it happen here?" and concerns in plant communities were elevated to new highs.

HOW THE INDUSTRY RESPONDED

In Canada, the chemical association board responded by raising its commitment to the Responsible Care program; it made signature to the program a mandatory requirement for membership.

In the U.S., the Chemical Manufacturers Association immediately surveyed its members' emergency response capabilities. The survey came back with an *OK* on corporate *internal* response plans and policy—but with low marks for external emergency response. Out of this need, CMA created CAER, the Community Awareness and Emergency Response program. Its goal was to help the manufacturer to work in unison with the community to plan for a coordinated response to any environmental incident. The CAER program was so successful that it was eventually borrowed by government regulators and written into law in the Right-to-Know Title III of SARA.

But the industry had more work to do. Despite the fact that the chemical industry had, according to EPA, done more than any other industry to promote and implement Title III, it had not convinced sufficient customer-publics of its commitment.

In June 1986, the Canadians conducted a poll of public attitudes, and the Decima Survey came back with results showing that 48 percent of Canadians still thought the chemical industry risks outweighed benefits.

Dave Buzzelli, then the head of Dow Canada and later CCPA chairman, said, "Decima turned the tide in CCPA. It made us realize that Responsible Care would have to move from being a philosophical statement to something with teeth." Those teeth would become known as the Codes of Practice.

Meanwhile the U.S. was busy with a number of activities. CMA Chairman and Du Pont Executive Vice President William Simeral urged members to take a look at industry through public eyes and suggested "adopting dumps" for cleanup. This suggestion was the origin of what later became known as Clean Sites, which we discuss in the partnering section of this book.

Louis Fernandez of Monsanto focused on trying to get companies to move away from litigation and confrontation as a way to solve conflicts and urged industry support of Superfund to make it work.

But perhaps the greatest impression made during that time came from a CMA task force. The Public Perception Committee was charged with gauging public distaste for the industry. The results were devastating, and CMA decided that Responsible Care was the answer. In September 1988, all but one member signed on voluntarily. Participation in Responsible Care is now a condition of membership in CMA.

CMA formed the framework, with each member company responsible for setting its own specific goals in each of the Management Practice Codes. This allowed smaller companies the needed leeway to meet the standards. Because peer competition is so stiff in the industry, self-regulation has not been a problem; nevertheless, the association has developed guides for measuring effective performance.

HOW IT WORKS

Responsible Care meets community concerns directly. It goes public with the intensive, *internal* program that chemical companies have long conducted to protect health, safety, and the environment. It pushes all the companies that participate in it toward the highest standard of industrial practice, with codes that spur progress toward that standard.

The program also provides a credible rationale for maintaining the company's independence from the codes of conduct, such as the *Valdez* Principles, developed by organizations outside the business community.

Companies have been able to point to Responsible Care as even more on the green than external model codes, providing better protection for the public and the environment, and setting *a company-specific commitment that can be quantified and tracked.*

The tracking starts immediately. Companies are required to report to CMA on a regular basis about their progress in carrying out each of the codes.

THE CODES OF RESPONSIBLE CARE

The six standards cover all aspects of chemical production, distribution, use, and disposal, and are detailed policy statements that companies apply to individual situations.

The codes are:

Community Awareness and Emergency Response

The Bhopal chemical-release incident was the solemn impetus for this code, which was developed independently by CMA prior to its adoption of the overall Responsible Care program.

The code requires companies to develop emergency response plans in cooperation with local governments and neighboring facilities. It includes requirements for community outreach to include neighbors in emergency training, and to provide information to them about the plant and its operations.

The code is intended to ensure that emergency response plans are in place, that all appropriate organizations and individuals know their roles in an emergency situation, and that lines of communication are open between the plant and the surrounding community.

CAER was needed to ensure an effective response to accidents. Even so, the industry realized that accident prevention was just as important as emergency response.

Process Safety

The Process Safety Code ensures that the participating company uses proper analysis and procedures to prevent fires, explosions, spills, releases, or other accidents.

The code provides a framework for companies to design, build, and operate plants safely. It encourages risk assessments, fault tree analyses, hazard and operability studies, and other techniques to identify potential plant failures, and to take measures to prevent them.

Pollution Prevention

The pollution prevention code consists of guidelines for release reduction and waste management.

Release Reduction. Under this code, chemical companies make a commitment to reduce the amount of chemicals that they release to the environment.

The goals are specific, achievable, and measurable. Companies must keep an inventory of all releases to the land, air, and water, and commit to reducing these by specified amounts—and within a specified time period—as determined by the individual companies.

Waste Management. This code goes beyond others to provide greater attention to solid waste. The waste management guidelines for management practice cover all residual material, whether hazardous or not, that remains after the firm carries out programs in source reduction, recycling, and reuse of material.

Companies are required to develop procedures for the safe handling and disposal of waste products where such waste cannot be eliminated.

Employee Health and Safety

CMA's Employee Health and Safety Code of Management Practice requires companies to carry out the best management practices to maintain a "safe and healthy work place."

Companies must implement an industrial hygiene program, set exposure limits for substances not regulated by OSHA, conduct medical surveillance for workers where appropriate, and ensure that procedures are carried out to protect employees from occupational injury and illness.

Distribution

All forms of transportation—road, rail, water, air, and pipelines—are covered by this code, along with chemical storage, transfer, packaging, and response to transportation emergencies.

The code pushes companies to use the most advanced techniques to prevent accidents during the transportation of chemicals, and to be prepared to respond to transportation emergencies involving chemicals wherever they occur.

Product Stewardship

This, the "no-loophole" code, covers everything not addressed above. It says the company assumes cradle-to-grave responsibility for its chemicals and chemical products.

Producers are required to ensure that their customers use chemicals correctly and have proper safeguards in chemical use, transportation, processing, and disposal.

Producers are encouraged to provide advice, training, and supervision for their customers to ensure that chemicals are used safely.

The ever-important downstream green communication comes into play here.

EXAMPLES OF COMPANY PROGRAMS

Responsible Care has become an international movement. The program varies from country to country, and from company to company for that matter, but the spirit and intent remain the same. Its first international workshop was held in 1991 in Rotterdam in conjunction with the Second World Industry Conference on Environmental Management (WICEM II).

Says CCPA president and founder of the plan, Jean Belanger, "Responsible Care is our *culture*, . . . not a *program*. Programs have beginnings and ends. Responsible Care must be our ongoing *way of life*." And industry needs to continue to communicate that philosophy, proving to the world that Responsible Care is not just a shell for executive cover.

Individually, here's how some companies have incorporated Responsible Care into their operations:

Phillips Petroleum's Katherine Powell was put in charge of Responsible Care in March 1989. Her first move was bottom-up communication (asking questions of customer-publics). She went into the field and interviewed plant employees to determine their fears and gain some advice on the best way to go about speeding up health, safety, and environment improvements. She found that, despite programs Phillips had implemented through CMA and American Petroleum Institute, employees did not identify with those groups. They identified with Phillips—their company. So Powell went about culling the best of the CMA and API programs, to integrate into Phillips' own interpretation of Responsible Care—including the codes of management practice—which it calls Principles of Performance. Periodic evaluations have rated Phillips high in environmental performance in comparison with its peers, especially in the areas of waste and release reduction.

Although **Monsanto**'s commitment to environmental protection predates Responsible Care, the company feels that the CMA program falls along many of its outstanding commitments and "legitimizes" on a national scale programs such as theirs. Vice President for Environment, Safety, and Health Michael Pierle says "Responsible Care is a positive companion in moving forward." He says it also broadens employee accountability beyond the company to the community and the public at large.

Companies such as **Eastman Kodak** have established consumer hot lines and established Community Advisory Panels.

J. Roger Hirl, president and CEO of **Occidental Chemical,** said of his company's efforts at the genesis of the Responsible Care program, "If we should err in execution or be misquoted or misunderstood in the public arena, we will lick our wounds and try again. What we can't do is let fear of the spotlight prevent us from giving this program our all-out effort."[2]

And finally, let's look at how **Union Carbide,** after lessons learned at Bhopal and initiation of Responsible Care, handled the March 12, 1991, explosion at its Seadrift Plant (Port Lavaca, TX) in which one person was killed and 19 injured. Within seven hours after the explosion, the fire was out and all surviving victims treated. Just a few hours later all community neighbors within a two-mile radius had been contacted (164 homes and businesses). Ninety-two percent of those contacted approved of the crisis handling.

Environmental group reactions to Responsible Care are diverse. The Audubon Society's Peter A. A. Berele calls Responsible Care "an important step in the right direction." On the other hand, Greenpeace national toxics campaign director Bill Walsh notes, "We don't think much of it, since I guess we hold the chemical industry responsible for much of the environmental damage we see today."

But Responsible Care has environmentalists on its very credible advisory board, the PAP—Public Advisory Panel—which also consists of a physician, a farmer, an ethicist, and a lobbyist, among others. One of its members represents an environmental group that is currently battling corporations that are signatories to Responsible Care. When asked how he could work with industry and still retain his integrity, he said, "I don't see a conflict. I can serve on the panel and then walk down the hall and argue for the upcoming RCRA reauthorization. If Responsible Care gives the industry more credibility and makes them a more powerful adversary, that's fine, especially if they really improve their act."

But perhaps the most notable Responsible Care endorser is former EPA Administrator Bill Reilly. He admits that his successful program, the 33/50 voluntary toxic emissions reduction program (meaning 33 percent reduction in emissions of 17 chemicals by 1992 and 50 percent by 1995 from a 1988 baseline year) was borrowed from Responsible Care. Reilly points to ambitious commitments in reductions of emissions by companies such as Monsanto and Du Pont and says that if government had mandated it, it would be ridiculous. If it's just a company PR campaign, it would be too risky.

Chapter Twenty-Seven

How a Corporation Communicated a New Environmental Ethic

Following is an excellent case study of how one of our clients, United Technologies Corp., on the heels of some negative publicity, successfully communicated their new dedication to environmental protection to a number of important customer-publics.

We have reprinted it here with the permission of PR News.

FIGURE 27–1
How a Corporation Communicated a New Environmental Ethic

While many companies have seized upon "green marketing" as a way to sell more products or increase market share, others have found that having a green image has other payoffs—with customers, local communities, and local and national press. Being environmentally irresponsible can hurt relations with all of these groups and can lead to punitive fines, as United Technologies Corp. (UTC) of Hartford, Conn., has found.

| CASE STUDY |
| No. 2294 |

In the mid- to late 1980s, the manufacturing company, with 50,000 employees in Connecticut and nearly 200,000 worldwide, was fined hundreds of thousands of dollars by the Environmental Protection Agency. In 1990, the firm received a $1.2 million fine—eventually settled for $730,000—for environmental violations.

At that time, company Chairman and CEO Robert F. Daniell decided that the company must take action to reform its philosophies and practices regarding the environment. "What we clearly lacked at UTC was a commitment to make environmental practices an essential consideration in all our business decisions," he said. He believed that the lack of a consistent environmental ethic or policy in the company was the root cause of the legal and negative environmental image problems facing the company.

The corporate communications department, working with E. Bruce Harrison Co. (Washington), developed a survey of legal, environmental, operating, and

FIGURE 27–1 *(continued)*
How a Corporation Communicated a New Environmental Ethic

communication managers at corporate headquarters and three operating units of UTC to assess the corporation's environmental commitment. Also analyzed was the level of environmental communications and the effectiveness of UTC's environmental organization.

Among the survey questions were:

—Have any of your business unit's employee communications contained information on environmental affairs?

—Are you aware of any company environmental training/education programs?

—How are line managers made aware of these programs?

As a result of the research, Daniell made several management changes, bringing in a top environmental officer for the company, and appointing a senior environmental officer at each of the company's operating units. These new managers also formed the company's new Environmental, Health, and Safety Council.

In January 1991, the company's new commitment to environmentally responsible behavior was announced to 1,400 UTC managers by Daniell in a videoconference broadcast via satellite to 14 UTC locations in the United States and Canada. Videotapes of the address were distributed to managers unable to attend and to external audiences, including the Connecticut news media and national business and trade press editors.

An editor from the *Hartford Courant*, the largest daily newspaper in Connecticut, was invited to the teleconference, and subsequently wrote an editorial favorably commenting on UTC's new environmental commitment. Selected public officials also received copies of the tape.

. . . Environmental Communications Council Formed

Communications policy and planning was given close attention early in the process. The company created an Environmental Communications Council, which identified environmental communications issues facing the company. Key communications staff on the council included Dandridge L. Harrison, UTC's director of public relations, and 14 other PR and communications professionals in corporate and divisional positions.

The council was charged with identifying environmental communications opportunities facing UTC, and crafting effective strategies. Broadly speaking, the goal for UTC's communications staff at corporate and division levels was to increase awareness of UTC's environmental effort among internal and external audiences: employees, regulators, legislators, and the news media.

Overall environmental communications was directed by the corporate public relations department, which worked closely with divisional communications staff on the full range of internal and external communications.

. . . Communications Staff Receives Environmental Issues Training

At this time, UTC's corporate public relations department retained ENSR Consulting and Engineering, of Acton, Mass., to assist communications staff. Caren Arnstein, director of environmental communications, was the project leader at ENSR. A key task of ENSR was to develop guidelines for environmental questions that communicators could use to better understand corporate

FIGURE 27–1 *(concluded)*
How a Corporation Communicated a New Environmental Ethic

environmental practices. ENSR also developed environmental awareness training and risk communications training programs for communications staff, as
well as for environmental and plant operating staff.

Topics covered included regulations, such as the Resource Conservation and
Recovery Act, Clean Water Act, Occupational Safety and Health Administration (OSHA), Toxic Substances Control Act, and others. Risk communications
sessions explained how to communicate statistical measures of risk and how
to understand public perceptions of environmental risk.

For internal communications, a brochure detailing UTC's commitment—and
the responsibility of each employee—to the environment, was distributed to
all employees. Environmental matters also began to receive coverage in almost
all issues of monthly corporate and divisional publications.

A subsequent survey of employees at Pratt & Whitney, UTC's largest division, found that the majority of employees rated the effectiveness of the company's environmental communications as "somewhat useful" or "very useful."

To prepare for communication with the media, UTC's various communications
departments prepared fact sheets, a primer on environmental regulations, a glos-
sary of environmental terms, and an environmental Q&A for both internal and
external audiences. Crisis communication plans also were developed for possible
environmental crises, such as lawsuits, fines, or plant accidents.

In media relations, communications personnel became "contrite," according to
PR Director Harrison, and acknowledged UTC's responsibility for past environmental "misdeeds" while emphasizing the company's promise to reform.

Frank W. McAbee, senior vice president/environmental and business practices,
was made available to the media as chief UTC spokesperson for the environment. Early in his tenure, he held a get-acquainted meeting with the environment reporter for the *Hartford Courant*.

At the same time, communications staff began to cite "success stories" that
showed how UTC was improving its environmental performance. For example,
the replacement of a solvent-based paint with a water-based paint at a UTC plant
in Tennessee was cited in news releases that then generated favorable publicity.

Published media tips regularly sent to reporters and editors also included a
number of UTC developments with beneficial environmental impacts. Reporters
also were regularly invited to UTC announcements with environmental significance, such as the dedication of the company's chemical milling maskant system
and a UTC-sponsored symposium on waste reduction.

To ensure that environmental communications remains a long-term and intrin-
sic part of the communications process, yearly strategic communications plans are
developed at the corporate and division levels. The plans include regularly sched-
uled coverage in internal publications. An awards program recognizing employee
environmental achievements is now in the planning stages. (United Technologies,
UTC Building, Hartford, CT 06101, 203/728-7956.)

Source: PR NEWS, Case Study No. 2294, April 6, 1992, Phillips Publishing, Inc., 7811
Montrose Road, Potomac, Md.

Chapter Twenty-Eight

Getting With the Program: A Sustainable Development Checklist for Your Organization

The broad, global concept *and* the leading-edge international business concept for getting on the green are the same. It is called *sustainable development*.

For nations, this means matching up economic goals with environmental goals. *Sustainable development*—a term that has been kicking around policy circles for two decades—was the theme of the Earth Summit, held in Rio de Janeiro in 1992. In the tremendous attention focused on that United Nations Conference on Environment and Development, involving tens of thousands of people from more than 178 nations, a process was set in motion to unify (or at least to align) any nation's economic commitment and its protection of the environment. That process will continue.

For the next decade at minimum, and perhaps for far longer, individual nations—developed and developing—will try to sort out the pros and cons of green moves and growth moves, drawing on the discussions and declarations from Rio 92.

This unified emphasis and the individualized decisions that flow from it will impact companies of virtually any size operating anywhere in the world.

Many companies, in the United States and throughout the industrialized world, have signed on to a "Business Charter on Sustainable Development" developed by the International Chamber of Commerce.

While this is not itself an enforced code—signers are expected to comply voluntarily—the fact that a company's name appears on the list committed to the Business Charter puts the company under special scrutiny. Companies signing on to the Business Charter realize that their publics, including government, employees, and activists, will see this commitment and expect the company to comply with the sustainable development principles suggested.

Should your company become associated with the Business Charter? You can decide for yourself. If your decision is that this is something you wish to do, you may be able to do so officially (you may contact the ICC to see how to qualify) or you may want to support the program unofficially—by simply stating in your publications or elsewhere your commitment to the goals of sustainable development described in the charter.

To help you make your decision, our firm has prepared a corporate checklist (at the end of this chapter), based on the ICC charter.

If you can answer *yes* to more than half of these questions, you are probably a good candidate for following the Business Charter. (In the U.S., contact the U.S. Council for International Business, Department of Environmental Affairs, in New York.)

I suggest that you don't sign up if you don't intend to make strong efforts, over time, to follow the principles stated in the charter. At the same time, recognize that some of these principles are already being picked up and put into law, so the chances are growing that your organization will be affected at some point, whether you sign on or not.

Companies that have agreed to be listed as supporters of the Business Charter generally feel there are benefits to being among those taking this step now, voluntarily committing to the sustainable development concept. This is a more positive and more progressive commitment than some alternative codes or principles offered by others.

FIGURE 28–1
Corporate Checklist on Sustainable Development

Has your company anticipated the challenges of commitment to sustainable development? Do you:

• Support the philosophy of sustainable development to meet the needs of the present generation without compromising the ability of future generations to meet their own needs?

• Promote the principles of sustainable development through environmental management, which works toward a "total quality management" approach, integrating environmental criteria into all corporate practices?

• Understand that true corporate commitment to environmental improvement must begin at the highest level of the company, the chief executive officer, and that environmental management must be among the highest corporate priorities?

• Know the environment, health, and safety reporting requirements; report environmental information to appropriate government agencies on a consistent and timely basis as required; and, where possible, exceed requirements?

• Regularly perform internal environmental audits to assess the quality of corporate environmental management and performance?

• Demonstrate how the company will improve energy efficiency and conservation to sustain the use of nonrenewable and renewable resources and to reduce the likelihood of global climate change?

• Assess the environmental impact of new and existing products and processes from a total-life-cycle approach and seek to reduce waste at the source, recycle and safely dispose of hazardous materials, basically in that priority?

• Demonstrate openness and dialogue about the environmental impact of products and processes and their relative risks with consumers, employees, surrounding communities, local media, shareholders, and government regulators?

• Regularly train and educate employees, contractors, and suppliers to enhance environmental awareness and protection?

• Develop and maintain operational emergency preparedness plans for facilities, employees, and consumers?

• Recognize that business and economic growth, at home and internationally, is essential to providing the financial and technical resources necessary for global environmental improvement?

• Support common environmental goals for all countries as well as a reasonable time frame for reaching those goals (taking into account the level of each country's relative development)?

• Share nonproprietary innovations and technologies with lesser-developed countries and other companies to increase their contribution toward sustainable development?

• Operate in foreign countries under standards that are equal or superior to those where you are headquartered?

FIGURE 28–1 *(concluded)*
Corporate Checklist on Sustainable Development

- Support policies that take into account the interrelationship of trade and global environmental improvement?
- Support a market economy approach to environmental improvement and encourage incentives (instead of command and control methods by government regulators) to reach agreed-upon environmental goals by the most efficient means?
- Encourage a partnership between government and industry in which government will work toward providing stable investment climates, solid infrastructure for research and development, and incentives for technology transfer, all necessary in the move toward sustainable development?

Source: Adapted by the E. Bruce Harrison Company from the Final Declaration of the Second World Industry Conference on Environmental Management and the International Chamber of Commerce Business Charter for Sustainable Development.

PART

V

ISSUES AHEAD

Chapter Twenty-Nine

Green Trends Point to Pressures on Every Business

Despite the success stories, the *other* news is that many companies have not yet begun to feel the impact of greenism. Yet pressures on individual companies show no sign of abating. In fact, as the big leading companies accommodate the external forces, the mid-size to small company will feel much more green pressure.

Signs along the road to the Green World of Business are worth reading by every businessperson. We've already talked about the Business Charter for Sustainable Development. Here are some others:

GREENING IS HIGHLY POLITICIZED

Politicians must have causes, and the environment is at or near the top of social and political agendas everywhere. While there are strong distinctions about greening from country to country, public support for greening is universal.

Environmental*ism*—that is, the ideology, if not the science—is embraced as a winning political issue all over the globe. The less-advantaged nations keep the pressure on the more industrialized nations, blaming them (us) for global pollution and asking that they (we) pay for their cleanup.

It's clear that for the foreseeable future you can expect only degrees of latitude or activism within the green platform of any party or candidate in any location.

NO ONE IS UNPLUGGED FROM GREENISM

As we've discussed, green activism is transnational. Information centered on business—that is to say, the greening of commerce or the lack thereof—is more widely accessible now than ever before. In North America, in Europe, and elsewhere, legal entitlements now encourage government officials, politicians, the news media, activist organizations, and any interested citizen to tap into a wide and deep pool of environmental data.

Thanks to computer databases and speed-of-light communication, situations that were once isolated are now brought easily into public view. There is instance access and connectibility with regard to environmental events.

As Browning-Ferris CEO William Ruckelshaus said at the WICEM meeting, "The global village is now a global phone booth. We are operating in each other's laps."

GREEN CLAIMS AND "OPENNESS" CAN ENTRAP BUSINESS

Business seems to be moving between a rock and a hard place. While striving to be "open" in their operations and communication, they dare not say too much.

The same green activists who have condemned business for not giving out enough technical (e.g., toxic release) information are now using some of the available information to criticize individual companies.

Green activists and government will increasingly team up to challenge companies' pro-environment claims or statements. This was started by state attorneys general blowing the whistle on misleading green marketing, and has been escalated by politicians, activist groups, and regulators at the state level.

You can look for challenges to any "self-serving" claim or company commitment regarding environmental cleanups. Yet the expectation of information and the concept of "openness" that now holds sway put pressure on each company to keep trying.

FIGURE 29–1
Market Model for Environmental Communication

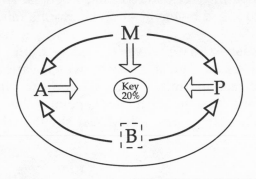

Source: © E. Bruce Harrision Company 1992

THE "AMP" SYNDROME IS IN HIGH GEAR

Greening and the public-policy impact of greenism are being propelled by what I refer to as the "AMP Syndrome"—a synergy of Activists + Media + Politicians.

Public scares about food safety, for example, have been stimulated by this syndrome. Activists stir up conflict, naming "victims" (various people or public sectors) and "villains" (very often, business interests). The news media respond to conflict and publicize it. Politicians respond to media and issues, moving to protect "victims" and punish "villains" with legislative and regulatory actions.

Recent green scares—Alar, dioxin, and others—were the direct result of this synergy, while business was at least initially boxed in, isolated from the action.

As greenism becomes more political and as activist groups look for causes to replenish funding (depleted by recent economic conditions), you will see AMP rise.

CONSUMERS AND COMMUNITIES ASK OTHERS FIRST

Despite strides and success by some businesses in becoming reliable sources of information, polls show that the people who buy products or who live near a business facility continue to trust others for information. A national poll conducted by Environment Opinion Study, Inc., concluded that "people tend to believe information supplied by environmental groups rather than business interests."

While we suspect that this varies widely from place to place, and has much to do with the way in which various companies "deliver" information (rather than "trade" it with customer-publics), there is little question that general publics are ready to believe the next negative word they hear about business from the AMP players.

INCREASE IN CITIZEN SUITS

Green litigation is increasing, as trial lawyers round up plaintiffs who have ever worked in or lived anywhere near certain companies—companies identified as polluters through the Toxic Release Inventory (TRI) or news stories.

More suits will be filed for violation of State Implementation Plans or other Clean Air Act requirements. Civil penalties of $25,000 per day for each violation will not be unusual.

Ironically, required industry self-reports will help identify targets for litigation and make prosecution easier.

CRIMINAL PENALTIES FOR COMPANY EXECUTIVES

Green-collar crime convictions (see Chapter Thirty) will continue a phenomenal rise, begun just a few years ago. Severity of prosecutions (more felonies) will also increase, as will penalties.

Company executives will not need to be "bad" to be convicted. "Knowingly" violating the Clean Air Act Amendments of 1990 can bring a personal fine of $250,000 and five years behind bars. But the definition of *knowing* is getting broader. Executives have been convicted of knowingly violating waste laws because they knew their firms were using particular waste-disposal facilities, even though they didn't know that the facilities lacked the proper permits.

FIGURE 29–2
Stockholder Votes

Favoring Valdez *Principles*	
Exxon	9.5%
American Express	8.5%
Atlantic Richfield	14.2%
Union Pacific	13.0%
Kerr-McGee	16.7%

Source: 1990 Annual Meetings

Corporate fines will run into the millions and jail sentences will lengthen. Many firms will settle out of court—or be convicted by press release.

RISING STOCKHOLDER ACTIVISM

For the publicly held company: Beware the agitated stockholders.

Urged on by groups such as CERES (discussed in Chapter Eleven), stockholders want stronger expressions of environmental commitment from corporations.

Look for more stockholder resolutions such as the CERES' *"Valdez* Principles"; demands for new board members from green organizations; pressure from institutional investors; and direct, personal challenges of corporate management at annual meetings, at board meetings, and in personal and professional confrontations. (Greens broke into one company's meeting, handed the CEO a "dirty globe award," and took photos for TV and newspapers.)

MEDIA COVERAGE WILL INTENSIFY

Just when you may be thinking that the press itself must be suffering green fatigue, there are indications that we haven't seen (or read or heard) anything yet!

News coverage of green topics rises every year, with the big news spike of the decade being the *Exxon Valdez* oil story. And the year 1992—with Earth Day, U.S. presidential politics, EC 92, 30th anniversary of the original environmental book, *Silent Spring*, moves to green Central and Eastern Europe, and many other important stories—lifted environmental news coverage to a new level of attention. That will continue. Many more reporters and editors have become conditioned to look for opportunities to investigate and interpret.

One positive result is that as more reporters are assigned to the environmental beat, coverage could be better balanced. Groups like the Society of Professional Journalists and the Radio, Television, and News Directors Association are holding seminars to educate editors and reporters.

Look for more local news—especially six o'clock TV—coverage of business greening.

These and other trends demonstrate that environmental fever can be expected to keep rising—and creating problems for any organization. In short, that's *why* green communication is more important than ever to you and your company.

Chapter Thirty

How It All Starts: A Guide to Green Crime's Humble Origins

An official from the Department of Justice began a talk to the National Association of Corporate Directors by saying, "It is a pleasure for me to be here to discuss a subject which should be of interest to you as corporate directors. Of course, if you are judgment-proof or would not be concerned with the possibility of spending time in a federal facility, then my talk may not be of much interest to you."

I am indebted to James A. Rogers, a very successful environmental lawyer (with the firm Wilmer, Cutler, and Pickering in Washington, D.C.), for telling me about this opening. "It was a little heavy-handed," said Jim, "but it got their attention."

And it was not a false alarm. There is no question that federal and state governments are increasingly inclined to use the criminal code to bring about what these prosecutors view as necessary changes in the way business approaches environmental compliance. They hold corporate directors and corporate officers and managers personally responsible for green performance and for strictly obeying rules.

Although criminal enforcement of green laws should be the court of last resort after civil and administrative routes are tried, in the years ahead you can expect more, not fewer, criminal charges against executives of companies large and small. There are three reasons:

First, government officials have discovered that nothing gets the attention of a business owner or senior executive like the threat of doing time for green crime.

Second, the public is either losing patience with, or failing to comprehend, any reasons for noncompliance with green laws. Abuse of the environment has replaced insider trading as the most-hated corporate crime.

In a 1991 survey conducted by A. D. Little, three out of four respondents said that corporate executives should be held personally liable for environmental offenses. An A. D. Little spokeswoman said, "It is clear that people are not just looking to industry for certain levels of performance. They also expect someone to take responsibility for a corporation's actions."

Finally, federal and state environmental laws increasingly spread a bigger net with smaller holes. The 1990 Clean Air Act amendments, for example, shattered the rule of thumb that a new law generates roughly 12 pages of regulations for every page of statute. The CAA weighs in with 700 pages of text and creates 55 wholly new regulations that will take many thousands of pages to express.

The CAA breaks ground in expanding liability by defining a facility's "operator" to mean any member of senior management. And you don't have to be a bad person to be convicted; managers need not even take part in or agree to a criminal action to be held accountable for it under the doctrine of "the responsible corporate officer" upheld by the Supreme Court.

Says Frank Friedman, vice president for health, environment, and safety for Occidental Petroleum Company, "Is it any wonder that some of the most dedicated environmental managers are leaving the field when a facility manager who inadvertently misses a regulatory deadline can be faced with criminal prosecution no different than a member of the Medellin cartel?"[1]

RAISING THE GREEN-CRIME ANTE

Jim Rogers got to know green rules from the inside, at the U.S. Environmental Protection Agency in the 1970s, when the agency was beginning to be challenged in federal court for its water and hazardous waste regulations. Before that, he was at the state level, as assistant attorney general in Wisconsin, involved in a number of environmental cases, including the federal court action against

Reserve Mining Company for taconite discharges to Lake Superior and against automakers for air pollution.

While at EPA, he kept a stable of 30 attorneys busy defending the federal agency's actions. Now he reminds his clients that modern court challenges are increasingly to the corporation's compliance position.

He accepts the record that each year for the past several years there has been about a 33 percent increase in the number of individuals and corporations pursued under the criminal provisions of the environmental laws—*but he insists that's not the full story.*

"The raw statistics on criminal prosecutions are misleading," Jim says, "in that many, if not most, criminal investigations are resolved through civil settlements that do not reveal the agonizing criminal investigations which preceded them."

Experienced attorneys like Jim Rogers firmly believe that the 1990s and beyond will be a totally new ball game for the American corporation. The possibility of criminal liabilities for environmental and other public health violations will pose a greater threat to corporate governance than virtually any other area of concern.

Green-collar crime vulnerability is much more intensive—and, as I will let Jim Rogers help me recount at the end of this chapter, much easier to take root and grow—than other management vulnerabilities, such as the possibility of a hostile corporate takeover.

Let's take a look at some of the evidence: four trends or vital points for the corporation with regard to environmental law, as presented by Rogers:

(1) *Both state and federal governments now impose obligations and penalties on the person or entity that could have avoided the complained-of activity.* "In the Superfund area," says Rogers, "we see the government increasingly suing the officers of a corporation under a theory that they were actual 'operators' of a Superfund site (i.e., they had an actual hand in decisions with respect to waste handling), or under a theory that through diligence and assertion of power within the corporation they could have avoided the problem by creating a system of compliance. We see increasingly creative efforts to pierce corporate veils, to use 'alter ego' theories to reach individuals and corporations that may be several layers above the actual entity carrying out the activity in question."

For example: Two officers and a director of a company in Canada were convicted of illegally discharging industrial waste in violation of Ontario law. It was the first case there in which a court had found company officers liable under a provision that specifically imposes duties on them.[2]

Though the company CEO was charged, he was exonerated because it was found that he hadn't ignored any problems that had been brought to his attention. On the other hand, the president had periodically visited the site in question and had been advised by employees of the problem months in advance of the charge.

Attorneys in the case said the facts considered were:

- nature of the environment affected;
- extent of the injury;
- deliberateness of the offense;
- attitude of the accused;
- size and wealth of the corporation;
- extent of attempts to comply; and
- the firm's criminal record.

There are also many new cases in which the government is attacking secured creditors under similar theories—that is, the creditor through use of economic power could have avoided the polluting activity. Indeed, even shareholders are being pursued when they have significant economic power over a corporation's day-to-day business. An environmental lawyer these days must be quite conversant with parent and successor corporation liability law, and the evolving federal common law addressing individual officer and director liability. This governmental preoccupation with control theories helps explain, in part, the surge in criminal prosecution.

(2) *Environmental laws are so complicated and voluminous that only the most sophisticated corporation can pretend to stay up to date, to keep the people that need to know truly informed of developments in the law.*

The process of taking the arcane information contained in the *Federal Register* and translating it for use by a plant manager (who may be trying to keep an eye on environmental compliance along with the many other tasks of running a business) has in many cases become hopeless. Environmental law is now very much like tax law. The rules are found in interwoven regulatory provisions, many of which can only be understood by reading the hundred-page preambles that accompany frequent changes in these rules. (The rules governing the Resource Conservation and Recovery Act program take up about 640 pages of the *Code of Federal Regulations*.)

"To a large extent," Rogers says, "the practice of environmental law is nothing more than selling discrete bits of information that come from rules too massive for in-house staff to master on a regular basis. Yet failure to understand the law is not a defense, even to a criminal prosecution."

(3) *"Paper" generated in connection with the day-to-day environmental compliance activities gets people into trouble more than the underlying violations!*

"A simple failure to meet a total-suspended-solids standard on a given day may not become as serious as the incorrect reporting of it," Rogers points out.

"Indeed, certification that the particular emission on that day was monitored a particular way may carry with it greater criminal implications than the actual violation. It is, by and large, far easier for a prosecutor to put a criminal case together that is based on inaccurate reporting, improper notification of the government, et cetera, than it is to show that a series of violations caused any real environmental harm."

Rogers believes this is why many of the criminal environmental cases begin by focusing on the so-called "pure" environmental violation (too much pollution up the stack in a given day) and end up as more traditional cases involving mail fraud, misleading a government investigator, failure to report releases, or the like.

Rogers' fourth point is one that he sees corporate officers most unwilling to accept, but it's true:

(4) *A corporation may be prosecuted under the criminal code even when no individual within that corporation acted in willful disregard of the law.*

In many respects it is useful to consider that the environmental laws are based on strict liability, even for criminal activity, Rogers observes. That is because corporate entities are charged with the *collective* knowledge of *all* the employees.

"If one employee knows that a material is being sent to a certain area of the plant site for disposal (but believes the activity to be perfectly OK), and another employee is aware that the substance is a waste and may be dangerous (but does *not* know how it is being handled)," says Rogers, "the *collective* information is enough on which to base a prosecution of the corporation."

There *are* limits on how far the government can go in imputing a criminal case, Rogers states; although the Justice Department and EPA have attempted to prosecute individual officers of a corporation merely on the basis that those officers had a duty to ensure environmental compliance, the few courts that have faced the question have been unwilling to accept the government's theory.

Small wonder corporate boards and top management are sending out the word in all directions: *Corporate environmentalism is a very serious matter.* Policy statements, internal guidelines, and careful coaching and interaction with employees are more critical areas for the corporation going green.

HOW GREEN PROBLEMS START

I want to close this chapter with the most interesting observation and the accompanying advice that lawyers all over the country, like Jim Rogers from Washington, are telling their corporate clients.

This has to do with the little things that turn into big problems, the apparently incidental, seemingly inconsequential ways in which a company can get into environmental legal action.

Rogers calls them "the humble origins of environmental criminal cases." He says that in the vast majority of situations (particularly involving larger corporations), green-crime culpability is not the result of some premeditated conspiracy to violate the laws. It doesn't involve the midnight release of deadly toxins. It has nothing to do with willful misdeeds or cooking the books.

More often than not, the problems arise in one of two categories: confused or inattentive insiders and angry or bumbling outsiders.

Well-meaning individuals in the corporation fail to understand the obligations placed on it by statute, implementing regulations, or the supposedly boilerplate provisions in an environmental permit.

In many of the green criminal prosecutions in recent years, the action was initiated or encouraged by disgruntled employees. Sometimes an outside consultant gets the company into trouble through bad advice or inept representation.

Some prosecutors routinely seek out recently terminated employees or former consultants as witnesses helpful in putting together criminal prosecutions.

Jim Rogers has provided me with four fictitious—but highly realistic—examples of the ways that individuals and corporations in the United States can get into big trouble. Through simple, relatively innocuous moves, the firm and its people can go tumbling down a path that leads into the awesome, powerful federal criminal justice system.

I give these cases to you as Rogers gave them to me:

CASE A: THE CREATIVE CONSULTANT

A company attempted to carry out its Clean Water Act monitoring in the most "efficient" way, and so it hired a local consultant to assume that chore—including preparation of discharge monitoring reports, verifying outside laboratory results, and advising on wastewater treatment. The consultant charged $39 per hour. The task was well beyond this person, who had less training than he had advertised. Rather than admit his inability to understand the rather delicate treatment system that was installed at this plant to handle electroplating wastes, this person began to undertake monitoring on a schedule that he assumed would lead to the lowest possible effluent levels. In an unfortunately not atypical scenario, he decided to monitor only when certain production lines were running and only when flows exceeded a certain level. Noncompliance became rare. (The consultant to this day swears that the creativity in monitoring was permissible under the permit.)

The corporation should have been aware of what was going on; a careful review of the information would have tipped off any well-trained environmental expert. But in fact no one in the corporation did have actual knowledge of the shortcuts the consultant was taking, or the true lack of comprehension this person had as to the fundamental operation of the wastewater treatment activities. Neither the consultant nor the company had seen written state directives on how monitoring should be done. The judge said the corporation was responsible for the acts of its agent. To make a long story short, this case started as a criminal investigation and resulted in the payment of a then-record civil penalty, a court injunction requiring the company to truck the waste rather than discharge to the stream, and the termination of the president and vice president after bondholders brought a class action over the failure to disclose this costly problem.

CASE B: THE STUMBLING START-UP

The problems began the day the corporation was formed. As one of the many entities that were created in the early 1980s through leveraged buy-outs, the survival of this corporation depended on preservation of a certain level of cash flow, no major dips in the demand for the product in question, and no unusual expenses. Cost-saving measures were instigated at every turn. These included the refusal by top management to allow subscriptions to environmental journals, reluctance to call an environmental lawyer on all but the most urgent of problems, allowing general deterioration of facilities, and insistence that environmental compliance be but one of many tasks of individuals at the various plants charged with that obligation. The result of this unwillingness and inability to stay current with environmental regulations was a major criminal prosecution at one of the facilities.

This action began by the government as a simple review of routine filings under Superfund and the Clean Water Act. Curiosity led to more information requests and then formal investigations. It turned out that the operators of the plant in question were unfamiliar with the boilerplate of the Resource Conservation and Recovery Act (RCRA) and Clean Water Act permits that applied to the facility and were repeatedly violating the terms of those permits. It also became clear that the many memoranda from high corporate officials encouraging cost savings were being interpreted by government prosecutors as virtual encouragement to low-level employees to sweep environmental problems under the rug. The company paid a then-record criminal penalty, and the plant in question remains closed because it cannot operate without frequently violating RCRA and the Clean Water Act permits. As a footnote, it should be said that at one point in the investigation the government threatened to investigate the role of the *lending banks*, on the theory that their due diligence investigation must have revealed the inadequate operations of the company in general and the particular plant specifically. That aspect of the prosecution went away, but not before gaining the undivided attention of high bank officials.

CASE C: HIDDEN DISCREPANCIES

The chaos began with the public complaints of a part-time employee who was disappointed at not receiving a full-time position. Channeling his resentment into unfocused allegations of improper use of certain tanks at a wastewater treatment plant, he caused enough fuss to interest a local reporter (this occurred in a community of about 100,000). The commotion was enough to prompt an inspection by the branch office of the state water pollution regulatory authority. That inspection revealed some other problems—still not out of the realm of the ordinary and still certainly not criminal in nature. However, the company's internal legal and technical staff descended on the plant and began a thorough inquiry. This corporation (one of the largest in the country) clearly did not want to find itself surprised by any new revelations. What it discovered through the internal investigation was that there had been a serious misunderstanding of the protocol to be followed in sampling and reporting discharges under the Clean Water Act permit issued to that facility. These discrepancies infected virtually all of the company's reports—as to which the plant manager had certified accuracy—for many years, and placed the company in an extremely exposed position. Following a multimillion dollar internal investigation and complete disclosure of the results to the state and federal governments, the corporation pleaded guilty to a relatively inconsequential misdemeanor and paid a significant civil penalty. A number of people were fired.

CASE D: TECHNICAL CREATIVITY

The principal participants were—as is often the case—experienced engineers and chemists who honestly believed that they knew how best to address environmental problems. It is all too often true that "technical" experts are guided by their own practical sense of what should be done to address environmental concerns rather than the perceived overly formalistic demands of EPA as expressed in *The Code of Federal Regulations*. Thus, a chemical engineer decided that the most effective way to address hazards of acids and bases is to mix them together and develop a rather neutral and far less harmful soup. It came as a surprise to him that the state and federal governments deemed such activity to be "treatment" of hazardous wastes under RCRA, for which a permit is required. Moreover, the most effective way to eliminate small quantities of residual solvents at this plant was to wash them out of virtually empty drums and let them volatilize in the hot afternoon sun in some remote part of a plant site. There is probably little actual danger attached to this activity, but it is illegal. These two activities, although probably not demonstrating the most venal of criminal minds, certainly were adequate to bring the full weight of the federal criminal environmental law down on the heads of the corporation in question. The implications were far-reaching on both an individual and a corporate basis.

Those are the fictitious examples, provided to me by Jim Rogers, environmental attorney. The scary part is that they aren't entirely fictional. They are based on fact patterns blended from real cases.

To reduce company exposure to environmental crime, the greening company in the 1990s will need to make sure it is relying on strong legal counsel to interpret requirements and to minimize the "humble origins."

Legal and technical know-how and execution are key factors in the corporate greening calculation. But Rogers's examples suggest that communication and relationships are also a big part of the equation.

"The environmental crime of the future," says Joel S. Hirschhorn, a former official of the U.S. Congress' Office of Technology Assistance, "will be a failure to act preventively and proactively, and a failure to measure performance, not failure to comply with regulations."

He defines *proactive* as "using technical innovation for environmental progress that can be measured, communicated, and used effectively as a marketing tool."[3]

Hirschhorn encourages in-house education and training programs that teach every employee—not just those with environmental jobs—about environmental issues, pollution prevention, and other aspects of environmental stewardship.

Well-informed employees, who understand and come to believe in the company's green commitment (and who in fact shape the company's green mentality), are the constant first line of defense against corporate green failure.

Beyond that line, public relationships are critical. Relationships developed with all customer-publics—neighbors, suppliers, regulators, consumers, and others, especially those who transact most closely and often with the company—will determine how well the company stays on the positive, public-interest green . . . and how quickly it can recover if circumstances go awry.

Chapter Thirty-One

Environmental Education Is a Key to Your Future

Why should business get involved in education? Because we have so much at stake. This certainly applies to greening and the future of companies going green.

Environmental illiteracy, fears and biases based on misinformation, lack of understanding about the costs and difficult choices regarding greening and growth—these have been the root of many problems for American business and the public. They have not only resulted in public confusion (and panic) and poorly formed public policy; they also hold back the kind of progress that might be made in environmental protection if people were better informed and better educated.

Samuel Johnson, chairman of S. C. Johnson & Son, Inc., put it this way in response to an executive survey I conducted: "Quality environmental education is necessary to form environmentally responsible attitudes and catalyze positive environmental behaviors." That education will be needed at many levels—primary and secondary schools; colleges teaching both business courses and communication or public relations courses; postgraduate studies; adult education courses; and classes that workers can attend.

One industry initiative addressing this need is the Learning and Environmental Action Program. LEAP evolved through sponsorship by the International Chamber of Commerce's Industry Advisory Board on Environmental Education in its efforts to implement the Business Charter on Sustainable Development. LEAP was launched at the Earth Summit in Rio de Janeiro in the summer of 1992 and consists of a student exchange with corporations, sharing of case studies from many enterprises, and the establishment of industry executives as environmental teachers.

SCARES THAT SHOULDN'T HAVE BEEN

Let me remind you of two situations that might not have happened—or, at least, might have been less damaging—if we had the benefit of widespread environmental understanding.

(1) *Alar, the chemical used by apple growers to strengthen the stem of the apple so it doesn't fall to the ground too soon and rot.*

In early 1989, activists raised fears that eating apples treated with Alar, or drinking apple juice made from such apples, increased the risks of cancer. The focus was on the alleged risks to children, who consume more apple products than other age groups. Parents panicked; school boards ordered apples out of school lunchrooms; millions of consumers stopped eating apples in any form; grocers, wholesalers, transporters were devastated. Apple growers reported losses of $100 million within a few months; several went out of business; several lost their farms. The drama climaxed in early June when the manufacturer withdrew the chemical from the market.

Subsequent, calmer, and more scientific assessment of the effect of Alar on apples showed that the risk was overblown. The panic was unnecessary. The damage to farmers and business and the residual fear and confusion among children and adults about eating apples were the result of environmental miscommunication and misunderstanding.

(2) *Dioxin, a by-product of many industrial processes that may be found in the environment wherever there are plants, incinerators, or waste sites.*

Dioxin has caused and continues to cause fear whenever it is mentioned. The best-known panic occurred in Times Beach, the small Missouri town evacuated in 1982 and 1983 because its dirt roads had been treated with waste oil containing dioxin. The federal government bought out all 2,240 residents and moved them elsewhere. The bill was $37 million. Many billions more have been spent by industry to clean up dioxin and prevent its release.

Was it worth it? A National Institute of Occupational Safety and Health study looked at more than 5,000 industrial workers exposed to high levels of dioxin from 1942 to 1984. Although the exposure to dioxin was as much as 90 times that of the general population, the workers showed no increased cancer risk. Further, many biologists now believe that dioxin contributes to cancer only indirectly.

Study has led to a round of revisionism by policymakers. "Given what we now know about this chemical's toxicity and its effects on human health," said Assistant Surgeon General Vernon Houk in *The New York Times*, "it looks as though the [Times Beach] evacuation was unnecessary. If [dioxin is] a carcinogen, it's a very weak carcinogen, and federal policy needs to reflect that."

Scares that shouldn't have been. Scares fed by a spurt of misinformation that can only succeed in the absence of persuasive, well-accepted, or well-entrenched understanding.

In this book, we try to help you communicate your environmental commitment. If you can identify for a moment with a company touched by a scare such as these two, you can readily appreciate the difficulty of communicating anything positive under such conditions. The *education* that occurred while these stories unfolded over time, finally reaching a point of true understanding, was very expensive education indeed, in many ways.

The media are a primary customer-public that became better-educated throughout the resolution of these scares.

Helping journalists to understand, and to report and interpret environmental topics is the goal of organizations such as the Society of Environmental Journalists, the Society of Professional Journalists, and the Radio and Television News Directors Association.

One of the pilots charting this important new course is Morris (Bud) Ward, whose newsletter "Environmental Writer" examines environmental news opportunities and explains some of the concepts that are basic to good reporting. Ward also reaches into journalism schools to interact with students and professors studying environmental issues.

Business needs to be involved in classroom education to try to raise the general-public understanding about environmental issues, to provide a bigger base of public awareness, so that scares like these can be minimized.

Business also needs to be involved to make sure kids are getting all the facts. There is a problem here. There is in fact a great deal of environmental education going on. Programs like the National Environmental Education Act of 1990 are spurring green teaching. The problem is what is being taught.

As Competitive Enterprise Institute policy analyst Jonathan Adler has pointed out, environmental education in schools sometimes mixes the sound with the "simple-minded and inaccurate." Curricula rarely make it clear that air quality, for example, is actually improving in the United States.

While some literature and teaching guides are available from business and industry, other guides, TV shows, comic books, and booklets give kids simplistic and frequently antibusiness information.

ENVIROCOMM EDUCATION

In the Q&A session after a speech to an industry group, I was asked, "What would you recommend to a university setting up a course in environmental communication?"

My response was to make sure the students in that course knew a lot about the real world before they started trying to "communicate."

I believe the foundation for a course in environmental communication ought to be history, science, economics, and government. On that foundation, students can then learn about current events, human behavior, and the applications of communication.

One framework that works well to give a theoretical foundation to what I've been saying in this book has been developed by James Grunig of the University of Maryland.[1]

Grunig has come up with four models of public relations. I would even call them stages, because I see them as getting progressively better and more attuned to modern realities. The first level is simple press agentry: An organization merely communicates in order to drum up publicity. Its information is largely propaganda and is often incomplete or even untrue.

The second model is called the public information model. The truth is respected but information flow is essentially one-way, from the organization to the public. Third is what Grunig calls the two-way asymmetric model, whose purpose is scientific persuasion. Information flows both ways, but data flowing to the organization are seen only as feedback and used to give the organization a better idea of how to persuade key publics.

Finally, there is the two-way symmetric model, in which public relations practitioners serve as mediators between publics and organizations. Each is amenable to the other's influence. Grunig rightly says that organizations practicing this model are best suited to respond to the demands of activist (e.g., environmental) groups and to survive attacks. And his model embodies what this book has been saying about the necessity to communicate, work with, and get on the same side of the table as one's key publics. The essence is dialogue, or multilogue, as I've discussed throughout this volume.

QUESTIONS TO ADDRESS

There are many questions that a progressive environmental literacy course should address. What are the failures and accomplishments, as viewed by specific publics and participants? What have various publics consistently expressed interest in? How have government, industry, green groups, churches, and others communicated with each other with regard to environmental concerns and action? How is green policy formed? What are the respective and interactive roles of science, economics, social behavior, consumer choices, and risk and benefit analysis in forming that policy? How are green partnerships formed? What are the trends and conditions likely to impact environmental decisions in the years ahead?

Sloan Fellows at General Motors were asked, "What do you wish you had learned but didn't?" and "What do you think should be taught now that will be needed 10 to 15 years down the road?"

Here are some of the responses:

- Leadership lessons on how to motivate, manage diverse work forces, integrate business cases, keep bureaucracies at bay, keep arrogance out, conduct global benchmarking, predict the next paradigm, orchestrate cultural change.

- Management lessons on how to downsize and rightsize, execute versus plan, deal with unions, work in teams, manage scarce resources, revitalize manufacturing facilities.

- Dr. Edwards Deming's principles on how to get quality ethics into organization.
- The elimination-of-waste principles learned from lean production. The elements of simplicity, learned from design for manufacturability. The elements of variety, learned from flexible manufacturing. The idea that manufacturing is a competitive weapon, and how to do it. Systems engineering, flow-down of requirements.
- Importance of excellence in all we do.

The traits and attitudes contained in these educational needs are being expressed in companies moving onto the green. They form the new green mentality in a growing number of companies operating all over the world.

ENVIRONMENTALISM GOES TO COLLEGE

It's heartening to note that America's post-secondary educational institutions are scrambling to fill the void in environmental education in four basic ways: teacher training, curriculum development, research and evaluation, and professional development.[2] But it is still a mixed picture.

Teacher Training.   Most institutions of higher learning in the United States that offer a degree program in education or natural resources offer at least one course in environmental education. But only a handful offer a specialization in environmental education at the undergraduate or graduate level. In general, undergraduate teaching programs place a low emphasis on preparing environmentally literate teachers capable of environmental instruction. A few states, such as Wisconsin, do require specific training in environmental education before a person can be licensed to teach.

Once in the classroom, teachers looking to improve their environmental teaching skills have a limited number of basic options. They can attend workshops at national, regional, or state environmental conferences; they can attend courses sponsored through university outreach and extension; or they can participate in specialized workshops. Often these courses and workshops provide "Continuing Education Units" or specific college credits that many teachers need to maintain certification to teach. A small number of teachers go on to specialize in environmental education by attending graduate programs, such as those offered at Ohio State University, Southern Illinois University, the University of Wisconsin-Stevens Point, and the University of Michigan.

Maintaining access to current environmental education materials is a challenge for most teachers. Current networks and clearinghouses of environmental information, such as the Educational Resources Information Center (ERIC) for science, math, and environmental education—affiliated with Ohio State University—are oriented to support teachers who already have the interest, initiative, scientific literacy, personal time, and other resources to use them.

Curriculum Development. Institutions of higher education have been actively involved in designing educational materials for the classroom. Most of these efforts have been directed at developing supplementary curriculum materials with a thematic focus, such as energy, water quality, or pollution. Much less work has been done on infusing environmental education into overall school curricula.

These supplementary curriculum materials frequently give teachers the basic information they need to teach the topic, provide student materials that can be copied by the teacher, and detail activities for teachers to conduct with their students. The materials are usually targeted at a range of grades. Their objectives are typically very similar to the learning objectives a teacher would use in class.

Research and Evaluation. A broad spectrum of environmental education research questions concerning environmental knowledge, skills, attitudes, and action have been investigated and reported in a variety of periodicals such as the *Journal of Environmental Education*, and conference proceedings and monographs such as those produced by the North American Association for Environmental Education. A healthy interest in the field is suggested by the numerous masters' theses and doctoral dissertations on environmental education that are defended each year. Through NAAEE's North American Commission on Environmental Education Research, faculty from nearly 20 universities have cooperated in identifying and addressing research needs in environmental education.

In general, environmental education programs have not received rigorous evaluation to determine their effectiveness. Several factors may contribute to this void, including the complexity of measuring long-term educational changes, broad program designs, and a lack of quantitative objectives.

Professional Development. Colleges, professional and graduate schools, University Cooperative Extension Services, and training institutes serve as the foundation for an environmentally educated work force and environmentally educated decision-makers in all sectors of society. In the early and mid-1970s, a surge of environmental studies programs appeared at U.S. colleges and universities. They were intended to bring an interdisciplinary approach to environmental training and management. Most of these programs are still operating. One survey found that 31 of 45 programs existing in 1978 survived 10 years later.

Tufts University's program shows that the movement has not run out of steam. With help from Allied-Signal Inc., Tufts launched its Environmental Literacy Institute in 1990. TELI seeks to incorporate environmental issues into a broad range of disciplines at both the undergraduate and graduate levels. TELI has begun to extend its efforts to other universities in the United States, Canada, and Brazil, with a five-year goal of reaching up to 100,000 students.

Arguing that "environmental issues are woven throughout business operations and the price of ignorance continues to escalate," the National Wildlife Federation's Corporate Conservation Council has helped to develop a model business school environmental curriculum that addresses the history of environmental concerns, ecological concepts and principles, environmental ethics, policy making, the issues themselves, and corporate environmental strategies. Three business schools—at Boston University, Loyola University of New Orleans, and the University of Minnesota—offered pilot courses in 1989 and 1990.

Technical training programs for environmental professionals have expanded in parallel with the widening scope of environmental regulations. Community and technical colleges have become increasingly active in providing training programs in the environmental field, offering specific degree programs for such careers as water/wastewater technician and course offerings on a variety of specific concerns. At present, these programs focus mainly on technical aspects of job performance and regulatory compliance, but the opportunity exists for a broader environmental education approach that also encompasses the nature of the environmental problems that prompt regulation.

It's a happy sign that business schools are beginning to upgrade their curricula to include elective courses in environmental management, as several dozen now do. For the foreseeable future, no graduate of a business program will step into a job anywhere that doesn't bring him or her face to face with environmental issues and/or problems in one form or another. Exploring the issues in a comprehensive way is a prerequisite to beginning to communicate about them. In fact, the exploration will open a path to the possibility of relationships that make communication meaningful.

Chapter Thirty-Two

Market Environmentalism: Better for Business, Better for the Environment

It's been more than 20 years since the first modern push for government protection of the environment began in the United States, and that effort has led to major changes in the nation's natural and regulatory landscapes.

Hardly anybody argues that the myriad laws and regulations haven't done any good—but there are sharp disagreements about going any further on this road. To many, it's clear that these early forms of regulation have done their job and ought to be let out to pasture—or put out if they won't go peaceably.

In place of the old command-and-control system, say these observers, we need to adopt a different theoretical basis for our environmental protection system. Thus it is that many environmentalists, citizens, and policymakers who once championed the strong hand of government protection are now grasping the invisible hand of Adam Smith's market.

This is good news for greening companies. By streamlining—without weakening—the means of regulating pollution and natural resource use and thereby reducing the drag on business, market-based environmentalism promotes sustainable development. And since greening companies are already leading the march toward SD, this trend brings government environmental policy into closer harmony with their goals. Environmental sparring partners for a quarter century, business and government thus move to emphasize partnering over sparring.

THE AUSTRIAN CONNECTION

Market-based environmental regulation has its deepest roots in the economic theories first discussed by Adam Smith and then elaborated by a group of Austrian economists, including Friedrich von Hayek and Ludwig von Mises.

Oversimplified, the idea was that allowing the market to allocate economic resources free of government interference leads to the greatest efficiency. Big deal, you say—but at the time, the Soviet Union and its eastern bloc allies were beginning their experiments in command-and-control economics, and they seemed like the wave of the future.

However, it didn't take all that long for their faults to appear—at least to objective observers. As the collapse of command-and-control economics approached, the theories of the Austrian free-market economists got a lot of thoughtful second looks.

In the United States, the 1970s ushered in a new environmental era and students of Hayek and Mises began to theorize about the market's ability to protect our natural, as well as political, heritage. Economists such as John Baden, Terry Anderson, and Richard Stroup posed the question, "If the market is the best arbiter of economic resources, shouldn't it also be the best arbiter and protector of natural resources?"

Market environmentalism as a political idea is now two schools of thought. Baden, Anderson, Stroup, and like-minded ideologues believe the proper role of government in the everyday lives of its citizens should be sharply limited. But other advocates of market solutions promote the theories mainly because of their economic efficiency in protecting the environment. These pragmatists believe that government must remain active in enforcing laws to protect the nation's natural resources—but that the laws should incorporate the least costly, least onerous methods possible for achieving this protection.

ENVIRONMENTAL REGS: LESS IS MORE

When the Environmental Protection Agency began developing rules to enforce the nation's environmental laws, the methods chosen allowed little flexibility or room for innovation. Command-

and-control methods dictate the level of allowable emissions, the specific technologies to be used to achieve them, and the deadlines for compliance. The same rules apply to everyone: Widget company A in Spokane must follow the same guidelines as frammitz factory B in Savannah. Regional differences—land aridity, air movements, dozens of other possibilities—don't count.

For a while, it worked. But the system has begun to choke on its own complexity and cost. As the range of environmental problems has widened, the command-and-control machinery to address them has become a vast Rube Goldberg contraption that clanks and wheezes and frequently breaks down. Working or not, it absorbs billions of dollars in compliance, reporting, permitting, and monitoring costs. The system discourages innovation and provides no incentive for cleaning up beyond the levels required by law.

Increasing frustration with command-and-control schemes has driven experiments with incentive-based regulations such as those first developed by Anderson, Baden, and Stroup. Some early successes, coupled with recent attempts to lessen the regulatory burden on American business, have piqued wider interest in market-based methods.

MARKET OPTIONS

Here are some examples of successful market-based environmental regulation:

Pollution charges levy taxes or fees on the amount of pollution generated, rather than monitoring a specific activity, such as manufacturing processes or purchasing of packaging. Examples include volume-based solid waste treatment pricing, which is gaining popularity among American cities, and water pollution taxes based on the amount of effluents released into local waterways, common in France, the Netherlands, and West Germany. Benefits include increased compliance flexibility, equalizing the incentives for different companies to produce less pollution, and minimizing the total costs of pollution control.

Marketable permit systems got a big boost during the debate over the 1990 Clean Air Act. In this system, the regulatory agency establishes a cap on total emissions and then "licenses" each affected company to produce a share of the total, via issuance of permits. Firms that keep emissions below their allotted level can sell unneeded permits to companies unable to meet their targets. This provides an economic incentive for firms to achieve maximum reductions, yet leaves an out for companies unable to meet the target reductions cost-effectively. The system allows firms to determine their own optimal levels of pollution reduction, encourages technological innovation by companies with ideas for economically reducing emission rates, and gives manufacturers the most control.

Tradeable permits have already shown they can work. For example, they were key to the successful phasing out of leaded gasoline in the United States in the early 1980s. Similar systems were established by the Congress for controlling acid rain pollutants.

Best known in connection with soda bottles, *deposit and refund systems* place a surcharge on products that might become pollutants. The surcharge is refunded when the consumer returns the product or its packaging, thus encouraging proper disposal. Deposit and refund systems have also been set up to encourage the recycling of lead-acid batteries and used motor oil.

Removal of market barriers, which are often erected regardless of their impact on environmental protection, can benefit both market and environment. Entrepreneurs hoping to use modern composting techniques in treating municipal yard wastes, for example, have often been thwarted by long-term contracts that prevent sending yard wastes anywhere other than the city-anointed choice. Although loosening such contractual arrangements might encourage innovative and more benign methods of waste treatment (such as composting), the current system not only discourages such innovation but often makes it illegal.

Finally, *ending government subsidies* where they work at cross purposes with national environmental policy would allow market forces to help protect the environment. Eliminating such subsidies could help preserve scarce resources.

COMMUNICATION VIA THE MARKET

The importance of these ideas to the greening company is that they are ultimately about communicating.

Command-and-control methods of protecting the environment distort the market. They cause fuzzy signals about the real costs of environmental protection and resource use to ricochet throughout the system, from company to consumer. Yet sustainable economic growth can't be pursued intelligently unless everyone knows what the score is.

Moreover, it can't be achieved unless resources are used with absolute maximum efficiency—and command-and-control methods, with their heritage of complexity, confusion, and contradiction, seem divinely designed to promote *in*efficiency.

Greening companies have a stake in market-based environmentalism because, to the extent that it catches on, they will become part of a transformation in which everybody wins.

Chapter Thirty-Three

Relating to Green Consumers: The Marketing Minefield

Kermit the Frog had to be in marketing. When he sang his famous song, "It's not easy being green," Kermit was singing the blues of the green marketeer. The job of positioning a product so its environmental benefits are part of the buying decision is like stepping through a minefield. At any moment there could be an explosion. Confused consumers, opportunistic competitors, eager regulators, and government enforcers—it's anything but easy for the company deciding to sell green products.

First let me stress that going green and selling green are tied together. While this chapter focuses on the green marketing minefield—with some guidance on getting through it—the scope of this book is environmental communication of any kind. The main theme here is that the company going green will be impacted (encouraged or denied) by various customer-publics, depending on the nature of the *relationship* with each group and each individual.

The company attempting to communicate its green commitment can be painfully, maybe mortally, wounded in the green-market minefield. This is because performance is vulnerable to perception. Good green performance (for example, the company may have reduced its solid-waste levels by a large percentage) communicated interactively with key customer-publics can create positive standing on the green. But, this green standing can be reduced—and reduced sharply—by a strong negative perception created in the customer-public marketplace (for example, the company is derided for a clumsy green advertisement or a misleading green label).

The company going green must usually build its credibility an inch at a time. That same credibility can be lost, by yards or even miles, virtually overnight.

The rate of loss and the nature of the loss will depend largely on the relationship that's been built with the firm's core customer-publics. It's like making multiple, reinforcing deposits in a bank; you hope there will be enough there to *sustain* you when the bad costly event occurs. Sustainable relationships, fed by sustainable communication, are the best way to figure out what, when, and how to conduct green marketing and promotion.

The greening company should think through the dynamics of the green-marketing minefield. There may be good things to communicate, but choose carefully. The timing, the terms, and the talk itself—the language you choose—can mean increasing risks of miscommunication. These risks go beyond consumers' baffled looks; they could cause disconnections with customer-publics, from employees to stockholders; they could run—as they already have in some cases—to legal action and loss of market share for the offered product.

SHADES OF GREEN CONSUMERISM

Are the risks worth it? The obvious place to find out is the market. What do your customer-publics think, what do they want, what will they support?

The Colgate-Palmolive Company uses a bottom-up approach to finding out their consumers' needs and wants. One tool, says Environmental Affairs Vice President Doug Wright, is their 800 number consumer hotline. Senior management regularly reviews, summarizes, and absorbs that data, and uses it to make sound management decisions based on the market.

In our QUALITY approach, we suggest that the company also ask questions of its own carefully quantified customer-publics. If you look at more general polls over the years, you come to the conclusion that about three-quarters of Americans think of themselves as environmentalists. Somewhere between 15 to 25 percent of all consumers actually spend money in support of their convictions. So you can expect to find some green shoppers, who will choose a product or service primarily or largely for its pro-environment connection—if they're convinced of the green benefit.

But you need to look closer at environmental consumers. They come in all shades.

A 1990 Roper poll was the first to sort out the "marketplace" of citizen opinion about the environment. It segmented consumers into five groupings:

- *True-blue Greens* represent 11 percent of the population. They have the highest average income and are environmental activists, with 52 percent of them reporting purchasing products based on environmental performance.

- *Greenback Greens* represent another 11 percent of the population. They are not active environmentalists, but are willing to pay extra for green products. Forty-three percent of these consumers report buying environmentally oriented products.

- *Sprouts* are 26 percent of the population. They are concerned about the environment but do not believe that individuals can make a difference. Forty-two percent of Sprouts reported making purchases because of a product's environmental characteristics.

- *Grousers* at 24 percent of the population do not believe that they can do much or that others are doing much either. Only 20 percent of this category reports buying products based on environmental claims.

- *Basic Browns,* 28 percent of the population, are the poorest group, and engage in virtually no environmental action. Eight percent of this group has bought environmentally advertised products.

Environmental consumerism is clearly not universal, but these categories represent tens of millions of consumers who have considered the green virtues of products when they shop.

That's hard to ignore. That's why many companies have acted to position their products or services as "environmentally friendly." The range of claims is wide, the definitions often vague and inconsistent. Some companies have stressed their recycled packaging, others superior biodegradability, and still others benefits ranging from protection of the stratospheric ozone layer to compactness in landfills. Predictably, the result has been confusion and cynicism about environmental marketing claims. Blame, boycotts, and charges of "greenwash" have been hurled at some companies.

TAKE MY DEFINITION, PLEASE

Several public, private, and business sector organizations have stepped in and tried to tease some order out of the chaos.

In November 1990, the attorneys general of 10 states brought together leaders from business, government, and environmental groups who hammered out a broad agreement on acceptable claim language and urged the federal government to write environmental marketing regulations for product labeling, packaging, and promotion.

The attorneys general task force also made four recommendations to companies, with the implication that although they weren't legally binding, they would be used as a guide to prosecution for deceptive practices:

1. Claims should be as specific as possible. Companies should avoid using terms like *environmentally safe* and should distinguish between the product and the packaging.

2. Claims of disposability should reflect current options available to consumers where the product is sold. The terms *compostable* and *recyclable* should be used only where these are realistic options.

3. Claims should be substantive, not trivial or irrelevant.

4. Claims should be supported by reliable scientific evidence.

Meanwhile, at least two private organizations have already begun offering guidance to consumers about environmentally acceptable products.

Green Seal is a nonprofit labeling organization established largely by environmental and public interest groups and initially led by Dennis Hayes, the executive director of Earth Day in 1970 and again the chief executive officer for Earth Day 1990. Green Seal set up an Environmental Standards Council, composed of independent scientists, to establish criteria for awarding the seal and to oversee product testing.

Green Seal said it intended to review light bulbs, laundry cleaners, house paints, toilet paper, and facial tissue. But the development of product categories and criteria has proceeded much more slowly than anticipated. Two years after its founding, Green Seal has yet to certify any product as environmentally acceptable.

Scientific Certification Systems, Inc. (formerly called Green Cross) certifies claims made by manufacturers about the environmental attributes of their products. Green Cross will verify, for instance, a claim that paper contains 50 percent recycled content. Areas eligible for certification include recycled content, biodegradability, energy efficiency, and use of sustainable resources. SCS has recently introduced the use of life-cycle analysis in its product evaluations, and is developing an Environmental Report Card for products.

THE G-MEN'S GREEN GUIDE

Most recently, the U.S. Federal Trade Commission has looked at the issue in cooperation with the Environmental Protection Agency and the U.S. Office of Consumer Affairs. The action was prompted by the state attorneys general report and by a petition brought by a coalition of industry groups, including the National Food Processors Association, the Cosmetic, Toiletry, and Fragrance Association, and the Nonprescription Drug Manufacturers Association.

The FTC held hearings and asked for public comment, and in July 1992 issued a set of guidelines—which are administrative interpretations of existing laws and not legally enforceable—to "help reduce consumer confusion and prevent the false or misleading use of environmental terms." The guidelines do not preempt state or local laws or regulations.

The FTC guidelines contain four general exhortations:

1. Qualifications and disclosures should be sufficiently clear and prominent to prevent deception.
2. Environmental claims should make clear whether they apply to the product, the package, or a component of either.
3. Claims should not overstate the environmental attribute or benefit.

4. A claim comparing the environmental attributes of one product with those of another should make the basis for the comparison clear and should be substantiated.

Using illustrative examples, the guidelines then discuss acceptable circumstances for use of the terms *degradable* (including *biodegradable* and *photodegradable*), *compostable, recyclable, recycled content, source reduction, refillable,* and *ozone-safe* and *ozone-friendly.*

THE BENEFITS OF CLEAN LANGUAGE

Environmentally progressive companies have an enormous interest in the next chapter of this story, as the original industry petition to the FTC suggests. With any luck, the commission's action will help to stabilize and standardize the language of green product features and the claims made about them. What does this mean to you?

First, it will level the communication playing field, or help clear the static out of the channels. If you are a company with a legitimate claim to make for a product, you should benefit by being able to communicate the good news in language that means something because its integrity is protected. A competitor, seeking quick green advantage without actual value, will be less able to give the good words a bad name.

Second, as the language catches on it may provide your company with a useful tool to reach its most important customer-public: the people who buy what you make. Earlier I said that one of your best moves is to get on the same side of the table with customer-publics. You need to see yourself as others see you. You need to understand. That is difficult unless everyone shares a common language and the confidence that they know what specific terms mean to everyone else. In a nutshell, the murkier the communication climate, the more dangerous it is to walk through the green marketing minefield.

There is a way to clear the air. If your firm has continuous give and take with key customer-publics (that is to say, *sustainable communication*), ask them what they think. First make sure your marketing intention and message will pass legal muster. Then go to your core support group. Try out ad copy, labels, or TV commercials on focus groups comprising representatives of your customer-publics. Ask them if they understand, and if they perceive what you are presenting as consistent with your green performance and your commitment to environmental stewardship. Once performance and perception are aligned, it's easier being green.

Chapter Thirty-Four

Green Gospel: The Industry Dilemma Over Religion, Science, and the Environment

Religious organizations and leaders from around the world are taking an increasing interest in environmental issues and are adding their moral and ecclesiastical authority to calls for greater and more rapid efforts to protect the global environment. To the extent that these efforts are based on incomplete or speculative science, industry faces a dilemma: how to caution restraint against rash action that might do more harm than good, without being seen as an opponent of a public-interest position taken by organized religion.

Businesses should seek to interact with church organizations, both locally and nationally, in order to promote honest exploration of these issues and avoid the role of obstructionist.

SPIRITUAL CRISIS?

The combining of religious and political forces to influence the environmental agenda has been going on for some time now.

- CERES (Coalition for Environmentally Responsible Economies) issued the *Valdez* Principles in 1989 with the help of church representatives.
- Catholic, Evangelical, Church of Christ, and Jewish leaders met in New York in 1991 intent on "crossing traditional reli-

gious and political lines" to influence public environmental policy.

- One hundred nations were represented at two meetings of the Global Forum of Spiritual and Parliamentary Leaders in Moscow in 1988 and in Oxford, England, in 1990.

Most recently a new twist was added when the Joint Appeal by Science and Religion for the Environment hosted a May, 1992 gathering in Washington. The meeting was cochaired by astronomer and science-popularizer Dr. Carl Sagan and The Very Reverend James Parks Morton, dean of the Cathedral of St. John the Divine in New York.

It assembled scientists and religious figures for the express purpose (in Sagan's words) of helping to "preserve the planetary environment on which our mutual well-being depends."

The gathering, held on Capitol Hill, also featured the political element. Senate sponsor—now vice-president—Al Gore told the audience, "As a person of faith I am convinced that [the environmental problem] is at bottom a spiritual crisis."

SCIENCE VS. POLICY

With religious leaders increasingly positioning themselves alongside some scientists and politicians as "pro-environmental" activists, business faces a dilemma. Many experts feel that environmental public policy has already outrun sound science in many instances, and there are fears that it is happening again with other issues, such as global warming. The new influence of religious organizations seems likely to accelerate this trend.

Yet if business and industry attempt to defend good science in an effort to head off unnecessary and costly political and economic decisions, they will find themselves once more on the defensive—but this time also risking the appearance of opposing "public-interest" positions taken by churches, church leaders, and religious organizations.

BRIDGES, NOT MOATS

The only winning position is interaction, not the usual uptight or defensive reaction. Business and industry cannot—and certainly will not wish to—fight churches. The alternative is to get involved. Business must seize opportunities at all levels to work with interested religious organizations and church groups toward honest exploration of troubling environmental questions.

Locally, for example, companies would do well to look for ways to interact with community church groups. Some are organizing committees to promote environmental stewardship, often at the urging of their national church organizations. Through local management and employees, companies can take part in the work of these committees, offering information and resources, and learning directly about the real concerns of the group and the community. This participation can help create a genuine public-interest benefit for the community and those who care about it.

Business also needs to think hard about exploring ways to work with national church organizations—perhaps by jointly developing educational materials for use by local communities, churches, and business groups. Other ideas would surely emerge through inquiry and interaction with church organizations.

As the "green gospel" converges with the mainstream of environmental public policy action, it is important that a firm grip be maintained on the principle of action based on good science. Business must add its strength to that effort.

VI

CONCLUSION

Chapter Thirty-Five

Sustainable Communication: Going Green, With Gusto!

Charlie Brown has put Lucy once again in center field. There is a long fly ball to center.[1] Lucy waits for it. The ball descends and, of course, Lucy drops it. Lucy always drops it. So we see her talking to Charlie Brown and she says, "I'm sorry, Manager. I thought for a minute I would catch it, and then I remembered all the ones I had missed before." There is a pause and we see her walking back to her position and she is saying to herself, "The past got in my eyes."

The past got in my eyes. It's easy to identify with hapless Lucy if you're in business and you look back selectively at the environmental game. How many have we really won?

Have we won in Congress? Congress enacted and President Bush signed the new clean air act in 1990. It's going to cost industry up to $35 billion, maybe as much as $50 billion, a year. Our firm has added up the probable costs of green laws and green regulations on business and industry by the year 2000. Our estimate is $200 billion a year. That's just federal. Not including state and in some cases local.

I recently met with executives in the chemical industry. That industry alone expects to be paying 3 to 4 percent of sales for environmental, health, and safety in the next decade. The chemical industry is a $250 billion industry. That's $10 billion a year in that industry alone.

Staggering costs! The oil industry says its pollution prevention costs will be up around $15 to $20 billion a year by the year 2000. Every business, large and small, is adding up its environmental expense and it is enormous. Would we have wished these expenses on ourselves?

How about the regulatory side? Have we won understanding and patience while we get into greening at higher and higher levels? Are they really putting businesspeople in jail for committing a green crime? Yes, and it's not that hard to do. You don't have to be a midnight dumper. We're not talking about plotting a scheme to pollute. We're not even talking about missing a compliance deadline. Your own compliance audit can do you in. It's rougher than *that*. A meeting, held in your company, at which environmental matters were discussed, can do you in. You can be done in, and get into deep trouble with the law, because of well-meaning employees and well-meaning consultants.

Did we drop the ball somewhere?

The trend is toward more, not fewer, criminal charges against company executives, in companies large and small.

Are we winning? Are we winning in public opinion? The polls keep showing that people blame business for pollution.

How about employees? EPA's criminal enforcement chief says his division gets tips on the companies that EPA targets for federal action from three sources: angry competitors, irate neighbors, and disgruntled workers.

Competitors will do you in. Community neighbors will do you in. Within the ranks of your own employees, there are those who will do you in. They've done it in the past!

Can't people be fair? Mobil Oil places an ad that says companies are "often criticized without any notice being taken of what we and our people do in a positive way for the environment." Unfair. Not based on the evidence. How can we win when the game is rigged?

"I thought for a minute I would catch it and then I remembered how often I had failed. The past got in my eyes."

STARTING OVER, AND WINNING

Vince Lombardi said, "Winning is not a sometime thing. It's an all-the-time thing. Winning is a habit. Unfortunately, so is losing."

Summarizing some of the points in this book, I want to suggest six steps to winning with regard to the environment, and the first step is to drop the losing habit.

1. **Don't let the past get in your eyes.** It's a new ball game. Develop a realistic green mentality. You are not alone. Since that 1990 conference in Rotterdam, where a few business leaders made the decision to take an innovative concept and make it work, more than 1,000 companies—big companies, American and other companies—have signed on to a "sustainable development" pledge. Sixteen guidelines now set the pace, worldwide, for companies to get on the green—to improve environmental performance within a business context, to measure progress, and to report.

We've come a long way from the days when company information was strictly proprietary, when a lot of information was classified secret, when information as sensitive and as complex as environmental data was made available only on a need-to-know basis.

We've moved from need-to-know to right-to-know. We've gone from proprietary secrets to the new Green Rule: Everybody knows everything most of the time. Our job is to help them understand the information to which they have ample access.

Obviously a new day has dawned with regard to health, safety, and product stewardship. We are on the verge of a new green mentality in American business.

2. **Watch what the winners are doing.** When it comes to greening, the leading companies have done four things: Comply with the law. Develop a public policy. Get into partnerships. Train employees.

Environmental management in the large companies ties communication into all levels of a company's operations: pollution prevention, product stewardships, life cycle analysis.

Large or small, companies going green must start with a written policy. Here is a four-step environmental policy that summarizes the essentials that I am seeing in such policies:

a. To take environmental protection measures as a positive challenge, not a hindrance to operations.

b. To solve problems at the source through innovative production measures.

c. To work continuously to achieve understanding with employees and various publics through open dialogue and interaction.

d. To seek cooperative relationships with public regulatory agencies.

A policy like this, obviously, can mean very little—another memo or framed certificate, an empty gesture, or, worse: a bomb that can explode in your face. But a statement like this, developed with full participation by representatives of all levels in the company, can be the road map for going green in a sustainable, win-win manner.

3. **Help employees to help you win.** Employees can put you into a court of law—but they can also help to pull you onto the green. In fact, you can't get there without them. By empowering those who are directly associated with the company so that they can achieve *personal satisfaction* of their individual environmental goals, the organization can move toward its green goals—and they will be the right goals.

4. **Help the community to win.** If the community wins, you win. While the national mood has been the gloomiest on record for at least two decades, the Roper Organization did a poll in 1992 that showed one small bright spot with regard to American business. Majorities said they feel a little better about business, big and small. The poll shows, in fact, that people want business to take over from the politicians. Just about everyone would greatly welcome more business involvement in the community— perhaps to pick up where the deficit-burdened government has left off.

We are not just talking about opportunities for you to spend more money. That opportunity is there, of course, but in fact I see in this polling data the opportunity to save money. Business has standing with the public. People are looking to business for answers. The Roper poll, for example, found that three out of four people would like companies to inform them about the environment, to tell them about the companies' view of environmental efforts, what works and what doesn't. They want to know what you are doing—and that's not a very long walk from the place where they may be ready to work with business to solve problems together.

Companies that have set up community advisory panels tell me they don't know how they ever got along without these partnership groups. Plant managers are now talking face-to-face about the environment with others in the community. The CEO of one company said: "They are telling us not only what they expect of us but what they are willing to do with us. We talk about plant improvements, emergency plans, training programs. We are learning from each other."

Learning from the community. Partnering with—or at least openly talking with—environmental activists. The name of the game is partnerships, getting on the same side of the table to look at specific green challenges together. A winning move. And the closer to home, the better. Your greatest strength is at the community level. It tends to erode as you leave home.

5. Get into the public policy game.

Most of our environmental laws started out as environmental theory, and theory is fine until practice proves that it is wrong. When environmental theory becomes law, it is time for people in business either to help make it practical or—if it is not practical—to help make it history.

When the polls are general—that is, when people are not asked who they blame for pollution, for example—90 percent of the American people say they feel moderately to highly favorable toward small businesses. That's in the Roper polling data. Ninety percent! Nearly 70 percent say the same thing about large businesses! Who are the critics of business? With numbers like these, why aren't we winning more?

Maybe we're not using this numerical advantage. Maybe we're not turning favorability potential into real clout.

6. Ask for action: keep looking ahead. Don't let the past get in your eyes.

The bottom line is *sustainable communication*, a term coined in this discussion to indicate that a new level of environmental communication is needed by the organization wishing to get on the green.

Sustainable communication is a results-driven process to be used by the organization wishing to benefit from the creation of long-term relationships with customer-publics.

It is continuous, open, interactive; it is consistent, with measurable results, and ever improving.

These characteristics make sustainable communication a total quality approach.

THREE STEPS TO THE GREEN

As the sustainable development era begins to touch every business, large and small, today's executive needs to understand the essential moves to place the company, and the individual as manager, in a positive environmental position—on the green of the public interest.

In addition to compliance with all green laws and regulations that apply to the organization, these moves are:

1. Commit to pollution prevention beyond what the current laws require of you;
2. Team up with people outside your organization to solve general environmental problems, including those you don't cause; and
3. Take the initiative in dialogue that ensures continuous environmental improvement.

While *compliance* is now given intense attention by most organizations, fewer organizations seem to have a handle on *communication*, and it is the latter that spells success or failure in your effective transition to a new Green World.

This book deals with the public perceptions that can support or devalue the company's green performance. Making the right moves in these three critical areas requires the attention of managers up to and including the chief executive.

KEY IDEAS OF THIS BOOK

Summarizing, here are some of the key ideas presented in this book:

1. Sustainable development (defined as the balancing of green and growth goals, and the recognition that today's actions and commitments will determine future environmental conditions) requires *sustainable communication;* that is, a continuous, multi-

level, and consistent exchange between the organization and its customer-publics.

2. Any notion of public relations as a short-term fix should be abandoned in the sustainable-development era; instead, we can usefully consider publics as customers to be created and sustained in a relationship that will benefit the environment, the general public, and the organization.

3. Green communication, to be sustainable, must be centered in the market of customer-publics; it involves a seven-step QUALITY model: questions, understanding, analysis, listening, interpreting, taking charge of an interactive process, and—*you*. The effective communicator need not be an accomplished *speaker*, but one who is ready to investigate, interpret, and initiate a dialogue.

4. Crises, environmental incidents, and performance problems are best handled through early acceptance of responsibility, shared concern, positive commitment to a resolution, continuous dialogue, and openness.

Environmental performance is full of frustrations for managers and executives. It's hard enough just to keep up with the proliferating, complex, and sometimes contradictory green laws and regulations. The new Clean Air Act has the effect of doubling and tripling the problem. And now we have the puzzle of global operations—of tracking rules in many lands.

To achieve 100 percent "compliance" can mean pushing the organization to such high levels of environmental performance that the economic viability of products and entire operations are threatened.

Companies comply at great cost—and yet get little public-interest credit. You can, in fact, be in compliance and still be clearly off the public-interest green when you are targeted by environmental activists, the news media, and elected officials and politicians. Activists + Media + Politicians: this AMP synergy is the most dynamic force in the creation of green opinion and green rules by which business must abide. It therefore makes sense for the business organization to get involved in this action—but that means breaking out of the traditional box (usually labeled "Villain") in which business and industry have so often been placed.

Employees and neighbors are customers just as surely as are the people who buy your product or service—and we've explored the value of looking back at your operations and your personal presentation from various customer perspectives.

To win in the sustainable-development era, you must create and sustain relationships that encourage your successful environmental performance and your organization's mission.

Here are some comparative characteristics of sustainable and unsustainable communication:

Sustainable communication	*Unsustainable communication*
manages expectations	manipulates emotions
acknowledges poor past performance as a serious matter	ignores or denies mistakes, or treats them lightly
looks for options that make sense to all stakeholders	looks out for number one only
presents evidence to support positions and ideas	does not disclose relevant raw data and backup work
asks and tries to answer questions	disseminates "news" and decisions
focuses on core publics to create relationships	"does PR" to "the public"
treats publics as customers who need to be understood	believes "publics" and "audiences" need "education"
interacts with customer-publics at their respective levels of awareness, with a consistent commitment	delivers a variable "message" to various publics
is always open	is open when convenient

After presenting my *sustainable communication* model to a business group in Brazil during the United Nations Conference in 1992, I was peppered with questions, beginning with the man who asked: "Can you give me an example of *un*sustainable communication?"

"An unsupported statement by a company about its green commitment is one example," I responded. "Or a meaningless claim on a product label."

"So you are really talking about not misleading the public?" asked the questioner.

My reply was yes—with the stipulation that this applies to any and every *customer-public*: internal (such as employees) or external (such as people who buy your product).

The questioner was satisfied, but later I realized that I had shortchanged him.

On one level, it is true that sustainable communication means *not misleading* any customer-public. But that level does not reach the deeper meaning of the concept.

In fact, you have to "not rest" while you are "not misleading." The thesis of this book is that the green scene is dynamic. I believe the organization's environmental communication must be in motion, moving toward the next green goal, as identified with your core customer-publics.

Not misleading the public is like saying that good environmental performance means *not being out of compliance;* in other words, not breaking the law.

As we've stressed in this book, *compliance* has come to mean the minimum condition of corporate greening. It's an okay shot, but short of the green. It is a *static* condition, in the sense that it is *not moving toward people's expectations.* The winning, *dynamic* condition is one in which the company is anticipating what key customer-publics will require, prefer, or expect, because the company has an honest desire to deal with these changing characteristics.

The organization that is going green will soon realize that the problems begin when the firm gets out of sync with the outside world, the worst-case extension of which is isolation: without core customer-public support and vulnerable to such things as legal action and consumer boycott.

To review the lesson: *Sustainable development* is the general goal of every country and every company that wants to be on the public-interest green. *Sustainable relationships* help the company and its customer-publics get there. And *sustainable communication* is the continuous process of creating and sustaining those relationships.

In the *quality* model for sustainable communication, the critical element is for the company to *understand* what the vital customer-publics know and wish (or need) to know. This produces options for mutually beneficial actions, by the company and by the customer-publics.

By going past the static and limiting condition of *compliance,* the company can put energy into keeping its relationships active. It can head off the fences of fear and mistrust that tend to get built at the exact point at which the company stops interacting with neighbors and other publics. The spirit of "150 percent compliance" goes beyond what the law requires. It gives the company an attitude of open exploration; in its best-case expression, it puts the company into an interactive commitment with customer-publics, looking for ways to work together for environmental and economic balance.

Sustainable communication is communication without significant gaps. If the company's primary goal is to gain understanding (and not "to be understood"), the company's managers and other representatives *must* interact with customer-publics continuously, in order to avoid and to close gaps in the communication link.

Sustainable communication lets the company reach past the unfriendly condition of mere compliance, to create and sustain the *relationships* that the company needs (and the customer-publics need) to ensure *sustainable development*.

*Un*sustainable communication, I should have said to the questioner in Brazil, is any communication that does not advance a good, lasting relationship.

"Not misleading" gets you teed up, but to make the drive to the green, we require a dynamic strategy that has staying power.

The corporate mentality necessary to get on the green is one that comprehends the longer time frame. The investment in communication may not return a dividend this quarter or this year, perhaps; but, over time, it sustains the relationships that pay off for all parties.

When do you start? In what direction?

I like the perspective expressed by Stephan Schmidheiny, chairman of UNOTEC, Switzerland, as he spoke to the Business Council on Sustainable Development: "Sustainable development, like business, is not a final destination, but a process. We know directions, but we do not know final destinations. This should not worry us overly; it certainly should not provide us with an excuse for delaying moves in the obvious directions."

This holds for sustainable communication as well. So don't delay! Pick a path in the direction of a critical customer-public and start moving in that obvious direction. **It is a winning move, so go with gusto!** The losing move—unsustainable communication—is not to move at all, and to miss all the benefits of going green.

Footnotes

Acknowledgments

[1]Rachel Carson, *Silent Spring* (Boston: Houghton Mifflin Company, 1962).

[2]Dan J. Forrestal, *The Story of Monsanto: Faith, Hope and $5,000* (New York: Simon & Schuster, 1977).

Chapter One

[1]International Chamber of Commerce Industry Forum, Rio de Janeiro, Brazil, May 27–29, 1992.

[2]Deputy Assistant Attorney General Roger B. Clegg.

[3]*United States Sentencing Commission Guidelines Manual.* U.S. Government Printing Office, November 1, 1991.

[4]Tim Bryant, *St. Louis Post-Dispatch*, July 23, 1991.

[5]Rachel Carson, *Silent Spring* (Boston: Houghton Mifflin Company, 1962).

[6]Stephan Schmidheiny with the Business Council on Sustainable Development (Cambridge, MA: The MIT Press, 1992).

[7]Jan-Olaf Willums/Ulrich Goluke, *From Ideas to Action: Business and Sustainable Development* (Oslo, Norway: ICC Publishing and Ad Notam Gyldendal, 1992).

Chapter Three

[1]Dorothy Sarnoff, *Speech Can Change Your Life* (New York: Dell Publishing Co., Inc., 1970).

Chapter Four

[1]Peter Drucker, *Management* (New York: Harper & Row, Publishers, Inc., 1973).

Chapter Five

[1]Vic Gold, *I Don't Need You When I'm Right: The Confessions of a Washington PR Man* (New York: William Morrow & Company, Inc., 1975).

Chapter Six

[1]Al Ries and Jack Trout, *Bottom-Up Marketing* (New York: Penguin Group, 1989).

Chapter Seven

[1]Max De Pree, *Leadership Is an Art* (New York: Doubleday, 1989).

[2]Remarks by E. S. Woolard, Jr., before the National Wildlife Federation Synergy '90 Conference, Washington, DC, January 30, 1990.

[3]"Bottom Line" (The Executive Committee [TEC], Summer 1992).

[4]"Managing the Global Environmental Challenge" (Business International Corporation, March 1992).

Chapter Eight

[1]William Safire, *Safire's Political Dictionary* (Latest edition of *The New Language of Politics*, 1968) (New York: Ballantine Books, 1980).

[2]Ernest and Elisabeth Wittenberg, *How To Win in Washington* (Cambridge, MA: Basil Blackwell, 1989).

Chapter Eleven

[1]1990 Annual Reports.

[2]Marc Epstein, "Corporate Shareholders Want Environmental Action" (Sy Symms School of Business, Yeshiva University, 1991).

[3]"Mobilizing Support to Eliminate An Environmental Menace," *PR News*. February 4, 1991.

Chapter Twelve

[1]Bill Gifford, "The Greening of the Golden Arches," *Rolling Stone*, August 22, 1991.

[2]Stephan Schmidheiny with the Business Council on Sustainable Development, *Changing Course: A Global Business Perspective on Environment and Development* (Cambridge, MA: The MIT Press, 1992).

[3]Jan-Olaf Willums/Ulrich Goluke, *From Ideas to Action: Business and Sustainable Development* (Oslo, Norway: ICC Publishing and Ad Notam Gyldendal, 1992).

[4]*Financial Times*, November 20, 1991.

[5]Jan-Olaf Willums/Ulrich Goluke, *From Ideas to Action: Business and Sustainable Development* (Oslo, Norway: ICC Publishing and Ad Notam Gyldendal, 1992).

Chapter Fifteen

[1]*PR News*, October 28, 1991.

[2]Al Ries and Jack Trout, *Bottom-Up Marketing* (New York: Penguin Group, 1989).

[3]Michael Abramowitz, "Oregon Governor Gets an Earful from the People," *The Washington Post*, April 10, 1992.

[4]Stephen Covey, *The Seven Habits of Highly Effective People* (New York: Simon & Schuster, 1989).

Chapter Sixteen

[1]*O'Dwyer's Washington Report*. J. R. O'Dwyer Co., July 20, 1992.

[2]Dorothy Sarnoff, *Speech Can Change Your Life* (New York: Dell Publishing Co., Inc., 1970).

[3]P. M. Sandman, David B. Sachsman, M. Greenberg, M. Jurkat, A. R. Gotsch, M. Gochfeld, "Environmental Risk Reporting in New Jersey Papers," The Environmental Risk Reporting Project (Brunswick, NJ: Rutgers—The State University of New Jersey and the University of Medicine and Dentistry of New Jersey—Rutgers Medical School: January 1986).

Chapter Seventeen

[1]Harold I. Sharlin, Environmental Protection Agency Study, 1980s (exact date unknown).

[2]Peter Sandman, "Explaining Environmental Risk" (Washington, DC: Office of Toxic Substances, TSCA Assistance Office, U.S. EPA, 1986).

[3]Vincent T. Covello, Peter M. Sandman, and Paul Slovic, "Risk Communication, Risk Statistics and Risk Comparisons: A Manual for Plant Managers" (Chemical Manufacturers Association, 1988).

[4]Vincent T. Covello and Frederick Allen, "Seven Cardinal Rules of Risk Communication" (Washington, DC: Office of Policy Analysis, U.S. EPA, 1988).

[5]Peter Sandman, "Explaining Environmental Risk" (Washington, DC: Office of Toxic Substances, TSCA Assistance Office, U.S. EPA, 1986).

Chapter Eighteen

[1]On March 24, 1989, the Exxon oil tanker *Valdez* ran aground on Bligh Reef in Prince William Sound, Alaska, spilling approximately 240,000 barrels of crude oil.

[2]Alan M. Webber, "Corporate Egotists Gone with the Wind," *The Wall Street Journal*, April 15, 1991.

Chapter Nineteen

[1]"Taste of Defeat Drives Effort for Thomas," *The Washington Post*, July 19, 1991.

[2]From his address to the World Congress of the International Public Relations Association, Toronto, Ontario, Canada, June 1991.

Chapter Twenty

[1]Associated Press/*Schenectady Gazette*, April 6, 1992.

[2]Interview with Robert Kennedy, CEO, Union Carbide. Danbury, CT, July 27, 1992.

[3]July/August 1992 issue.

Chapter Twenty-One

[1]*Getting to Yes: Negotiating Agreement Without Giving In* (New York: Penguin Books Ltd, 1981).

Chapter Twenty-Two

[1]*PR Reporter*, November 11, 1991.

Chapter Twenty-Three

[1]Bill Gifford, "The Greening of the Golden Arches," *Rolling Stone*, August 22, 1991.

[2]From the author's interview of First Brands CEO Al Dudley and company materials.

[3]Clean Sites, Inc.; Clean Sites 1989 and 1990 annual reports; *Environmental Forum*, May/June 1989; *Holden (MO) Review*, July 6, 1988; *The New York Times*, December 26, 1988 and September 1, 1991; *NAPEC Quarterly*, March 1991.

[4]*The Christian Science Monitor,* October 3, 1991; *Environment Ohio,* July/August, 1991; *Los Angeles Times,* November 1, 1991; *PR Newswire,* October 31, 1991; *San Francisco Chronicle,* October 31, 1991; *The Washington Post,* August 4, 1991.

Chapter Twenty-Four

[1]Dick Siebert/NAM and Steve Hellem and George Eliades/NEDA, *The Washington Post,* July 9, 1992.

Chapter Twenty-Five

[1]*The Washington Post,* July 21, 1992.

Chapter Twenty-Six

[1]*Chemical Week,* November 28, 1990; *Chemical Week,* July 17, 1991.

[2]*Chemical Week,* July 17, 1991.

Chapter Thirty

[1]"Is This Job Worth it?" *The Environmental Forum,* May/June 1991.

[2]"Directors and Officers Convicted in Canadian Toxics Case," *Environment, Health and Safety Management,* August 3, 1992. The Environment Group Inc. 1992.

[3]"Environmental Quality Is in the Doing, Not the Words," *Total Quality Environmental Management,* Summer 1992.

Chapter Thirty-One

[1]James E. Grunig and Todd Hunt, *Managing Public Relations* (New York: CBS College Publishing, 1984).

[2]Draft report by EPA's Environmental Education Advisory Committee, Summer 1992.

Chapter Thirty-Five

[1]"Peanuts" characters created by Charles M. Shultz.

Index

A

Accountability, as executive trait, 125
Activists, 82, 103–104
  attacks by, 180–189
  leaders of, 195
Adler, Jonathan, 295
Air pollution
  Monsanto and, 238
  Ohio Edison and, 238
  Pacific Gas & Electric Co. and, 238–239
Alar, 293
Alaska, Prince William Sound oil spill in, 159, 166–167. *See also Exxon Valdez*
Alcoa, 10
Allen, Frederick, 151
Allied-Signal Inc., 12, 299
Alyeska Pipeline Service Company, 166
American Chemical Society, 151
AMP Syndrome, 277
Anderson, Terry, 302
Anheuser-Busch Companies, water conservation by, 232
Apple juice, Alar scare and, 293
Arctic National Wildlife Refuge oil exploration, 167
Aristech Chemical plant, 198
Arrogance, public speaking and, 146
Ashland Chemical, Inc., Responsible Care Management System of, 232
Ashland Oil, 93, 127, 166
AT&T, 113
  CFC emissions control by, 232–233
  compliance goals of, 206
  environmental policy statement of, 208–209
Attitudes, toward greening, 15–26
Audiences, 38. *See also* Public speaking
Audubon, 218
Awards programs, 242–256

B

Baden, John, 302
Barkley, Alben, 74
Belanger, Jean, 258, 263
Bell Labs, 232
Berele, Pete A.A., 264
Bhopal, India, 23, 258
Bioreserve idea, 228–229
"Blue Bag" recycling system, 221–223
Borden Inc., waste disposal and, 233
Boston University, 299
Bottom-Up Marketing, 40
Brook Furniture Rental, 124
Browning-Ferris, 276
"Bubble-up," 12
Bulletin boards, 62
Bureaucrats, 73–74
Bush, George, 9
Business
  employee success by, 67–68
  greening and, 5–14
  ratings of, 108–109
Business Charter on Sustainable Development, 124, 269, 270, 292
  as policy statement, 208
Business Council on Sustainable Development, 10, 12
Business International Corporation, 67
Buzzelli, Dave, 259

C

CAER. *See* Community Awareness and Emergency Response program
Canada, convictions in, 284
Canadian Chemical Producers' Association (CCPA), 258, 263
Canadian Pacific Hotels & Resorts, 114
Carcinogen, dioxin as, 294
Carpenter, Richard, 115

Carpet Policy Dialogue, 75
Carson, Rachel, 257
Carter, Jimmy, 8
CCPA. *See* Canadian Chemical
   Producers' Association
CEO. *See* Executive
CERES. *See* Coalition for
   Environmentally Responsible
   Economies
CFC emissions, control of, 232–233
*Changing Course: A Global Business
   Perspective on Development and the
   Environment*, 12, 114
Chanson, Robert, 108
Chapman, Clark R., 150
Chemical industry, 105–106
Chemical Manufacturers Association
   (CMA), 126, 223
   Responsible Care program of,
      197–198, 240, 257–265
Chemicals. *See* Hazardous materials
Chevron Corporation, Environmental
   Compliance Program of, 233
Chittick, David, 113
Ciba-Geigy, green credo of, 204–205
Citgo, wetlands and, 239
Citicorp, 86–87
Citizen's Clearinghouse for Hazardous
   Wastes, 219
Clean Air Act (1990), 125, 303
Clean Air Act amendments (1990), 5, 9,
   282
   violation of, 278
Clean Sites, Inc., 223–227, 259
   and Rose Chemicals Company, 226
Clean Water Act, 286, 287
Clorox Company, The, recycling and,
   233
Coalition for Environmentally
   Responsible Economies (CERES),
   104–106, 131, 279, 313
Coalitions. *See* Partners
Code of ethics, 203
Code of Federal Regulations, The, 290
Cognitive dissonance, 130
Colgate-Palmolive Company
   bottom-up approach of, 307
   environmental policy statement of,
      209–210

packaging of, 233–234
Colleges and universities, environmental
   education in, 297–300
Commitment, as executive trait, 126
Communication, 34–37, 133. *See also*
   Envirocomm process; Laws;
   Listening; Public speaking;
   QUALITY model
   basics of, 169–170
   crisis, 158–167, 168–179
   environmental, 195–197
   horizontal, 57–58
   jargon and, 145–146
   listening and, 41–43
   by lobbyists, 90
   via market, 304–305
   means of, 60–63
   negative, 17–19
   of new environmental ethic, 266–268
   partners and, 190–199
   process-driven and problem-driven,
      34–37
   QUALITY model for, 36–37, 38–46
   with regulatory agency, 72–73
   about risk, 148–157
   sustainable, 14, 311, 323, 324–329
Communication risk, technical
   assessments and, 153–157
Community
   crisis management in, 177–178
   neighbor concerns and, 132, 134–136
   opinion leaders in, 193–195
   relations with, 190–199
Community Awareness and Emergency
   Response program, 259, 261
Community-Industry Forum, 225
Competitive Enterprise Institute, 295
Compliance, 7–8, 69–71, 325. *See also*
   Crime
   cost of, 16
   policy statements and, 206
Concern, evidencing, 133–136. *See also*
   Listening
Conduct, of lobbyists, 87–88
Confrontation principles, 188–189
Congress, and Alaska oil spill, 166–167
Connectability, as executive trait, 125–126
Conservation groups, public lands and,
   227–230

Consolidated Coal, wetlands and, 234
Consumers
  marketing to, 306–312
  Roper groupings of, 308–309
Continental Pipeline Co., wetlands and, 239
Corbett, Bill, 170–172
CORE program, 237
Corporate codes of ethics, 203
Corporations, environmental policy statements of, 208–215
Correction, of problems, 117–119
Cosmair, Inc., A.W.A.R.E. program of, 234
Courage, as executive trait, 127–128
Covello, Vincent, 140–141, 151
Covey, Stephen, 132, 133
Cowper, Steve, 166
Crawford, Bob, 124
Crime
  green-collar, 278–279
  origins of green, 281–291
Criminalization, environment and, 6–7
Crisis communication, 158–167
  basics of, 169–170
  dos and don'ts of, 168–179
  profile for, 172–178
Crisis management
  activist groups attacks and, 180–189
  assessment of plan for, 172–178
  facility and operations for, 177
  planning questionnaire for, 179
Crown Rancho Pipeline, wetlands and, 239
CSI. See Clean Sites, Inc.
Customer-publics, 29–33, 192
  listening to, 131–133
  quantifying leaders and, 194–195
  questions from, 134
Customers
  sustainable, 31
  types of, 31–33

D

Daggett, Christopher, 225
Dalton, Jerry, 130
Daniell, Robert F., 93, 124, 208, 266, 267

Data, interpreting, 43–44
Decima Survey, 259
Deere, John, Company, 237
Defect prevention, 48
Demand-side management (DSM) techniques, 115–116
Deming, Edward, 297
Depolarization, and activist attacks, 185–186
DePree, Max, 47
"Design for Environment" (AT&T), 113
Development. See Sustainable development
Dialogue, 123–124
  media coverage of, 198–199
  and risk communication, 153
Dioxin panic, 293–294
Direct mail, 62–63
Disclosure, lobbyists and, 88
Distribution
  concerns of chain members, 132
  Responsible Care program and, 262
Doe Run Company, 66
Dow Brands, environmental policy statement of, 210–211
Dow Chemical, 10, 124
  waste disposal and, 235
  wetlands and, 239
Dow Corning, waste disposal and, 235
Drucker, Peter, 30
DSM. See Demand-side management techniques
Duke Power Company, environmental policy statement of, 211
DuPont, 10, 13, 50
  environmental policy statement of, 211–212
  managerial evaluation by, 126–127

E

Earth Day, 309
Earth Summit (1992), 10–11, 105, 189, 292
  sustainable development and, 269
Eastern Europe, greening in, 4
Eastman Kodak, 264
EC, green legislation and, 4–5

Ecology. *See* Environment; Greening
Economists, 302
  Austrian, 302
Eco-Rating International, 108–109
"Ecosystem management," 228
Ecosystems, preservation of, 241
EDF. *See* Environmental Defense Fund
Education
  employees and, 49–50
  environmental, 292–300
Educational Resources Information
  Center (ERIC), 298
Elections, of 1976, 8–9
Eliades, George, 232n
Emergency Planning and Community
  Right-to-Know-Act (EPCRA) (1986),
  11–12, 53, 191
Emergency response, plans for, 261. *See
  also* Hazardous materials
Employee communication, supervisor
  and, 58–59
Employee Health and Safety Code of
  Management Practice, of CMA, 262
Employees, 47–68
  checklist for, 67–68
  concerns of, 131, 134
  education, training, and, 49–50, 64–66
  information provided to, 50–53
Engineering studies, 157
Envirocomm process, 16, 34, 35, 119
  education and, 295–296
  initiative in, 197–198
  QUALITY model and, 38–46
  relationships and, 44–45
  stockholder relations and, 110–112
Environment
  activists and, 82, 103–104
  compliance and, 7–8, 16
  and employee relations, 47–48
  laws and, 6–7, 17
  news about, 231–241
  news media and, 92–94
  winning strategies for, 321–329
Environmental activist groups, dealing
  with, 180–189
Environmental awards, 242–256
  listing of selected, 244–256
Environmental communication. *See also*
  Envirocomm

factors affecting, 195–197
  as interactive process, 56–63
  market model for, 277
Environmental Defense Fund, 126
  General Motors and, 236
  McDonald's and, 189, 216–220
Environmental disasters. *See* Crisis
  communication
Environmental education, 292–300
  post-secondary, 297–300
  questions to address, 296–297
Environmentalism, 4
  politicization of, 275
Environmental laws, 281–291
Environmental Literacy Institute, 299
Environmental policy, 321–322
  of business, 16–20
Environmental policy statements, 203–215
  of leading corporations, 208–215
Environmental Protection Agency, 282,
  302. *See also* EPA
  Clean Sites, Inc., and, 223–227
Environmental regulations, 302–303
Environmental Report Card, 310
Environmental scares, 293–295
Environmental Standards Council, 309
Environmental trends, 319–320
"Environmental Writer" newsletter, 294
Environment movement, 8–11
EPA, 6, 7, 12
  Green Lights program, 115
  hazardous materials and, 53
  voluntary toxics release inventory
  reduction program of, 125
EPCRA. *See* Emergency Planning and
  Community Right-to-Know-Act
Epstein, Marc, 107
ERIC. *See* Educational Resources
  Information Center
Ethics
  codes of, 203
  United Technologies and, 266–268
Europe, greening in, 4
Executives
  public concerns of, 163–164
  traits of, 123–128
Exxon Valdez, 15, 104
  crisis communication and, 158–167

Exxon Valdez Principles, 104–105, 279, 313

F

Face-to-face communication, 60–61
Federal Trade Commission, 310
"Feebates," 115
Feedback, 118
Fellows, Sloan, 296
Fernandez, Louis, 259
First Brands Corporation, Glad partnership and, 220–223
Fisher, Roger, 191
Florida Power Corporation, waste disposal and, 235
Forest products industry, 105–106
4/40 rule, 222
Friedman, Frank, 282
Friedman, Steve, 95
From Ideas to Action, 13
Fuller, H.B., Co., environmental efforts of, 236

G

General Motors
  environmental policy statement of, 212–213
  environmental programs of, 235–236
Gifford, Bill, 219
Gillett, John, 115
Glad trash bags, and First Brands Corporation, 220–223
Glick, Dennis, 228
Global Environmental Management Initiative, 109
Global Forum of Spiritual and Parliamentary Leaders, 314
Goals, 30
  company involvement as, 57
Gore, Al, 314
Government, 69–80. *See also* Laws
  subsidies, 304
Greater Yellowstone Tomorrow Project, 228
Green activists, business and, 276
Green consumerism, 306–312
Green crime, 278–279

origins of, 281–291
Green Cross, 310
Green executive. *See* Executive
Greenfield, Meg, 127–128
Green Goals, of Dow Brands, 210–211
Greening
  Americanization of, 4–5
  attitudes toward, 15–26
  business and, 5–14
  customer-publics and, 29–33
  definition of, 3–4
  globalization of, 4
  mental, 21–26
  trends in, 275–280
Green Lights program, 115, 243
Green marketing, 306–312
Greenpeace, 189
  Responsible Care programs and, 264
Green Seal, 309–310
Grumbly, Thomas, 224, 227
Grunig, James, 295
Guest Services Inc., waste disposal and, 236

H

Haas, Robert, 57–58
Hall, John, 93, 127, 166
Harrison, E. Bruce, Co., 266, 272, 277
Harvard Negotiation Project, 191
Hayek, Friedrich von, 302
Hayes, Dennis, 309
Hazardous materials, 51
  OSHA requirements and, 51–52
  SARA requirements and, 53
Health, 48
Hearperson. *See* Listening
Heinz, H.J., Company, environmental protection by, 236–237
Hellem, Steve, 232n
Hirl, J. Roger, 264
Hirschhorn, Joel S., 290
Hobson, Tina, 242–243
Hooker Chemical Company, 15, 165
Houk, Vernon, 294
How to Win in Washington, 77
Huntsman Chemical Corporation, CORE program of, 237

I

Iacocca, Lee, 164
IBM, 114–115
  environmental policy statement of,
    213
ICI, 54–56
Industrial managers, 87
Industry, environmental programs of,
    105–106
Industry Cooperative for Ozone Layer
    Protection, 233
Industry groups, 310
Information. *See also* Environmental
    education; Listening
  consumer/community sources of, 278
  disseminating to employees, 60–63
  interpreting, 43–44
  sources of, 40–41
Information sources, and news, 92–94
Inspection, 117–119
Interactive process, 45
  environmental communication as,
    56–63
International Chamber of Commerce
  Business Charter on Sustainable
    Development, 106
  Industry Advisory Board on
    Environmental Education, 292
  Industry Forum, 10, 12–13
  policy statement of, 208
  Rotterdam meeting and, 123–124
Interpretation, of data, 43–44
Interviews, managing, 97–101
Intitiative, in envirocomm, 197–198
Investment firms, ratings by, 108–109
Investor Responsibility Research Center
    (IRRC), 109
Investors, communicating with, 102–112
IRRC. *See* Investor Responsibility
    Research Center
Irvine, Robert, 166, 167

J

Jackson, Patrick, 36
Jargon, 145–146
Jenner, Bruce, 13
John Deere Company, 237

Johnson & Johnson, Tylenol crisis and,
    168
Johnson, S.C., 115, 292
Johnson, Samuel, 292
Johnson, Samuel C., 6
Johnson Wax, 6
Joint Appeal by Science and Religion
    for the Environment, 314
Journalism. *See* Environment; News
    media
Justice Department, 6

K

Kennedy, Robert D., 10, 11, 23, 24, 49,
    187
Kerr-McGee, 105
Kiam, Victor, 164
Krupp, Fred, 217–218, 220

L

Labeling, safety and, 52
Lancaster, John, 228
Land management, conservationists
    and, 227–230
Language
  in product claims, 310–311
  standardizing, 311–312
"Last Great Places" program, 229
Laws. *See also* Crime; Politicians
  compliance with, 7–8
  environmental cases and, 281–291
  environmental violation and, 6–7
  growth of U.S., 17
  hazardous materials and, 50–54
  lobbying and, 81–91
Law suits, 278
Leaders
  activist-group, 195
  community, 193–195
Leadership, 47
Leadership Is an Art, 47
LEAP. *See* Learning and Environmental
    Action Program
Learning and Environmental Action
    Program (LEAP), 292
Leighton, Tony, 189
Lesly, Philip, 67

Leverage, employees and, 66–68
Levi Strauss & Co., 57
LIMB (Limestone Injection Multi-State Burner), 238
Lincoln, Abraham, as public speaker, 147
Linde Division, of Union Carbide Industrial Gases Inc., 239–240
Listening, 129–136
  by lobbyists, 91
  strategy for, 41–43
Litigation, 278
Lobbying, 81–91
Lombardi, Vince, 320
Long, Earl, 34
Love Canal, 15, 165
Loyola University of New Orleans, 299
LTV Corporation, 130

M

Mahoney, Richard, 127
Management, and public interest, 87
Management goal, 30
Manufacturing, 113–116
Marketable permit systems, 303–304
Market barriers, removal of, 304
Market environmentalism, 301–305
Marketing, 130, 306–312
Material safety data sheets (MSDSs), 52
McAbee, Frank, 208
McDonald's, 114, 126
  and Environmental Defense Fund partnership, 189, 216–220
McGuire, William, 146
Media. See News media
Meetings, 60
Mennen Company, 237–238
Mental greening, 21–26
Mills, C. Wright, 74
Minnesota, University of, 299
Mises, Ludwig von, 302
Monongahela River oil spill, 127
Monsanto, 127
  compliance goals of, 206
  environmental policy statement of, 213–214
  Responsible Care program and, 264
  toxic air emissions reduction by, 238

Monsanto Pledge, as greening manifesto, 127
Moore, Dudley, 158
Morrison, David, 150
Morton, James Parks, 314
MSDSs. See Material safety data sheets
Multilogue, 45

N

NAFTA talks, 4
National Environmental Education Act (1990), 294
National parks, 228
National Park Service, waste disposal and, 236
National Wildlife Federation, Corporate Conservation Council, 299
Nature Conservancy, The, 227–230
Neighbors
  communication with, 154
  concerns of, 132, 134–136
New England Power Company, ecologically significant sites and, 238
New Language of Politics, The, 74
News, lobbying and, 82–83
News media, 39, 82
  and activist attacks, 186
  crisis management and, 178
  education and, 294
  environmental coverage by, 280
  environmental news and, 231–232
  interacting with, 92–101
  interviews by, 97–101
  news sources and, 96–97
Nexis, 182
Nimbyism. See "Not-in-My-Backyard" syndrome
North American Association for Environmental Education (NAAEE), 298–299
"Not-in-My-Backyard" (Nimbyism) syndrome, 153

O

Occidental Chemical, 238
  Responsible Care program at, 264

Occupational Safety and Health
    Administration (OSHA), 51–52
Office of Consumer Affairs, 310
Ohio Edison, air pollution reduction by,
    238
Oil spill. *See Exxon Valdez*
Ombudsmen, regulation and, 75
150-percent-plus compliance, 7
O'Neill, Paul, 10
O'Neill, Thomas P. (Tip), 78
Openness, 123–124
Operational goal, 30
Options, and community partners, 191
Oregon, bottom-up marketing in,
    130–131
OSHA. *See* Occupational Safety and
    Health Administration
OSHA Voluntary Protection Program,
    209
Ozone layer, protection of, 232–233

P

Pacific Gas & Electric Co., air pollution
    and, 238–239
PAP. *See* Public Advisory Panel
Partnering, practices of, 126, 216–230
Partners, community, 190–199
Patton, George, 42
Pennwalt, 15
Periodicals, research and evaluation,
    298–299
Permits, 74
Permit systems, 303–304
Peters, Tom, 41
    listening strategy and, 133
Petitto, Laura Ann, 133
PET plastic, 233–234
Phillips Petroleum, 20
    Responsible Care program at, 263
    wetlands and, 239
Pierle, Michael, 264
Piller, Charles, 153
Planning. *See also* Crisis management
    crisis management questionnaire and,
    179
    by lobbyists, 91
Plans, for handling environmental crisis
    communication, 160–163

Plaut, Jon, 12
Policy statements, 203–215
    content of, 205–206
    implementation and, 206–208
    intent of, 204–205
    objectives of, 204
Political Action Committees (PACs), 78–79
Political contributions, 78–79
Politicians, 82, 83–84
    and environmentalism, 275
    public interest and, 85–87
    and regulators, 73–74
Politics, lobbyists and, 88–89
Pollution, 8, 114. *See also* Environment;
    Greening; Waste disposal
    air, 238
    prevention code, 261
Pollution Prevention Act, 51
Popoff, Frank, 10, 124
Powell, Katherine, 263
Preparation, and crisis communication,
    170–172
Presidential candidates, greening and,
    127–128
Presidential elections, 8–9
Press conferences, 82–83
Prince William Sound, 159
Printed materials, 60
Print journalists, 95
Proactive process, 45
Problem-driven communication, 34–37,
    40
Process-driven communication, 34–37
Process Safety Code, 261
Procter & Gamble, 193–194, 214
Product claims, 309–311
Product stewardship, and Responsible
    Care program, 262–263
Professional development, 199–300
PR Reporter, 36
Public, general, 155–156
Public Advisory Panel (PAP), 264
Publications, policy statements and, 208
Public interest, politicians and, 85–87
Public Perception Committee, of CMA,
    259
Public relations
    and crisis communications, 168–169.
    See also Crisis communications

Public relations—Continued
  models, 295–296
  professionals, 34–35
  programs, 34–35
Public relationships, listening and, 132
Publics
  customer, 29–33
  as customers, 32
  informing critical, 186–188
  questions from, 134
Public speaking, pointers for, 137–147.
    See also Communication
Purdue, Frank, 164
PVC plastic, 233–234
Pyramid Mountain, 237

Q

Quality control circles, 60
Quality ethics, 297
QUALITY model, 36–37, 38–46, 117,
    118, 119, 307
  and environmental communication,
    56
  listening and, 129
Quality programs, greening and, 48
Quantification, 56
  of community leaders, 194–195

R

Raspberry, William, awards programs
    and, 242–243
Ratings, environmental, 108–109
RCRA. *See* Resource Conservation and
    Recovery Act
Reactive process, 45
Recycling. *See also* Solid waste disposal
  Glad bags and, 220–223
  of used motor oil, 240
Regulation, 69–80, 302–303. *See also*
    Government; Laws
  market-based environmental, 303–304
  ombudsmen and, 75
  politicians and, 73–74
  testifying and, 76
Regulatory negotiation (reg-neg), 75
Reilly, William, 223, 224, 265
Relationships

creating, 44–45
customer, 31
regulation and, 77–80
Religion, and environmental policy,
    313–314
Renew America, awards by, 242–243
Reporters, 94–95. *See also* Interviews;
    Media
Research, activist attacks and, 182
Resource Conservation and Recovery
    Act (RCRA), rules governing, 285,
    288
Resource management, 236
Responsible Care program, 45, 105, 240
  codes of, 260–263
  company programs and, 263–265
  operation of, 260
Ries, Al, 40
"Right to know" (Sunshine) laws, 146
Rio de Janeiro, Earth Summit in. *See*
    Earth Summit
Risk communication, 148–157
  cardinal rules of, 151–152
River and Harbors Act (1899), 16
Roberts, Barbara, 130
Rogers, James A., 281, 282, 285–286
Rooting for America, 239
Rose Chemicals, 226
Ruckelshaus, William, 148, 276

S

Safety communication, 48
Safire, William, 74
Safire's Political Dictionary, 74
Sagan, Carl, 314
Sandman, Peter, 146, 152–153
  risk and, 150
Sandoz Group, 241
SARA. *See* Superfund Amendments
    and Reauthorization Act
Sawhill, John C., 228
Schmidheiny, Stephan, 3, 10, 12, 114,
    328
Science, and environmental policy, 314
Scientific Certification Systems, Inc.,
    310
SEADOCK, 239
Seadrift Plant, of Union Carbide, 264

"Searching for Success" awards,
242–243
Second World Industry Conference on
Environmental Management
(WICEM II), 9–10, 208, 263
Security analysts, 110
Seven Habits of Highly Effective People,
The, 132
Shell Oil, wetlands and, 239
Siebert, Dick, 232n
Silas, Pete, 10
Silent Spring, 8, 257, 280
Silvers, Phil, 92
Simeral, William, 259
Simpson Paper, waste disposal and, 239
Slovic, Paul, 151
Smith, Adam, 301, 302
Smith & Hawken, 114
Solid waste disposal, 234–235, 236–237
Southern California Edison, 116
Speeches, making, 137–147. See also
Public speaking
Standard and Poor directory, 109
State government, Oregon, 130–131
Stevens, Ross, 13
Stockbrokers, 110
Stockholders
activism of, 279
communicating with, 102–112
concerns of, 131, 134
study of, 107–108
Strategies, 40, 42
Strong, Maurice, 12
Stroup, Richard, 302
Subsidies, government, 304
Sunshine laws, 146
Superfund Amendments and
Reauthorization Act (SARA), 51, 53,
71, 224
chemical release risks and, 151
questions from community neighbors
and, 135–136
Title III emissions data of, 125, 258
Supervisor, role of, 58–59
Suppliers, 113–116
concerns of, 132
Sustainable communication, 14, 311,
323, 324–329
Sustainable customers, 31

Sustainable development, 9–10, 124,
324–329
international progress toward, 12–14
organization checklist for, 269–272

T

Teacher training, 297–298
Technical assessments, in public
domain, 153–157
Television. See also News media
and employee communication, 62
news coverage and, 95
TELI. See Environmental Literacy
Institute
Testimony, before government agencies,
76–77
Texaco Chemical, nesting sites and, 239
Textile industry, compliance goals of,
206
33/50 plan, 12, 265
3M, compliance goals of, 206
Total Quality Management (TQM), 8,
36, 113, 258
Toxic emissions, reduction program, 265
Toxics Release Inventory (TRI), 258, 278
Toxics Release Inventory, 53, 71
Toxics Substances Control Act, 75
TQM. See Total Quality Management
Train, Russell, 227
Training, employees and, 49–50, 64–66
Transnational activity, green activism
as, 276
Transparency, as executive trait, 123–125
Trash bags. See Recycling
Tree planting program, 239–240
Trends, 275–280, 319–320
Trout, Jack, 40
Trout & Ries, 130
Truman, Harry, 73
Tufts University, 299
Tylenol, handling of crisis, 168

U

UNCED. See United Nations
Conference on Environment and
Development
Union Carbide, 10, 11, 49, 187

Union Carbide—Continued
  Bhopal tragedy and, 23, 258
  Responsible Care program at, 264
Union Carbide Chemicals and Plastics,
    environmental policy statement of,
    214–215
Union Carbide Industrial Gases Inc.,
    239–240
Uniroyal Chemical Company, The, 240
United Nations Conference on
    Environment and Development
    (UNCED), 10, 12. *See also* Earth
    Summit
United Nations Earth Summit, 10–11, 105
United Technologies, 93, 124
  communication of new environmental
    ethic by, 266–268
  policy statements of, 208
Universities, environmental education
    in, 297–300. *See also* state
    universities by state name
Unocal Corporation, waste disposal
    and, 240
Ury, William, 191
U.S. Council for International Business,
    270
U.S. government agencies, 310
U.S. Steel, 198
Utilities industry, demand-side
    management techniques in, 115–116

V

Valdez. See Exxon Valdez
Valvoline, used motor oil and, 240
Video. *See* Television
Virginia Coast Reserve, 227–230
Visualization techniques, 22–24

W

Walsh, Bill, 264
Ward, Morris (Bud), 294
Washington, D.C., lobbying in, 81–91
Washington Post, The, 127
Waste, 114
Waste disposal, 234–235, 236–237, 239,
    240. *See also* Responsible Care
    program
Waste management, and Responsible
    Care program, 262
Webber, Alan, 163
Wetlands, 239
WICEM II. *See* Second World Industry
    Conference on Environmental
    Management
WIIFM (what's in it for me?) rules,
    155–157
Wilderness Act (1964), 16
Willow Lake project, 236
Wills, Garry, 147
Wittenberg, Ernie, 77–78
Woolard, Edgar S., Jr., 10, 50, 127, 211
World Conservation Strategy, 229
World Industry Conference on
    Environmental Management, 24
WRAP (Waste Reduction Always Pays)
    program, 235
Wright, Doug, 307
Writing. *See* Public speaking

Y

Yastrow, Shelby, 217–218

Z

Zelms, Jeffrey, 66
Zoecon Corporation, ecosystems and,
    241